PROLOGUE—THE WANDERERS

ARGUMENT

Certain gentlemen and mariners of Norway, having considered all that they had heard of the Earthly Paradise, set sail to find it, and after many troubles and the lapse of many years came old men to some Western land, of which they had never before heard: there they died, when they had dwelt there certain years, much honoured of the strange people.

Forget six counties overhung with smoke,
Forget the snorting steam and piston stroke,
Forget the spreading of the hideous town;
Think rather of the pack-horse on the down,
And dream of London, small, and white, and clean,
The clear Thames bordered by its gardens green;
Think, that below bridge the green lapping waves
Smite some few keels that bear Levantine staves,
Cut from the yew wood on the burnt-up hill,
And pointed jars that Greek hands toiled to fill,
And treasured scanty spice from some far sea,
Florence gold cloth, and Ypres napery,
And cloth of Bruges, and hogsheads of Guienne;
While nigh the thronged wharf Geoffrey Chaucer's pen
Moves over bills of lading—mid such times
Shall dwell the hollow puppets of my rhymes.

  A nameless city in a distant sea,
White as the changing walls of faërie,
Thronged with much people clad in ancient guise
I now am fain to set before your eyes;
There, leave the clear green water and the quays,
And pass betwixt its marble palaces,
Until ye come unto the chiefest square;
A bubbling conduit is set midmost there,
And round about it now the maidens throng,
With jest and laughter, and sweet broken song,
Making but light of labour new begun
While in their vessels gleams the morning sun.
  On one side of the square a temple stands,
Wherein the gods worshipped in ancient lands
Still have their altars, a great market-place
Upon two other sides fills all the space,
And thence the busy hum of men comes forth;
But on the cold side looking toward the north
A pillared council-house may you behold,
Within whose porch are images of gold,
Gods of the nations who dwelt anciently
About the borders of the Grecian sea.

Pass now between them, push the brazen door,
And standing on the polished marble floor
Leave all the noises of the square behind;
Most calm that reverent chamber shall ye find,
Silent at first, but for the noise you made
When on the brazen door your hand you laid
To shut it after you—but now behold
The city rulers on their thrones of gold,
Clad in most fair attire, and in their hands
Long carven silver-banded ebony wands;
Then from the dais drop your eyes and see
Soldiers and peasants standing reverently
Before those elders, round a little band
Who bear such arms as guard the English land,
But battered, rent, and rusted sore, and they,
The men themselves, are shrivelled, bent, and grey;
And as they lean with pain upon their spears
Their brows seem furrowed deep with more than years;
For sorrow dulls their heavy sunken eyes,
Bent are they less with time than miseries.

    Pondering on them the city grey-beards gaze
Through kindly eyes, midst thoughts of other days,
And pity for poor souls, and vague regret
For all the things that might have happened yet,
Until, their wonder gathering to a head,
The wisest man, who long that land has led,
Breaks the deep silence, unto whom again
A wanderer answers. Slowly as in pain,
And with a hollow voice as from a tomb
At first he tells the story of his doom,
But as it grows and once more hopes and fears,
Both measureless, are ringing round his ears,
His eyes grow bright, his seeming days decrease,
For grief once told brings somewhat back of peace.

THE ELDER OF THE CITY
    From what unheard-of world, in what strange keel,
Have ye come hither to our commonweal?
No barbarous race, as these our peasants say,
But learned in memories of a long-past day,
Speaking, some few at least, the ancient tongue
That through the lapse of ages still has clung
To us, the seed of the Ionian race.
    Speak out and fear not; if ye need a place
Wherein to pass the end of life away,
That shall ye gain from us from this same day,
Unless the enemies of God ye are;
We fear not you and yours to bear us war,
And scarce can think that ye will try again

The Earthly Paradise by William Morris

A Poem

Part I

William Morris was born in Walthamstow, London on 24th March 1834 he is regarded today as a foremost poet, writer, textile designer, artist and libertarian.

Morris began to publish poetry and short stories in 1856 through the Oxford and Cambridge Magazine which he founded with his friends and financed while at university. His first volume, in 1858, The Defence of Guenevere and Other Poems, was the first published book of Pre-Raphaelite poetry. Due to its luke warm reception he was discouraged from poetry writing for a number of years.

His return to poetry was with the great success of The Life and Death of Jason in 1867, which was followed by The Earthly Paradise, themed around a group of medieval wanderers searching for a land of everlasting life; after much disillusion, they discover a surviving colony of Greeks with whom they exchange stories. In the collection are retellings of Icelandic sagas. From then until his Socialist period Morris's fascination with the ancient Germanic and Norse peoples dominated his writing being the first to translate many of the Icelandic sagas into English; the epic retelling of the story of Sigurd the Volsung being his favourite.

 In 1884 he founded the Socialist League but with the rise of the Anarchists in the party he left it in 1890.

In 1891 he founded the Kelmscott Press publishing limited edition illuminated style books. His design for The Works of Geoffrey Chaucer is a masterpiece.

Morris was quietly approached with an offer of the Poet Laureateship after the death of Tennyson in 1892, but declined.

William Morris died at age 62 on 3rd October 1896 in London.

Index Of Contents

An Apology

Of Heaven or Hell I have no power to sing,
I cannot ease the burden of your fears,
Or make quick-coming death a little thing,
Or bring again the pleasure of past years,
Nor for my words shall ye forget your tears,
Or hope again for aught that I can say,
The idle singer of an empty day.

But rather, when aweary of your mirth,
From full hearts still unsatisfied ye sigh,
And, feeling kindly unto all the earth,
Grudge every minute as it passes by,
Made the more mindful that the sweet days die—
Remember me a little then I pray,
The idle singer of an empty day.

The heavy trouble, the bewildering care
That weighs us down who live and earn our bread,
These idle verses have no power to bear;
So let me sing of names remembered,
Because they, living not, can ne'er be dead,
Or long time take their memory quite away
From us poor singers of an empty day.

Dreamer of dreams, born out of my due time,
Why should I strive to set the crooked straight?
Let it suffice me that my murmuring rhyme
Beats with light wing against the ivory gate,
Telling a tale not too importunate
To those who in the sleepy region stay,
Lulled by the singer of an empty day.

Folk say, a wizard to a northern king
At Christmas-tide such wondrous things did show,
That through one window men beheld the spring,
And through another saw the summer glow,
And through a third the fruited vines a-row,
While still, unheard, but in its wonted way,
Piped the drear wind of that December day.

So with this Earthly Paradise it is,
If ye will read aright, and pardon me,
Who strive to build a shadowy isle of bliss
Midmost the beating of the steely sea,
Where tossed about all hearts of men must be;
Whose ravening monsters mighty men shall slay,
Not the poor singer of an empty day.

Across the perils of the shifting plain
To seek your own land whereso that may be:
For folk of ours bearing the memory
Of our old land, in days past oft have striven
To reach it, unto none of whom was given
To come again and tell us of the tale,
Therefore our ships are now content to sail,
About these happy islands that we know.

THE WANDERER.
Masters, I have to tell a tale of woe,
A tale of folly and of wasted life,
Hope against hope, the bitter dregs of strife,
Ending, where all things end, in death at last:
So if I tell the story of the past,
Let it be worth some little rest, I pray,
A little slumber ere the end of day.

No wonder if the Grecian tongue I know,
Since at Byzantium many a year ago
My father bore the twibil valiantly;
There did he marry, and get me, and die,
And I went back to Norway to my kin,
Long ere this beard ye see did first begin
To shade my mouth, but nathless not before
Among the Greeks I gathered some small lore,
And standing midst the Væringers, still heard
From this or that man many a wondrous word;
For ye shall know that though we worshipped God,
And heard mass duly, still of Swithiod
The Greater, Odin and his house of gold,
The noble stories ceased not to be told;
These moved me more than words of mine can say
E'en while at Micklegarth my folks did stay;
But when I reached one dying autumn-tide
My uncle's dwelling near the forest side,
And saw the land so scanty and so bare,
And all the hard things men contend with there,
A little and unworthy land it seemed,
And yet the more of Asagard I dreamed,
And worthier seemed the ancient faith of praise.

But now, but now—when one of all those days
Like Lazarus' finger on my heart should be
Breaking the fiery fixed eternity,
But for one moment—could I see once more
The grey-roofed sea-port sloping towards the shore,
Or note the brown boats standing in from sea,
Or the great dromond swinging from the quay,
Or in the beech-woods watch the screaming jay
Shoot up betwixt the tall trunks, smooth and grey—

Yea, could I see the days before distress
When very longing was but happiness.

   Within our house there was a Breton squire
Well learned, who fail'd not to fan the fire
That evermore unholpen burned in me
Strange lands and things beyond belief to see;
Much lore of many lands this Breton knew;
And for one tale I told, he told me two.
He, counting Asagard a new-told thing,
Yet spoke of gardens ever blossoming
Across the western sea where none grew old,
E'en as the books at Micklegarth had told,
And said moreover that an English knight
Had had the Earthly Paradise in sight,
And heard the songs of those that dwelt therein,
But entered not, being hindered by his sin.
Shortly, so much of this and that he said
That in my heart the sharp barb entered,
And like real life would empty stories seem,
And life from day to day an empty dream.
   Another man there was, a Swabian priest,
Who knew the maladies of man and beast,
And what things helped them; he the stone still sought
Whereby base metal into gold is brought,
And strove to gain the precious draught, whereby
Men live midst mortal men yet never die;
Tales of the Kaiser Redbeard could he tell
Who neither went to Heaven nor yet to Hell,
When from that fight upon the Asian plain
He vanished, but still lives to come again
Men know not how or when; but I listening
Unto this tale thought it a certain thing
That in some hidden vale of Swithiod
Across the golden pavement still he trod.

   But while our longing for such things so grew,
And ever more and more we deemed them true,
Upon the land a pestilence there fell
Unheard-of yet in any chronicle,
And, as the people died full fast of it,
With these two men it chanced me once to sit,
This learned squire whose name was Nicholas,
And Swabian Laurence, as our manner was;
For could we help it scarcely did we part
From dawn to dusk: so heavy, sad at heart,
We from the castle yard beheld the bay
Upon that ne'er-to-be-forgotten day;
Little we said amidst that dreary mood
And certes nought that we could say was good.
   It was a bright September afternoon,

The parched-up beech trees would be yellowing soon;
The yellow flowers grown deeper with the sun
Were letting fall their petals one by one;
No wind there was, a haze was gathering o'er
The furthest bound of the faint yellow shore;
And in the oily waters of the bay
Scarce moving aught some fisher-cobles lay,
And all seemed peace; and had been peace indeed
But that we young men of our life had need,
And to our listening ears a sound was borne
That made the sunlight wretched and forlorn—
The heavy tolling of the minster bell—
And nigher yet a tinkling sound did tell
That through the streets they bore our Saviour Christ
By dying lips in anguish to be kissed.

　At last spoke Nicholas, "How long shall we
Abide here, looking forth into the sea
Expecting when our turn shall come to die?
Fair fellows, will ye come with me and try
Now at our worst that long desired quest,
Now—when our worst is death, and life our best."
　"Nay, but thou know'st," I said, "that I but wait
The coming of some man, the turn of fate,
To make this voyage—but I die meanwhile
For I am poor, though my blood be not vile,
Nor yet for all his lore doth Laurence hold
Within his crucibles aught like to gold;
And what hast thou, whose father driven forth
By Charles of Blois, found shelter in the North?
But little riches as I needs must deem."
　"Well," said he, "things are better than they seem,
For 'neath my bed an iron chest I have
That holdeth things I have made shift to save
E'en for this end; moreover, hark to this,
In the next firth a fair long ship there is
Well victualled, ready even now for sea,
And I may say it 'longeth unto me;
Since Marcus Erling, late its owner, lies
Dead at the end of many miseries,
And little Kirstin, as thou well mayst know,
Would be content throughout the world to go
If I but took her hand, and now still more
Hath heart to leave this poor death-stricken shore.
Therefore my gold shall buy us Bordeaux swords
And Bordeaux wine as we go oceanwards.
　"What say ye, will ye go with me to-night,
Setting your faces to undreamed delight,
Turning your backs unto this troublous hell,
Or is the time too short to say farewell?

"Not so," I said, "rather would I depart
Now while thou speakest, never has my heart
Been set on anything within this land."
   Then said the Swabian, "Let us now take hand
And swear to follow evermore this quest
Till death or life have set our hearts at rest."
   So with joined hands we swore, and Nicholas said,
"To-night, fair friends, be ye apparelled
To leave this land, bring all the arms ye can
And such men as ye trust, my own good man
Guards the small postern looking towards St. Bride,
And good it were ye should not be espied,
Since mayhap freely ye should not go hence,
Thou Rolf in special, for this pestilence
Makes all men hard and cruel, nor are they
Willing that folk should 'scape if they must stay:
Be wise; I bid you for a while farewell,
Leave ye this stronghold when St. Peter's bell
Strikes midnight, all will surely then be still,
And I will bide you at King Tryggve's hill
Outside the city gates."
                    Each went his way
Therewith, and I the remnant of that day
Gained for the quest three men that I deemed true,
And did such other things as I must do,
And still was ever listening for the chime
Half maddened by the lazy lapse of time,
Yea, scarce I thought indeed that I should live
Till the great tower the joyful sound should give
That set us free: and so the hours went past,
Till startled by the echoing clang at last
That told of midnight, armed from head to heel
Down to the open postern did I steal,
Bearing small wealth—this sword that yet hangs here
Worn thin and narrow with so many a year,
My father's axe that from Byzantium,
With some few gems my pouch yet held, had come,
Nought else that shone with silver or with gold.
   But by the postern gate could I behold
Laurence the priest all armed as if for war,
And my three men were standing not right far
From off the town-wall, having some small store
Of arms and furs and raiment: then once more
I turned, and saw the autumn moonlight fall
Upon the new-built bastions of the wall,
Strange with black shadow and grey flood of light,
And further off I saw the lead shine bright
On tower and turret-roof against the sky,
And looking down I saw the old town lie
Black in the shade of the o'er-hanging hill,
Stricken with death, and dreary, but all still

Until it reached the water of the bay,
That in the dead night smote against the quay
Not all unheard, though there was little wind.
But as I turned to leave the place behind,
The wind's light sound, the slowly falling swell,
Were hushed at once by that shrill-tinkling bell,
That in that stillness jarring on mine ears,
With sudden jangle checked the rising tears,
And now the freshness of the open sea
Seemed ease and joy and very life to me.
  So greeting my new mates with little sound,
We made good haste to reach King Tryggve's mound,
And there the Breton Nicholas beheld.
Who by the hand fair Kirstin Erling held,
And round about them twenty men there stood,
Of whom the more part on the holy rood
Were sworn till death to follow up the quest,
And Kirstin was the mistress of the rest.
  Again betwixt us was there little speech,
But swiftly did we set on toward the beach, .
And coming there our keel, the Fighting Man,
We boarded, and the long oars out we ran,
And swept from out the firth, and sped so well
That scarcely could we hear St. Peter's bell
Toll one, although the light wind blew from land;
Then hoisting sail southward we 'gan to stand,
And much I joyed beneath the moon to see
The lessening land that might have been to me
A kindly giver of wife, child, and friend,
And happy life, or at the worser end
A quiet grave till doomsday rend the earth.

Night passed, day dawned, and we grew full of mirth
As with the ever-rising morning wind
Still further lay our threatened death behind,
Or so we thought: some eighty men we were,
Of whom but fifty knew the shipman's gear,
The rest were uplanders; midst such of these
As knew not of our quest, with promises
Went Nicholas dealing florins round about,
With still a fresh tale for each new man's doubt,
Till all were fairly won or seemed to be
To that strange desperate voyage o'er the sea.

Now if ye ask me from what land I come
With all my folly, Viken is my home
Where Tryggve Olaf's son and Olaf's sire
Lit to the ancient Gods the sacred fire,
Unto whose line am I myself akin,
Through him who Astrid in old time did win,
King Olaf's widow: let all that go by,

Since I was born at least to misery.

  Now Nicholas came to Laurence and to me
To talk of what he deemed our course should be,
To whom agape I listened, since I knew
Nought but old tales, nor aught of false and true
Amid these, for but one kind seemed to be
The Vineland voyage o'er the unknown sea
And Swegder's search for Godheim, when he found
The entrance to a new world underground;
But Nicholas o'er many books had pored
And this and that thing in his mind had stored,
And idle tales from true report he knew.
—Would he were living now, to tell to you
This story that my feeble lips must tell!
  Now he indeed of Vineland knew full well,
Both from my tales where truth perchance touched lies,
And from the ancient written histories;
But now he said, "The land was good enow
That Leif the son of Eric came unto,
But this was not our world, nay scarce could be
The door into a place so heavenly
As that we seek, therefore my rede is this,
That we to gain that sure abode of bliss
Risk dying in an unknown landless sea;
Although full certainly it seems to me
All that we long for there we needs must find.

  "Therefore, O friends, if ye are of my mind,
When we are passed the French and English strait
Let us seek news of that desired gate
To immortality and blessed rest
Within the landless waters of the west,
But still a little to the southward steer.
Certes no Greenland winter waits us there,
No year-long night, but rather we shall find
Spice-trees set waving by the western wind,
And gentle folk who know no guile at least,
And many a bright-winged bird and soft-skinned beast,
For gently must the year upon them fall.

  "Now since the Fighting Man is over small
To hold the mighty stores that we shall need,
To turn as now to Bremen is my rede,
And there to buy a new keel with my gold,
And fill her with such things as she may hold;
And thou thenceforward, Rolf, her lord shalt be,
Since thou art not unskilled upon the sea."

But unto me most fair his saying seemed,
For of a land unknown to all I dreamed,
And certainly by some warm sea I thought
That we the soonest thereto should be brought.

Therefore with mirth enow passed every day
Till in the Weser stream at last we lay
Hearkening the bells of Bremen ring to mass,
For on a Sunday morn our coming was.
   There in a while to chaffer did we fall,
And of the merchants bought a dromond tall
They called the Rose-Garland, and her we stored
With such like victuals as we well might hoard,
And arms and raiment; also there we gained
Some few men more by stories true and feigned,
And by that time, now needing nought at all,
We weighed, well armed, with good hope not to fall
Into the hands of rovers of the sea,
Since at that time had we heard certainly
Edward of England drew all men to him,
And that his fleet held whatso keel could swim
From Jutland to Land's End; for all that, we
Thought it but wise to keep the open sea
And give to warring lands a full wide berth;
Since unto all of us our lives seemed worth
A better purchase than they erst had been.

   So it befell that we no sail had seen
Till the sixth day at morn, when we drew near
The land at last and saw the French coast clear,
The high land over Guines our pilot said.
There at the day-break, we, apparelled
Like merchant ships in seeming, now perforce
Must meet a navy drawing thwart our course,
Whose sails and painted hulls not far away
Rolled slowly o'er the leaden sea and grey,
Beneath the night-clouds by no sun yet cleared;
But we with anxious hearts this navy neared,
For we sailed deep and heavy, and to fly
Would nought avail since we were drawn so nigh,
And fighting, must we meet but certain death.
   Soon with amazement did I hold my breath
As from the wide bows of the Rose-Garland,
I saw the sun, new risen o'er the land,
Light up the shield-hung side of keel on keel,
Their sails like knights' coats, and the points of steel
Glittering from waist and castle and high top.
And well indeed awhile my heart might stop
As heading all the crowded van I saw,
Huge, swelling out without a crease or flaw,
A sail where, on the quartered blue and red,
In silk and gold right well apparelled,
The lilies gleamed, the thin gaunt leopards glared
Out toward the land where even now there flared
The dying beacons. Ah, with such an one
Could I from town to town of France have run

To end my life upon some glorious day
Where stand the banners brighter than the May
Above the deeds of men, as certainly
This king himself has full oft wished to die.
  And who knows now beneath what field he lies,
Amidst what mighty bones of enemies?
Ah, surely it had been a glorious thing
From such a field to lead forth such a king,
That he might live again with happy days,
And more than ever win the people's praise.
Nor had it been an evil lot to stand
On the worse side, with people of the land
'Gainst such a man, when even this might fall,
That it might be my luck some day to call
My battle-cry o'er his low lying head,
And I be evermore remembered.
  Well as we neared and neared, such thoughts I had
Whereby perchance I was the less a-drad
Of what might come, and at the worst we deemed
They would not scorn our swords; but as I dreamed
Of fair towns won and desperate feats of war,
And my old follies now were driven afar
By that most glorious sight, a loud halloo
Came down the wind, and one by me who knew
The English tongue cried that they bade us run
Close up and board, nor was there any one
Who durst say nay to that, so presently
Both keels were underneath the big ship's lee;
While Nicholas and I together passed
Betwixt the crowd of archers by the mast
Unto the poop, where 'neath his canopy
The king sat, eyeing us as we drew nigh.

  Broad-browed he was, hook-nosed, with wide grey eyes
No longer eager for the coming prize,
But keen and steadfast, many an ageing line,
Half hidden by his sweeping beard and fine,
Ploughed his thin cheeks, his hair was more than grey,
And like to one he seemed whose better day
Is over to himself, though foolish fame
Shouts louder year by year his empty name.
Unarmed he was, nor clad upon that morn
Much like a king, an ivory hunting-horn
Was slung about him, rich with gems and gold,
And a great white ger-falcon did he hold
Upon his fist; before his feet there sat
A scrivener making notes of this or that
As the king bade him, and behind his chair
His captains stood in armour rich and fair;
And by his side unhelmed, but armed, stood one
I deemed none other than the prince his son;

For in a coat of England was he clad,
And on his head a coronel he had.
Tall was he, slim, made apt for feats of war,
A splendid lord, yea, he seemed prouder far
Than was his sire, yet his eyes therewithal
With languid careless glance seemed wont to fall
On things about, as though he deemed that nought
Could fail unbidden to do all his thought.
But close by him stood a war-beaten knight,
Whose coat of war bore on a field of white
A sharp red pile, and he of all men there
Methought would be the one that I should fear
If I led men.

       But midst my thoughts I heard
The king's voice as the high seat now we neared,
And knew his speech because in French it was,
That erewhile I had learnt of Nicholas.
"Fair sirs, what are ye? for on this one day,
I rule the narrow seas mine ancient way.
Me seemeth in the highest bark I know
The Flemish handiwork, but yet ye show
Unlike to merchants, though your ships are deep
And slowly through the water do ye creep;
And thou, fair sir, seem'st journeying from the north
With peltries Bordeaux-ward? Nay then go forth
Thou wilt not harm us: yet if ye be men
Well-born and warlike, these are fair days, when
The good heart wins more than the merchant keeps,
And safest still in steel the young head sleeps;
And here are banners thou mayest stand beneath
And not be shamed either in life or death—
What, man, thou reddenest, wouldst thou say me no,
If underneath my banner thou shouldst go?
Nay, thou mayest speak, or let thy fellow say
What he is stuffed with, be it yea or nay."
  For as he spoke my fellow gazed on me
With something like to fear, and hurriedly
As I bent forward, thrust me on one side,
And scarce the king's last word would he abide
But 'gan to say, "Sire, from the north we come,
Though as for me far nigher is my home.
Thy foes, my Lord, drove out my kin and me,
Ere yet thine armed hand was upon the sea;
Chandos shall surely know my father's name,
Loys of Dinan, which ill-luck, sword, and flame,
Lord Charles of Blois, the French king, and the pest
In this and that land now have laid to rest,
Except for me alone. And now, my Lord,
If I shall seem to speak an idle word
To such as thou art, pardon me therefore;

But we, part taught by ancient books and lore,
And part by what, nor yet so long ago,
This man's own countrymen have come to do,
Have gathered hope to find across the sea
A land where we shall gain felicity
Past tongue of man to tell of; and our life
Is not so sweet here, or so free from strife,
Or glorious deeds so common, that, if we
Should think a certain path at last to see
To such a place, men then could think us wise
To turn away therefrom, and shut our eyes,
Because at many a turning here and there
Swift death might lurk, or unaccustomed fear.
O King, I pray thee in this young man's face
Flash not thy banner, nor with thy frank grace
Tear him from life; but go thy way, let us
Find hidden death, or life more glorious
Than thou durst think of, knowing not the gate
Whereby to flee from that all-shadowing fate.
　　"O King, since I could walk a yard or twain,
Or utter anything but cries of pain,
Death was before me; yea, on the first morn
That I remember aught, among the corn
I wandered with my nurse, behind us lay
The walls of Vannes, white in the summer day,
The reapers whistled, the brown maidens sung,
As on the wain the topmost sheaf they hung,
The swallow wheeled above high up in air,
And midst the labour all was sweet and fair;
When on the winding road between the fields
I saw a glittering line of spears and shields,
And pleased therewith called out to some one by
E'en as I could; he scarce for fear could cry
'The French, the French!' and turned and ran his best
Toward the town gates, and we ran with the rest,
I wailing loud who knew not why at all,
But ere we reached the gates my nurse did fall,
I with her, and I wondered much that she
Just as she fell should still lie quietly;
Nor did the coloured feathers that I found
Stuck in her side, as frightened I crawled round,
Tell me the tale, though I was sore afeard
At all the cries and wailing that I heard.
　　"I say, my Lord, that arrow-flight now seems
The first thing rising clear from feeble dreams,
And that was death; and the next thing was death,
For through our house all spoke with bated breath
And wore black clothes, withal they came to me
A little child, and did off hastily
My shoon and hosen, and with that I heard
The sound of doleful singing, and afeard

Forebore to question, when I saw the feet
Of all were bare, like mine, as toward the street
We passed, and joined a crowd in such-like guise
Who through the town sang woeful litanies,
Pressing the stones with feet unused and soft,
And bearing images of saints aloft,
In hope 'gainst hope to save us from the rage
Of that fell pest, that as an unseen cage
Hemmed France about, and me and such as me
They made partakers of their misery.
　"Lo death again, and if the time served now
Full many another picture could I show
Of death and death, and men who ever strive
Through every misery at least to live.
The priest within the minster preaches it,
And brooding o'er it doth the wise man sit
Letting life's joys go by. Well, blame me then,
If I who love this changing life of men,
And every minute of whose life were bliss
Too great to long for greater, but for this—
Mock me, who take this death-bound life in hand
And risk the rag to find a happy land,
Where at the worst death is so far away
No man need think of him from day to day—
Mock me, but let us go, for I am fain
Our restless road, the landless sea, to gain."
　His words nigh made me weep, but while he spoke
I noted how a mocking smile just broke
The thin line of the Prince's lips, and he
Who carried the afore-named armoury
Puffed out his wind-beat cheeks and whistled low:
But the king smiled, and said, "Can it be so?
I know not, and ye twain are such as find
The things whereto old kings must needs be blind.
For you the world is wide—but not for me,
Who once had dreams of one great victory
Wherein that world lay vanquished by my throne,
And now, the victor in so many an one,
Find that in Asia Alexander died
And will not live again; the world is wide
For you I say,—for me a narrow space
Betwixt the four walls of a fighting place.
　"Poor man, why should I stay thee; live thy fill,
Of that fair life, wherein thou seest no ill
But fear of that fair rest I hope to win
One day, when I have purged me of my sin.
　"Farewell, it yet may hap that I a king
Shall be remembered but by this one thing,
That on the morn before ye crossed the sea
Ye gave and took in common talk with me;
But with this ring keep memory of the morn,

O Breton, and thou Northman, by this horn
Remember me, who am of Odin's blood,
As heralds say: moreover it were good
Ye had some lines of writing 'neath my seal,
Or ye might find it somewhat hard to deal
With some of mine, who pass not for a word
Whate'er they deem may hold a hostile sword."

   So as we kneeled this royal man to thank,
A clerk brought forth two passes sealed and blank,
And when we had them, with the horn and ring,
With few words did we leave the noble king,
And as adown the gangway steps we passed,
We saw the yards swing creaking round the mast,
And heard the shipman's ho, for one by one
The van outsailed before, by him had run
E'en as he stayed for us, and now indeed
Of his main battle must he take good heed:
But as from off the mighty side we pushed,
And in between us the green water rushed,
I heard his scalds strike up triumphantly
Some song that told not of the weary sea,
But rather of the mead and fair green-wood,
And as we leaned o'er to the wind, I stood
And saw the bright sails leave us, and soon lost
The pensive music by the strong wind tossed
From wave to wave, then turning I espied
Glittering and white upon the weather side
The land he came from, o'er the bright green sea,
Scarce duller than the land upon our lee,
For now the clouds had fled before the sun
And the bright autumn day was well begun.
Then I cried out for music too, and heard
The minstrels sing some well-remembered word,
And while they sung, before me still I gazed,
Silent with thought of many things, and mazed
With many longings; when I looked again
To see those lands, nought but the restless plain
With some far-off small fisher-boat was left;
A little hour for evermore had reft
The sight of Europe from my helpless eyes,
And crowned my store of hapless memories.

THE ELDER OF THE CITY
   Sit friends, and tell your tale which seems to us
Shall be a strange tale and a piteous,
Nor shall it lack our pity for its woe,
Nor ye due thanks for all the things ye show
Of kingdoms nigh forgot that once were great,
And small lands come to glorious estate.
   But, sirs, ye faint, behold these maidens stand

Bearing the blood of this our sunburnt land
In well-wrought cups,—drink now of this, that while
Ye poor folk wandered, had from fortune's smile
Abode your coming, hidden none the less
Below the earth from summer's happiness.

THE WANDERERS
  Fair sirs, we thank you, hoping we have cone
Through many wanderings to a quiet home
Befitting dying men—Good health and peace
To you and to this land, and fair increase
Of everything that ye can wish to have!

  But to my tale: A fair south-east wind drave
Our ships for ten days more, and ever we
Sailed mile for mile together steadily,
But the tenth day I saw the Fighting Man
Brought up to wait me, and when nigh I ran
Her captain hailed me, saying that he thought
That we too far to northward had been brought,
And we must do our southing while we could,
So as his will to me was ever good
In such like things, we changed our course straightway,
And as we might till the eleventh day
Stretched somewhat south, then baffling grew the wind,
But as we still were ignorant and blind
Nor knew our port, we sailed on helplessly
O'er a smooth sea, beneath a lovely sky,
And westward ever, but no signs of land
All through these days we saw on either hand,
Nor indeed hoped to see, because we knew
Some watery desert we must journey through,
That had been huge enough to keep all men
From gaining that we sought for until then.

  Yet when I grew downcast, I did not fail
To call to mind, how from our land set sail
A certain man, and, after he had passed
Through many unknown seas, did reach at last
A rocky island's shore one foggy day,
And while a little off the land he lay
As in a dream he heard the folk call out
In his own tongue, but mazed and all in doubt
He turned therefrom, and afterwards in strife
With winds and waters, much of precious life
He wasted utterly, for when again
He reached his port after long months of pain,
Unto Biarmeland he chanced to go,
And there the isle he left so long ago
He knew at once, where many Northmen were.
  And such a fate I could not choose but fear

For us sometimes; and sometimes when at night
Beneath the moon I watched the foam fly white
From off our bows, and thought how weak and small
Showed the Rose-Garland's mast that looked so tall
Beside the quays of Bremen; when I saw
With measured steps the watch on toward me draw,
And in the moon the helmsman's peering face,
And 'twixt the cordage strained across my place
Beheld the white sail of the Fighting Man
Lead down the pathway of the moonlight wan—
Then when the ocean seemed so measureless
The very sky itself might well be less,
When midst the changeless piping of the wind,
The intertwined slow waves pressed on behind
Rolled o'er our wake and made it nought again,
Then would it seem an ill thing and a vain
To leave the hopeful world that we had known,
When all was o'er, hopeless to die alone
Within this changeless world of waters grey.

But hope would come back to me with the day,
The talk of men, the viol's quivering strings,
Would bring my heart to think of better things.
Nor were our folk down-hearted through all this;
For partly with the hope of that vague bliss
Were they made happy, partly the soft air
And idle days wherethrough we then did fare
Were joy enow to rude sea-faring folk.

But this our ease at last a tempest broke
And we must scud before it helplessly,
Fearing each moment lest some climbing sea
Should topple o'er our poop and end us there,
Nathless we 'scaped, and still the wind blew fair
For what we deemed was our right course; but when
On the third eve, we, as delivered men,
Took breath because the gale was now blown out,
And from our rolling deck we looked about
Over the ridges of the dark grey seas,
And saw the sun, setting in golden ease,
Smile out at last from out the just-cleared sky
Over the ocean's weltering misery,
Still nothing of the Fighting Man we saw,
Which last was seen when the first gusty flaw
Smote them and us; but nothing would avail
To mend the thing, so onward did we sail,
But slowly, through the moonlit night and fair,
With all sails set that we could hoist in air,
And rolling heavily at first, for still
Each wave came on a glittering rippled hill,
And lifting us aloft, showed from its height
The waste of waves, and then to lightless night

Dropped us adown, and much ado had we
To ride unspilt the wallow of the sea.
   But the sun rose up in a cloudless sky,
And from the east the wind blew cheerily,
And southwest still we steered; till on a day
As nigh the mast deep in dull thoughts I lay,
I heard a shout, and turning could I see
One of the shipmen hurrying fast to me
With something in his 1 and, who cast adown
Close to my hand a mass of sea-weed brown
Without more words, then knew I certainly
The wrack, that oft before I had seen lie
In sandy bights of Norway, and that eve
Just as the sun the ridgy sea would leave,
Shore birds we saw, that flew so nigh, we heard
Their hoarse loud voice that seemed a heavenly word.
   Then all were glad, but I a fool and young
Slept not that night, but walked the deck and sung
Snatches of songs, and verily I think
I thought next morn of some fresh stream to drink.
What say I? next morn did I think to be
Set in my godless fair eternity.

   Sirs, ye are old, and ye have seen perchance
Some little child for very gladness dance
Over a scarcely-noticed worthless thing,
Worth more to him than ransom of a king,
Did not a pang of more than pity take
Your heart thereat, not for the youngling's sake,
But for your own, for man that passes by,
So like to God, so like the beasts that die. —
Lo, sirs, my pity for myself is such,
When like an image that my hand can touch
My old self grows unto myself grown old.
Sirs, I forget my story is not told.

   Next morn more wrack we saw, more birds, but still
No land as yet either for good or ill,
But with the light increased the favouring breeze,
And smoothly did we mount the ridgy seas.
Then as a-nigh the good ship's stern I stood
Gazing adown, a piece of rough-hewn wood
On a wave's crest I saw, and loud I cried,
"Drift-wood! drift-wood!" and one from by my side,
Maddened with joy, made for the shrouds, and clomb
Up to the top to look on his new home,
For sure he thought the green earth soon to see;
But gazing thence about him, presently
He shouted out, "a sail astern, a sail!"
Freshening the hope that now had 'gun to fail
Of seeing our fellows with the earth new found;

Wherefore we shortened sail, and sweeping round
The hazy edges of the sea and sky
Soon from the deck could see that sail draw nigh,
Half fearful lest she yet might chance to be
The floating house of some strange enemy,
Till on her sail we could at last behold
The ruddy lion with the axe of gold,
And Marcus Erling's sign set corner-wise,
The green, gold-fruited tree of Paradise.
Ah, what a meeting as she drew anigh,
Greeted with ringing shouts and minstrelsy;
Alas, the joyful fever of that day,
When all we met still told of land that lay
Not far ahead! Yet at our joyous feast
A word of warning spoke the Swabian priest
To me and Nicholas, for, "O friends," he said,
"Right welcome is the land that lies ahead
To us who cannot turn, and in this air,
Washed by this sea, it cannot but be fair,
And good for us poor men I make no doubt;
Yet, fellows, must I warn you not to shout
Ere we have left the troublous wood behind
Wherein we wander desperate and blind:
Think what may dwell there! Call to mind the tale
We heard last winter o'er the Yule-tide ale,
When that small, withered, black-eyed Genoese
Told of the island in the outer seas
He and his fellows reached upon a tide,
And how, as lying by a streamlet's side,
With ripe fruits ready unto every hand,
They lacked not for fair women of the land,
The devils came and slew them, all but him,
Who, how he scarce knew, made a shift to swim
Off to his ship: nor must ye, fellows, fear
Such things alone, for mayhap men dwell here
Who worship dreadful gods, and sacrifice
Poor travellers to them in such horrid wise
As I have heard of; or let this go by,
Yet we may chance to come to slavery,
Or all our strength and weapons be too poor
To conquer such beasts as the unknown shore
May breed; or set all these ill things aside,
It yet may be our lot to wander wide
Through many lands before at last we come
Unto the gates of our enduring home."

But what availed such warning unto us
Who by this change made nigh delirious
Spake wisdom outward from the teeth, but thought
That in a little hour we should be brought
Unto that bliss our hearts were set upon,

That more than very Heaven we now had won.

    Well, the next morn unto our land we came,
And even now my cheeks grow red with shame,
To think what words I said to Nicholas,
(Since on that night in the great ship I was,)
Asking him questions, as if he were God,
Or at the least in that fair land had trod,
And knew it well, and still he answered me
As some great doctor in theology
Might his poor scholar, asking him of heaven.
    But unto me next morn the grace was given
To see land first, and when men certainly
That blessed sight of all sights could descry,
All hearts were melted, and with happy tears,
Born of the death of all our doubts and fears,
Yea, with loud weeping, each did each embrace
For joy that we had gained the glorious place.
Then must the minstrels sing, then must they play
Some joyous strain to welcome in the day,
But for hot tears could see nor bow nor string,
Nor for the rising sobs make shift to sing;
Yea, some of us in that first ecstasy
For joy of 'scaping death went near to die.
    Then might be seen how hard is this world's lot
When such a marvel was our grief forgot,
And what a thing the world's joy is to bear,
When on our hearts the broken bonds of care
Had left such scars, no man of us could say
The burning words upon his lips that lay;
Since, trained to hide the depths of misery,
Amidst that joy no more our tongues were free.
Ah, then it was indeed when first I knew,
When all our wildest dreams seemed coming true,
And we had reached the gates of Paradise
And endless bliss, at what unmeasured price
Man sets his life, and drawing happy breath,
I shuddered at the once familiar death.
    Alas, the happy day! the foolish day!
Alas, the sweet time, too soon passed away!

    Well, in a while I gained the Rose Garland,
And as toward shore we steadily did stand
With all sail set, the wind, which had been light,
Since the beginning of the just past night,
Failed utterly, and the sharp ripple slept,
Then toiling hard forward our keels we swept,
Making small way, until night fell again,
And then, although of landing we were fain,
Needs must we wait, but when the sun was set
Then the cool night a light air did beget,

And 'neath the stars slowly we moved along,
And found ourselves within a current strong
At daybreak, and the land beneath our lee.
  There a long line of breakers could we see,
That on a yellow sandy beach did fall,
And then a belt of grass, and then a wall
Of green trees, rising dark against the sky.
Not long we looked, but anchored presently
A furlong from the shore, and then, all armed,
Into the boats the most part of us swarmed,
And pulled with eager hands unto the beach,
But when the seething surf our prow did reach
From off the bows I leapt into the sea
Waist deep, and, wading, was the first to be
Upon that land; then to the flowers I ran,
And cried aloud like to a drunken man
Words without meaning, whereof none took heed,
For all across the yellow beach made speed
To roll among the fair flowers and the grass.
  But when our folly somewhat tempered was,
And we could talk like men, we thought it good
To try if we could pierce the thick black wood,
And see what men might dwell in that new land;
But when we entered it, on either hand
Uprose the trunks, with underwood entwined
Making one thicket, thorny, dense, and blind;
Where with our axes, labouring half the day,
We scarcely made some half a rod of way;
  Therefore, we left that place and tried again,
Yea, many times, but yet was all in vain;
So to the ships we went, when we had been
A long way in our arms, nor yet had seen
A sign of man, but as for living things,
Gay birds with many-coloured crests and wings,
Conies anigh the beach, and while we hacked
Within the wood, grey serpents, yellow-backed,
And monstrous lizards; yea, and one man said
That 'midst the thorns he saw a dragon's head;
And keeping still his eyes on it he felt
For a stout shaft he had within his belt;
But just as he had got it to the string
And drawn his hand aback, the loathly thing
Vanished away, and how he could not tell.

  Now spite of all, little our courage fell,
For this day's work, nay rather, all things seemed
To show that we no foolish dream had dreamed—
The pathless, fearful sea, the land that lay
So strange, so hard to find, so far away,
The lovely summer air, the while we knew
That unto winter now at home it grew,

The flowery shore, the dragon-guarded wood,
So hard to pierce—each one of these made good
The foolish hope that led us from our home,
That we to other misery might come.

  Now next morn when the tide began to flow
We weighed, and somewhat northward did we go
Coasting that land, and every now and then
We went ashore to try the woods again,
But little change we found in them, until
Inland we saw a bare and scarped white hill
Rise o'er their tops, and going further on
Until a broad green river's mouth we won,
And entering there ran up it with the flood,
For it was deep although 'twixt walls of wood
Darkly enough its shaded stream did flow,
And high trees hid the hill we saw just now.
  So as we peered about from side to side
A path upon the right bank we espied
Through the thick wood, and mooring hastily
Our ships unto the trunks of trees thereby,
Laurence and I with sixty men took land
With bow or cutting sword or bill in hand,
And bearing food to last till the third day;
  But with the others there did Nicholas stay
To guard the ships, with whom was Kirstin still,
Who now seemed pining for old things and ill,
Spite of the sea-breeze and the lovely air.
But as for us, we followed up with care
A winding path, looking from left to right
Lest any deadly thing should come in sight;
And certainly our path a dragon crossed
That in the thicket presently we lost;
And some men said a leopard they espied,.
And further on we heard a beast that cried;
Serpents we saw, like those we erst had seen,,
And many-coloured birds, and lizards green,
And apes that chattered from amidst the trees..
  So on we went until a dying breeze
We felt upon our faces, and soon grew
The forest thinner, till at last we knew .
The great scarped hill, which if we now could scale
The sight of much far country would avail;
But coming there we climbed it easily,
For though escarped and rough toward the sea,
The beaten path we followed led us round
To where a soft and grassy slope we found,
And there it forked, one arm led up the hill
Another through the forest wound on still;
Which last we left, in good hope soon to see
Some signs of man, which happened presently;

For two-thirds up the hill we reached a space
Levelled by man's hand in the mountain's face,
And there a rude shrine stood, of unhewn stones
Both walls and roof, with a great heap of bones
Piled up outside it: there awhile we stood
In doubt, for something there made cold our blood,
Till brother Laurence, with a whispered word,
Crossed himself thrice, and drawing forth his sword
Entered alone, but therewith presently
From the inside called out aloud to me
To follow, so I trembling, yet went in
To that abode of unknown monstrous sin,
And others followed: therein could we see,
Amidst the gloom by peering steadily,
An altar of rough stones, and over it
We saw a god of yellow metal sit,
A cubit long, which Laurence with his tongue
Had touched and found pure gold; withal there hung
Against the wall men's bodies brown and dry,
Which gaudy rags of raiment wretchedly
Did wrap about, and all their heads were wreathed
With golden chaplets; and meanwhile we breathed
A heavy, faint, and sweet spice-laden air,
As though that incense late were scattered there.
    But from that house of devils soon we passed
Trembling and pale, Laurence the priest, the last,
And got away in haste, nor durst we take
Those golden chaplets for their wearers' sake,
Or that grim golden devil whose they were;
Yet for the rest, although they brought us fear
They did but seem to show our heaven anigh
Because we deemed these might have come to die
In seeking it, being slain for fatal sin.
    And now we set ourselves in haste to win
Up to that mountain's top, and on the way
Looked backward oft upon the land that lay
Beneath the hill, and still on every hand
The forest seemed to cover all the land,
But that some four leagues off we saw a space
Cleared of the trees, and in that open place
Houses we seemed to see, and rising smoke
That told where dwelt the unknown, unseen folk.
    But when at last the utmost top we won
A dismal sight our eyes must look upon;
The mountain's summit, levelled by man's art,
Was hedged by high stones set some yard apart
All round a smooth paved space, and midst of these
We saw a group of well-wrought images,
Or so they seemed at first, who stood around
An old hoar man laid on the rocky ground
Who seemed to live as yet; now drawing near

We saw indeed what things these figures were;
Dead corpses, by some deft embalmer dried,
And on this mountain after they had died
Set up like players on a yule-tide feast;
Here stood a hunter, with a spotted beast
Most like a leopard, writhing up his spear;
Nigh the old man stood one as if drawn near
To give him drink, and on each side his head
Two damsels daintily apparelled;
And then again, nigh him who bore the cup,
Were two who 'twixt them bore a litter up
As though upon a journey he should go,
And round about stood men with spear and bow,
And painted targets as the guard to all,
Headed by one beyond man's stature tall,
Who, half turned round, as though he gave the word;
Seemed as he once had been a mighty lord.
   But the live man amid the corpses laid,
Turning from side to side, some faint word said
Now and again, but kept his eyes shut fast,
And we when from the green slope we had passed
On to this dreadful stage, awe-struck and scared,
Awhile upon the ghastly puppets stared,
Then trembling, with drawn swords, came close anigh
To where the hapless ancient man did lie,
Who at the noise we made now oped his eyes
And fixing them upon us did uprise,
And with a fearful scream stretched out his hand,
While upright on his head his hair did stand
For very terror, while we none the less
Were rooted to the ground for fearfulness,
And scarce our weapons could make shift to hold.
But as we stood and gazed, over he rolled
Like a death-stricken bull, and there he lay,
With his long-hoarded life quite past away.
   Then in our hearts did wonder conquer fear,
And to the dead men did we draw anear
And found them such-like things as I have said,
But he, their master, was apparelled
Like to those others that we saw e'en now
Hung up within the dreary house below.

   Right little courage had we there to stay,
So down the hill again we took our way,
When looking landward thence we had but seen,
All round about, the forest dull and green,
Pierced by the river where our ships we left,
And bounded by far-off blue mountains, cleft
By passes here and there; but we went by
The chapel of the gold god silently,
For doubts had risen in our hearts at last

If yet the bitterness of death were past.
  But having come again into the wood,
We there took council whether it were good
To turn back to the ships, or push on still
Till we had reached the place that from the hill
We had beheld, and since the last seemed best
Onward we marched, scarce staying to take rest
And eat some food, for feverish did we grow
For haste the best or worst of all to know.
  Along the path that, as I said before,
Led from the hill, we went, and laboured sore
To gain the open ere the night should fall,
But yet in vain, for like a dreary pall
Cast o'er the world, the darkness hemmed us in,
And though we struggled desperately to win
From out the forest through the very night,
Yet did that labour so abate our might,
We thought it good to rest among the trees,
Nor come on those who might be enemies
In the thick darkness, neither did we dare
To light a fire lest folk should slay us there
Mazed and defenceless; so the one half slept
As they might do, the while the others kept
Good guard in turn; and as we watched we heard
Sounds that might well have made bold men afeard,
And cowards die of fear, but we, alone,
Apart from all, such desperate men were grown,
If we should fail to win our Paradise,
That common life we now might well despise.
  So by the day-break on our way we were
When we had seen to all our fighting gear;
And soon we came unto that open space,
And here and there about a grassy place
Saw houses scattered, neither great nor fair,
For they were framed of trees as they grew there,
And walled with wattle-work from tree to tree;
And thereabout beasts unknown did we see,
Four-footed, tame; and soon a man came out
From the first house, and with a startled shout
Took to his heels, and soon from far and near,
The folk swarmed out, and still as in great fear
Gave us no second look, but ran their best,
And they being clad but lightly for the rest,
To follow them seemed little mastery. .
So to their houses gat we speedily
To see if we might take some loiterer;
And some few feeble folk we did find there,
Though most had fled, and unto these with pain
We made some little of our meaning plain,
And sent an old man forth into the wood
To show his fellows that our will was good.

Who going from us came back presently
His message done, and with him two or three
The boldest of his folk, and they in turn
A little of us by our signs did learn,
Then went their way: and so at last all fear
Was laid aside, and thronging they drew near
To look upon us; and at last came one
Who had upon his breast a golden sun,
And in strange glittering gay attire was clad;
He let us know our coming made him glad,
And bade us come with him; so thereon we,
Thinking him some one in authority,
Rose up and followed him, who with glad face
Led us through closer streets of that strange place,
And brought us lastly to a shapely hall
Round and high-roofed, held up with tree trunks tall,
And midst his lords the barbarous king sat there.
Gold-crowned, in strange apparel rich and fair,
Whereat we shuddered, for we saw that he
Was clad like him that erewhile we did see
Upon the hill, and like those other ones
Hung in the dismal shrine of unhewn stones.

   Yet nought of evil did he seem to think,
But bade us sit by him and eat and drink,
So eating did we speak by signs meanwhile
Each unto each, and they would laugh and smile
As folk well-pleased; and with them all that day
Well feasted, learning some things did we stay.
And sure of all the folk I ever saw
These were the gentlest: if they had a law
We knew not then, but still they seemed to be
Like the gold people of antiquity.

   Now when we tried to ask for that good land,
Eastward and seaward did they point the hand;
Yet if they knew what thing we meant thereby
We knew not; but when we for our reply
Said that we came thence, they made signs to say
They knew it well, and kneeling down they lay
Before our feet, as people worshipping.

   But we, though somewhat troubled at this thing,
Failed not to hope, because it seemed to us
That this so simple folk and virtuous,
So happy midst their dreary forest bowers,
Showed at the least a better land than ours,
And some yet better thing far onward lay.

   Amidst all this we made a shift to pray
That some of them would go with us, to be
Our fellows on the perilous green sea,
And much did they rejoice when this they knew,
And straightway midst their young men lots they drew,
And the next morn of these they gave us ten,

And wept at our departing.

                  Now these men,
Though brown indeed through dint of that hot sun,
Were comely and well-knit, as any one
I saw in Greece, and fit for deeds of war,
Though as I said of all men gentlest far;
Their arms were axe and spear, and shield and bow,
But nought of iron did they seem to know,
For all their cutting tools were edged with flint,
Or with soft copper, that soon turned and bent;
With cloths of cotton were their bodies clad,
But other raiment for delight they had
Most fairly woven of some unknown thing;
And all of them from little child to king
Had many ornaments of beaten gold:
Certes, we might have gathered wealth untold
Amongst them, had that then been in our thought,
But none the glittering evil valued aught.
   Now of these foresters, we learned, that they
Hemmed by the woods, went seldom a long way
From where we saw them, and no boat they had,
Or much of other people good or bad
They knew, and ever had they little war:
But now and then a folk would come from far
In ships unlike to ours, and for their gold
Would give them goods; and some men over bold
Who dwelt beyond the great hill we had seen,
Had waged them war, but these all slain had been
Among the tangled woods by men who knew
What tracks of beasts the thicket might pierce through.
   Such things they told us whom we brought away,
But after this, for certes on that day
Not much we gathered of their way of life.
   So to the ships we came at last, and rife
With many things new learned, we told them all,
And though our courage might begin to fall
A little now, yet each to other we
Made countenance of great felicity,
And spoke as if the prize were well-nigh won.

   Behold then, sirs, how fortune led us on,
Little by little till we reached the worst,
And still our lives grew more and more accurst.

THE ELDER OF THE CITY.
   Nay, friends, believe your worser life now past,
And that a little bliss is reached at last;
Take heart, therefore, for like a tale so told
Is each man's life: and ye, who have been bold
To see and suffer such unheard-of things,

Henceforth shall be more worshipped than the kings
We hear you name; then since ye reach this day
How are ye worse for what has passed away?

THE WANDERER.
   Kind folk, what words of ours can give you praise
That fits your kindness; yet for those past days,
If we bemoan our lot, think this at least:
We are as men, who cast aside a feast
Amidst their lowly fellows, that they may
Eat with the king, and who at end of day, .
Bearing sore stripes, with great humility
Must pray the bedesmen of those men to be
They scorned that day while yet the sun was high.

   Not long within the river did we lie,
But put to sea intending as before
To coast with watchful eyes the unknown shore,
And strive to pierce the woods: three days we sailed,
And little all our watchfulness availed,
Though all that time the wind was fair enow;
But on the fourth day it began to blow
From off the land, and still increased on us
Until the storm grown wild and furious,
Although at anchor still we strove to ride,
Had blown us out into the ocean wide,
Far out of sight of land; and when at last,
After three days, its fury was o'erpast,
Of all our counsels this one was the best
To beat back blindly to the longed-for west;
Baffling the wind was, toilsome was the way,
Nor did we make land till the thirtieth day,
When both flesh-meat and water were nigh spent,
But anchoring at last, ashore we went,
And found the land far better than the first.
For this with no thick forest was accurst,
Though here and there were scattered clumps of wood.
The air was cooler, too, but soft and good,
Fair streams we saw, and herds of goats and deer,
But nothing noisome for a man to fear.
   So since at anchor safe our good ships lay
Within the long horns of a sandy bay,
We thought it good ashore to take our ease,
And pitched our tents anigh some maple-trees
Not far from shore, and there with little pain
Enough of venison quickly did we gain
To feast us all, and high feast did we hold
Lighting great fires, for now the nights were cold,
And we were fain a noble roast to eat;
Nor did we lack for drink to better meat,
For from the dark hold of the Rose Garland

A well-hooped cask our shipmen brought aland,
That knew some white-walled city of the Rhine.
   There crowned with flowers, and flushed with noble wine,
Hearkening the distant murmur of the main,
And safe upon our promised land again,
What wonder if our vain hopes rose once more
And Heaven seemed dull beside that twice-won shore.
   By midnight in our tents were we asleep,
And little watch that night did any keep,
For as our pleasance that fair land we deemed.
But in my sleep of lovely things I dreamed,
For I was back at Micklegarth once more,
But not a court-man's son there as of yore,
But the Greek king, or so I seemed to be,
Set on the throne whose awe and majesty
Gold lions guard; before whose moveless feet
A damsel knelt, praying in words so sweet
For what I know not now, that both mine eyes
Grew full of tears, and I must bid her rise
And sit beside me; step by step she came
Up the gold stair, setting my heart a-flame
With all her beauty, till she reached the throne
And there sat down, but as with her alone
In that vast hall, my hand her hand did seek,
And on my face I felt her balmy cheek,
Throughout my heart there shot a dreadful pang,
And down below us, with a sudden clang
The golden lions rose, and roared aloud,
And in at every door did armed men crowd,
Shouting out death and curses, and I fell
Dreaming indeed that this at last was hell.

   But therewithal I woke, and through the night
Heard shrieks and shouts and clamour as of fight,
And snatching up my axe, unarmed beside
Nor scarce awaked, my rallying cry I cried,
And with good haste unto the hubbub went;
But even in the entry of the tent
Some dark mass hid the star-besprinkled sky,
And whistling past my head a spear did fly,
And striking out I saw a naked man
Fall 'neath my blow, nor heeded him, but ran
Unto the captain's tent, for there indeed
I saw my fellows stand at desperate need,
Beset with foes, nor yet armed more than I,
Though on the way I rallied hastily
Some better armed, with whom I straightway fell
Upon the foe, who with a hideous yell
Turned round upon us; but we desperate
And fresh, and dangerous for our axes' weight,
Fought so that they must needs give back a pace

And yield our fellows some small breathing space;
Then gathering all together, side by side
We laid our weapons, and our cries we cried
And rushed upon them, who abode no more
Our levelled points, but scattering from the shore
Ran here and there, but when some two or three
We in the chase had slain right easily,
We held our hands, nor followed more their flight,
Fearing the many chances of the night.
   Then did we light our watch-fires up again
And armed us all, and found three good men slain;
Ten wounded, among whom was Nicholas,
Though little heedful of these things he was,
For in his tent he sat upon the ground,
Holding fair Kirstin's hand, whom he had found
Dead, with a feathered javelin in her breast.
   But taking counsel now, we thought it best
To gather up our goods and get away
Unto the ships, and there to wait the day;
Nor did we loiter, fearful lest the foe,
Who somewhat now our feebleness must know,
Should come on us with force made manifold,
And all our story quickly should be told.
So to our boats in haste the others gat,
But in his tent, not speaking, Nicholas sat,
Nor moved when o'er his head we struck the tent..
But when all things were ready, then I went
And raised the body up, and silently
Walked with it down the beach unto the sea;
Then he arose and followed me, and when
He reached at last the now embarking men,
And in a boat my burden I had laid,
He sat beside; but no word had he said
Since first he knew her slain. Such ending had
The night at whose beginning all were glad.

   One wounded man of theirs we brought with us
Hoping for news, but he grew furious
When he awoke aboard from out his swoon,
And tore his wounds, and smote himself, and soon.
Died outright, though his hurts were slight enow,
So nought from him of that land could we know.
But now as we that luckless country scanned,
Just at the daybreak did we see a band
Of these barbarians come with shout and yell
Across the place where all these things befell,
Down to the very edges of the sea;
But though armed now, by day, we easily
Had made a shift no few of them to slay,
It seemed to us the better course to weigh
And try another entry to that land;

So southward with a light wind did we stand,
Not losing sight of shore, and now and then
I led ashore the more part of our men
Well armed, by daylight, and the barbarous folk
Once and again from bushments on us broke,
Whom without loss of men we brushed away.
But in our turn it happed to us one day
Upon a knot of them unwares to come,
These we bore back with us, the most of whom
Would neither eat nor drink, but sullenly
Sat in a corner of the ship to die;
But 'mongst them was a woman, who at last,
Won by the glitter of some toy we cast
About her neck, by soft words and by wine,
Began to answer us by sign to sign;
Of whom we learned not much indeed, but when
We set on shore those tameless savage men,
And would have left her too, she seemed to pray,
For terror of her folk, with us to stay:
Therefore we took her back with us, and she,
Though learning not our tongue too easily,
Unto the forest-folk began to speak.

   Now midst all this passed many a weary week,
And we no nigher all the time had come
Unto the portal of our blissful home,
And needs our bright hope somewhat must decay;
Yet none the less as dull day passed by day,
Still onward by our folly were we led,
And still with lies our wavering hearts we fed.
   Happy we were in this, that still the wind
Blew as we wished, and still the air was kind;
Nor failed we of fresh water as we went
Along the coast, and oft our bows we bent
On beast and fowl, and had no lack of food.
   Upon a day it chanced, that as we stood
Somewhat off shore to fetch about a ness,
Although the wind was blowing less and less,
We were entrapped into a fearful sea,
And carried by a current furiously
Away from shore, and there were we so tost
That for awhile we deemed ourselves but lost
Amid those tumbling waves; but now at last,
When out of sight of land we long had passed,
The sea fell, and again toward land we stood,
Which, reached upon the tenth day, seemed right good,
But still untilled, and mountains rose up high
Far inland, mingling with the cloudy sky.
   Once more we took the land, and since we found
That, more than ever, beasts did there abound,
We pitched our camp beside a little stream,

But scarcely there of Paradise did dream
As heretofore. Our camp we fortified
With wall and dyke, and then the land we tried,
And found the people most untaught and wild,
Nigh void of arts, but harmless, good, and mild,
Nor fearing us: with some of these we went
Back to our camp and people, with intent
To question them, by her we last had got.
But when she heard their tongue she knew it not,
Nor did those others: but they seemed to say,
That o'er the mountains other lands there lay
Where folk dwelt, clothed and armed like unto us,
But made withal as they were timorous
And feared them much. Then we made signs that we,
So little feared by all that tumbling sea,
Would go to seek them; but they still would stay
Our journey; nathless what they meant to say
We scarce knew yet: howbeit, since these men
Were friendly, and the weather, which till then
Had been most fair, now grew to storm and rain,
And the wind blew on land, and not in vain
To us poor fools, that tale, half understood
Those folk had told: midst all, we thought it good
To haul our ships ashore, and build us there
A place where we might dwell, till we could fare
Along the coast, or inland it might be,
That fertile realm, those goodly men to see.
    Right foul the weather was a dreary space
While we abode with people of that place,
And built them huts, as well we could, for we
Who dwell in Norway have great mastery
In woodwright's craft; but they in turn would bring
Wild fruits to us, and many a woodland thing,
And catch us fish, and show us how to take
The smaller beasts, and meanwhile for our sake
They learned our tongue, and we too somewhat learned
Of words of theirs; but day by day we yearned
To cross those mountains, and I woke no morn,
To find myself lost, wretched, and forlorn,
But those far-off white summits gave me heart;
Now too those folk their story could impart
Concerning them, and that in short was this—
Beyond them lay a fair abode of bliss
Where dwelt men like the Gods, and clad as we,
Who doubtless lived on through eternity
Unless the very world should come to nought;
But never had they had the impious thought
To scale those mountains, since most surely, none
Could follow over them the fearful sun
And live, of men they knew; but as for us
They said, who were so wise and glorious

It might not be so.

Thus they spoke one eve
When the black rain-clouds for a while did leave
Upon the fresh and teeming earth to frown,
And we they spoke to, had just set us down
Midmost their village: from the resting earth
Sweet odours rose, and in their noisy mirth
The women played, as rising from the brook
Off their long locks the glittering drops they shook;
Betwixt the huts the children raced along;
Some man was singing a wild barbarous song
Anigh us, and these folk possessing nought,
And lacking nought, lived happy, free from thought,
Or so it seemed—but we, what thing could pay
For all that we had left so far away?
  Such thoughts as these I uttered murmuringly,
But lifting up mine eyes, against the sky
Beheld the snowy peaks brought near to us
By a strange sunset, red and glorious,
That seemed as through the much-praised land it lit,
And would do, long hours after we must sit
Beneath the twinkling stars with none to heed:
And though I knew it was not so indeed,
Yet did it seem to answer me, as though
It called us once more on our quest to go.
  Then springing up I raised my voice and said,—
"What is it fellows, fear ye to be dead
Upon those peaks, when, if ye loiter here
Half dead, with very death still drawing near,
Your lives are wasted all the more for this,
That ye in this world thought to garner bliss;
Unless indeed ye chance to think it well
With this unclad and barbarous folk to dwell,
Deedless and hopeless; ye, to whom the land,
That o'er the world has sent so many a band
Of conquering men, was not yet good enough.
  "Did ye then deem the way would not be rough
Unto the lovely land ye so desire?
Did ye not rather swear through blood and fire,
And all ill things to follow up this quest
Till life or death your longing laid to rest?
  "Let us not linger here then, until fate
Make longing unavailing, hope too late,
And turn to lamentations all our prayers,
But with to-morrow cast aside your cares,
And stout of heart make ready for the strife
'Twixt this short time of dreaming and real life.
  "Lo now, if but the half will come with me,
The summit of those mountains will I see,
Or, else die first, yea, if but twenty men

Will follow me; nor will I stay if ten
Will share my trouble or felicity
What do I say? alone, O friends, will I
Seek for my life, for no man can die twice,
And death or life may give me Paradise!"

  Then Nicholas said, "Rolf, I will go with thee,
For desperate do I think the quest to be,
And I shall die, and that to me is well,
Or else I may forget, I cannot tell
Still I will go."
            Then Laurence said, "I too
Will go remembering what I said to you,
When any land, the first to which we came
Seemed that we sought, and set your hearts aflame,
And all seemed won to you: but still I think,
Perchance years hence, the fount of life to drink,
Unless by some ill chance I first am slain,
But boundless risk must pay for boundless gain."
  So most men said, but yet a few there were
Who said, "Nay, soothly let us live on here,
We have been fools and we must pay therefore
With this dull life, and labour very sore
Until we die; yet are we grown too wise
Upon this earth to seek for Paradise;
Leave us, but ye may yet come back again
When ye have found your trouble nought and vain."

  Well, in three days we left those men behind,
To dwell among the simple folk and kind
Who were our guides at first, until that we
Reached the green hills clustered confusedly
About the mountains, then they turned, right glad
That till that time no horrors they had had;
But we still hopeful, making nought of time,
The rugged rocks now set ourselves to climb,
And lonely there for days and days and days
We stumbled through the blind and bitter ways,
Now rising to the never-melting snow,
Now beaten thence, and fain to try below
Another kingdom of that world of stone.
  At last when all our means of life were gone
And some of us had fallen in the fight
With cold and weariness, we came in sight
Of what we hungered for—what then—what then?
A savage land, a land untilled again,
No lack of food while lasted shaft or bow,
But folk the worst of all we came to know;
Scarce like to men, yea, worse than most of beasts,
For of men slain they made their impious feasts;
These, as I deem for our fresh blood athirst

From out the thick wood often on us burst.
Not heeding death, and in confused fight
We spent full many a wretched day and night,
That yet were happiest of the times we knew,
For with our grief such fearful foes we grew,
That Odin's gods had hardly scared men more
As fearless through the naked press we bore.
  At first indeed some prisoners did we take,
Asking them questions for our fair land's sake,
Hoping 'gainst hope; but when in vain had been
Our questioning, and we one day had seen
Their way of banqueting, then axe and spear
Ended the wretched life and sullen fear
Of any wild man wounded in the fight.
  So with the failing of our hoped delight
We grew to be like devils—then I knew
At my own cost, what each man cometh to
When every pleasure from his life is gone,
And hunger and desire of life alone,
That still beget dull rage and bestial fears,
Like gnawing serpents through the world he bears.
  What time we spent there? nay, I do not know:
For happy folk no time can pass too slow
Because they die; because at last they die
And are at rest, no time too fast can fly
For wretches; but eternity of woe
Had hemmed us in, and neither fast or slow
Passed the dull time as we held reckoning.
  Yet midst so many a wretched, hopeless thing
One hope there was, if it was still a hope,
At last, at last, to turn, and scale the cope
Of those dread mountains we had clambered o'er.
And we did turn, and with what labour sore,
What thirst, what hunger, and what wretchedness
We struggled daily, how can words express?
Yet amidst all, the kind God led us on
Until at last a high raised pass we won
And like grey clouds afar beheld the sea,
And weakened with our toil and misery
Wept at that sight, that like a friend did seem
Forgotten long, beheld but in a dream
When we know not if he be still alive.
  But thence descending, we with rocks did strive,
Till dwindled, weary, did we reach the plain
And came unto our untaught friends again,
And those we left, who yet alive and well,
Wedded to brown wives, fain would have us tell
The story of our woes, which when they heard,
The country people wondered at our word,
But not our fellows; and so all being said
A little there we gathered lustihead

Still talking over what was best to do.
And we the leaders yet were fain to go
From sea to sea and take what God might send,
Who at the worst our hopes and griefs would end
With that same death we once had hoped to stay,
Or even yet might send us such a day,
That our past troubles should but make us glad
As men rejoice in pensive songs and sad.

  This was our counsel; those that we had left
Said, that they once before had been bereft
Of friends and country by a sick man's dream,
That this their life not evil did they deem
Nor would they rashly cast it down the wind;
But whoso went, that they would stay behind.

  Others there were who said, whate'er might come
They would at least seek for the happy home
They had forgotten once, and there at last
In penitence for sins and follies past
Wait for the death that they in vain had fled.

  Well, when all things by all sides had been said
We drew the ships again unto the sea,
Which those who went not with us, carefully
Had tended for those years we were away
(Which still they said was ten months and a day);
And these we rigged, and in a little while
The Fighting Man looked o'er the false sea's smile
Unto the land of Norway, and our band
Across the bulwarks of the Rose Garland,
Amidst of tears and doubt and misery
Sent after them a feeble farewell cry,
And they returned a tremulous faint cheer,
While from the sandy shell-strewn beach anear
The soft west wind across the waves bore out
A strange confused noise of wail and shout,
For there the dark line of the outland folk
A few familiar grey-eyed faces broke,
That minded us of Norway left astern,
Ere we began our heavy task to learn.

THE ELDER OF THE CITY
  Sirs, by my deeming had ye still gone on
When ye had crossed the mountains, ye had won
Unto another sea at last, and there
Had found clad folk, and cities great and fair
Though not the deathless country of your thought.

THE WANDERER
  Yea, sirs, and short of that we had deemed nought,
Ere yet our hope of life had fully died,
And for those cities scarce should we have tried,

E'en had we known of them, and certainly
Nought but those bestial people did we see:
But let me hasten now unto the end.

  Fair wind and lovely weather God did send
To us deserted men, who but two score
Now mustered, so we stood off from the shore
Still stretching south till we lost land again,
Because we deemed our labour would be vain
Upon the land too near where we had been,
Where nine of us as yet a sign had seen
Of that which we desired. And now we few,
Thus left alone, each unto other grew
The dearer friends, and less accursed we seemed
As still the less of 'scaping death we dreamed,
And knew the lot of all men should be ours,
A chequered day of sunshine and of showers
Fading to twilight and dark night at last.
  Those forest folk with ours their lot had cast,
And ever unto us were leal and true,
And now when all our tongue at last they knew
They told us tales, too long to tell as now;
Yet this one thing I fain to you would show
About the dying man our sight did kill
Amidst the corpses on that dreary hill:
Namely, that when their king drew nigh to death,
But still had left in him some little breath,
They bore him to that hill, when they had slain,
By a wild root that killed with little pain,
His servants and his wives like as we saw,
Thinking that thence the gods his soul would draw
To heaven; but the king being dead at last,
The servants dead being taken down, they cast
Into the river, but the king they hung
I Embalmed within that chapel, where they sung
Some office over him in solemn wise,
Amidst the smoke of plenteous sacrifice.

  Well, though wild hope no longer in us burned,
Unto the land within a while we turned,
And found it much the same, and still untilled,
And still its people of all arts unskilled;
And some were dangerous and some were kind;
But midst them no more tidings did we find
Of what we once had deemed well-won, but now
Was like the dream of some past kingly show.
  What shall I say of all these savages,
Of these wide plains beset with unsown trees,
Through which untamed man-fearing beasts did range?
To us at least there seemed but little change,
For we were growing weary of the world.

Whiles did we dwell ashore, whiles were we hurled
Out to the landless ocean, whiles we lay
Long time within some river or deep bay;
And so the months went by, until at last,
When now three years were fully overpast
Since we had left our fellows, and grown old
Our leaky ship along the water rolled,
Upon a day unto a land we came
Whose people spoke a tongue well-nigh the same
As that our forest people used, and who
A little of the arts of mankind knew,
And tilled the kind earth, certes not in vain;
For wealth of melons we saw there, and grain
Strange unto us. Now battered as we were,
Grown old before our time, in worn-out gear,
These people, when we first set foot ashore,
Garlands of flowers and fruits unto us bore,
And worshipped us as gods, and for no words
That we could say would cease to call us Lords,
And pray our help to give them bliss and peace,
And fruitful seasons of the earth's increase.
    Withal at last, they, when in talk they fell
With our good forest-folk, to them did tell
That they were subject to a mighty king,
Who, as they said, ruled over everything,
And, dwelling in a glorious city, had
All things that men desire to make them glad.
"He," said they, "none the less shall be but slave
Unto your lords, and all that he may have
Will he but take as free gifts at their hands,
If they will deign henceforth to bless his lands
With their most godlike presence."
                        Ye can think
How we poor wretched souls outworn might shrink
From such strange worship, that like mocking seemed
To us, who of a godlike state had dreamed,
And missed it in such wise; yet none the less
An earthly haven to our wretchedness
This city seemed, therefore we 'gan to pray
That some of them would guide us on our way,
Which words of ours they heard most joyously,
And brought us to their houses nigh the sea,
And feasted us with such things as they might.
    But almost ere the ending of the night
We started on our journey, being up-borne
In litters, like to kings, who so forlorn
Had been erewhile; so in some ten days' space
They brought us nigh their king's abiding place;
And as we went the land seemed fair enough,
Though sometimes did we pass through forests rough,
Deserts and fens, yet for the most, the way

Through ordered villages and tilled land lay,
Which after all the squalid miseries
We had beheld, seemed heaven unto our eyes,
Though strange to us it was.

             But now when we
From a hill-side the city well could see,
Our guides there prayed us to abide awhile,
Wherefore we stayed, though eager to beguile
Our downcast hearts from brooding o'er our woe
By all the new things that abode might show;
So while we bided on that flowery down
The swiftest of them sped on toward the town
To bear them news of this unhoped-for bliss;
And we, who now some little happiness
Could find in that fair place and pleasant air,
Sat 'neath strange trees, on new flowers growing there
Of scent unlike to those we knew of old,
While unfamiliar tales the strange birds told.
But certes seemed that city fair enow
That spread out o'er the well-tilled vale below,
Though nowise built like such as we had seen;
Walled with white walls it was, and gardens green
Were set between the houses everywhere;
And now and then rose up a tower foursquare
Lessening in stage on stage: with many a hue
The house walls glowed, of red and green and blue,
And some with gold were well adorned, and one
From roofs of gold flashed back the noontide sun.
Had we seen such a place not long ago
We should have made great haste to get thereto,
Deeming that it must be the heaven we sought.
  But now while quietly we sat, and thought
Of many things, the gate wherein that road
Had end, was opened wide, and thereout flowed
A glittering throng of people, young and old,
And men and women, much adorned with gold;
Wherefore we rose to meet them, who stood still
When they beheld us winding down the hill,
And lined both sides of the grey road, but we
Now drawing nigh them, first of all could see
Old men in venerable raiment clad,
White bearded, who sweet flowering branches had
In their right hands, then young men armed right well
After their way, which now were long to tell,
Then damsels clad in radiant gold array,
Who with sweet-smelling blossoms strewed the way
Before our feet, then men with gleaming swords
And glittering robes, and crowned like mighty lords,
And last of all; within the very gate
The king himself, round whom our guides did wait,

Kneeling with humble faces downward bent.
   What wonder if, as 'twixt these folk we went,
Hearkening their singing and sweet minstrelsy,
A little nigher seemed our heaven to be—
Alas, a fair folk, a sweet spot of earth,
A land where many a lovely thing has birth,
But where all fair things come at last to die.
   Now when we three unto the king drew nigh
Before our fellows, he, adored of all,
Spared not before us on his knees to fall,
And as we deemed who knew his speech but ill,
Began to pray us to bide with him still,
Speaking withal of some old prophecy
Which seemed to say that there we should not die.
   What could we do amidst these splendid lords?
No time it was to doubt or make long words,
Nor with a short but happy life at hand
Durst we to ask about the perfect land,
Though well we felt the life whereof he spoke,
Could never be among those mortal folk.
Therefore we way-worn, disappointed men,
So richly dowered with three-score years and ten,
Vouchsafed to grant the king his whole request,
Thinking within that town awhile to rest,
And gather news about the hope that fled
Still on before us, risen from the dead,
From out its tomb of toil and misery,
That held it while we saw but sea and sky,
Or untilled lands and people void of bliss,
And our own faces heavy with distress.

   But entering now that town, what huge delight
We had therein, how lovely to our sight
Was the well-ordered life of people there,
Who on that night within a palace fair
Made us a feast with great solemnity,
Till we forgot that we came there to die
If we should leave our quest, for as great kings
They treated us, and whatsoever things
We asked for, or could think of, those were ours.
   Houses we had, noble with walls and towers,
Lovely with gardens, cooled with running streams,
And rich with gold beyond a miser's dreams,
And men and women slaves, whose very lives
Were in our hands; and fair and princely wives
If so we would; and all things for delight,
Good to the taste or beautiful to sight
The land might yield. They taught us of their law,
The muster of their men-at-arms we saw,
As men who owned them; in their judgment-place
Our lightest word made glad the pleader's face,

And the judge trembled at our faintest frown.
  Think then, if we, late driven up and down
Upon the uncertain sea, or struggling sore
With barbarous men upon an untilled shore,
Or at the best, midst people ignorant
Of arts and letters, fighting against want
Of very food—think if we now were glad
From day to day, and as folk crazed and mad
Deemed our old selves, the wanderers on the sea.
  And if at whiles midst our felicity
We yet remembered us of that past day
When in the long swell off the land we lay,
Weeping for joy at our accomplished dream,
And each to each a very god did seem,
For fear was dead—if we remembered this,
Yet after all, was this our life of bliss,
A little thing that we had gained at last?
And must we sorrow for the idle past,
Or think it ill that thither we were led?
Thus seemed our old desire quite quenched and dead.
  You must remember though, that we were young,
Five years had passed since the grey fieldfare sung
To me a dreaming youth laid 'neath the thorn,
And though while we were wandering and forlorn
I seemed grown old and withered suddenly,
But twenty summers had I seen go by
When I left Viken on that desperate cruise.
But now again our wrinkles did we lose
With memory of our ills, and like a dream
Our fevered quest with its bad days did seem,
And many things grew fresh again, forgot
While in our hearts that wild desire was hot:
Yea, though at thought of Norway we might sigh,
Small was the pain which that sweet memory
Brought with its images seen fresh and clear,
And many an old familiar thing grown dear,
We loved but little while we lived with it.

  So smoothly o'er our heads the days did flit,
Yet not eventless either, for we taught
Such lore as we from our own land had brought
Unto this folk, who when they wrote must draw
Such draughts as erst at Micklegarth I saw,
Writ for the evil Pharaoh-kings of old;
Their arms were edged with copper or with gold,
Whereof they had great plenty, or with flint;
No armour had they fit to bear the dint
Of tools like ours, and little could avail
Their archer craft; their boats knew nought of sail,
And many a feat of building could we show,
Which midst their splendour still they did not know.

And midst of all, war fell upon the land,
And in forefront of battle must we stand,
To do our best, though little mastery
We thought it then to make such foemen flee
As there we met; but when again we came
Into the town, with something like to shame
We took the worship of that simple folk
Rejoicing for their freedom from the yoke
That round about their necks had hung so long.

For thus that war began: some monarch strong
Conquered their land of old, and thereon laid
A dreadful tribute, which they still had paid
With tears and curses; for as each fifth year
Came round, this heavy shame they needs must bear:
Ten youths, ten maidens must they choose by lot
Among the fairest that they then had got.
Who a long journey o'er the hills must go
Unto the tyrant, nor with signs of woe
Enter his city, but in bright array,
And harbingered by songs and carols gay,
Betake them to the temple of his god;
But when the streets their weary feet had trod
Their wails must crown the long festivity,
For on the golden altar must they die.

Such was the sentence till the year we came,
And counselled them to put away this shame
If they must die therefore, so on that year
Barren of blood the devil's altars were,
Wherefore a herald clad in strange attire
The tyrant sent them, and but blood and fire
His best words were; him they sent back again
Defied by us, who made his threats but vain,
When face to face with those ill folk we stood
Ready to seal our counsel with our blood.

Past all belief they loved us for all this,
And if it would have added to our bliss
That they should die, this surely they had done;
So smoothly slipped the years past one by one,
And we had lived and died as happy there
As any men the labouring earth may bear,
But for the poison of that wickedness
That led us on God's edicts to redress.
At first indeed death seemed so far away,
So sweet in our new home was every day,
That we forgot death like the most of men
Who cannot count the threescore years and ten;
Yet we grew fearful as the time drew on,
And needs must think of all we might have won,
Yea, by so much the happier that we were
By just so much increased on us our fear,
And those old times of our past misery

Seemed not so evil as the days went by
Faster and faster with the year's increase,
For loss of youth to us was loss of peace.

   Two gates unto the road of life there are,
And to the happy youth both seem afar,
Both seem afar, so far the past one seems,
The gate of birth, made dim with many dreams,
Bright with remembered hopes, beset with flowers;
So far it seems he cannot count the hours
That to this midway path have led him on
Where every joy of life now seemeth won—
So far, he thinks not of the other gate,
Within whose shade the ghosts of dead hopes wait
To call upon him as he draws anear,
Despoiled, alone, and dull with many a fear,
"Where is thy work? how little thou hast done,
Where are my friends, why art thou so alone?"
   How shall he weigh his life? slow goes the time
The while the fresh dew-sprinkled hill we climb,
Thinking of what shall be the other side,
Slow pass perchance the minutes we abide
On the gained summit, blinking at the sun;
But when the downward journey is begun
No more our feet may loiter, past our ears
Shrieks the harsh wind scarce noted midst our fears,
And battling with the hostile things we meet
Till, ere we know it, our weak shrinking feet
Have brought us to the end and all is done.

   And so with us it was, when youth twice won
Now for the second time had passed away,
And we unwitting were grown old and grey,
And one by one, the death of some dear friend,
Some cherished hope, brought to a troublous end
Our joyous life; as in a dawn of June
The lover, dreaming of the brown bird's tune
And longing lips unto his own brought near,
Wakes up the crashing thunder-peal to hear.
So, sirs, when this world's pleasures came to nought
Not upon God we set our wayward thought,
But on the folly our own hearts had made;
Once more the stories of the past we weighed
With what we hitherto had found, once more
We longed to be by some unknown far shore,
Once more our life seemed trivial, poor, and vain,
Till we our lost fool's paradise might gain,
And we were like the felon doomed to die,
Who when unto the sword he draws anigh
Struggles and cries, though erewhile in his cell
He heard the priest of heaven and pardon tell,

Weeping and half-contented to be slain.

   Was I the first who thought of this again?
Perchance I was, but howsoe'er that be
Long time I thought of these things certainly
Ere I durst stir my fellows to the quest,
Though secretly myself, with little rest
For tidings of our lovely land I sought.
Should prisoners from another folk be brought
Unto our town, I questioned them of this;
I asked the wandering merchants of a bliss
They dreamed not of, in chaffering for their goods;
The hunter in the far-off lonely woods,
The fisher in the rivers nigh the sea,
Must tell their wild strange stories unto me.
Within the temples books of records lay
Such as I told of, thereon day by day
I pored, and got long stories from the priests
Of many-handed gods with heads of beasts,
And such like dreariness; and still, midst all
Sometimes a glimmering light would seem to fall
Upon my ignorance, and less content
As time went on I grew, and ever went
About my daily life distractedly,
Until at last I felt that I must die
Or to my fellows tell what in me was.
   So on a day I came to Nicholas
And trembling 'gan to tell of this and that,
And as I spoke with downcast eyes I sat
Fearing to see some scorn within his eyes,
Or horror at unhappy memories;
But now, when mine eyes could no longer keep
The tears from falling, he too, nigh to weep,
Spoke out, "O Rolf; why hast thou come to me,
Who thinking I was happy, now must see
That only with the ending of our breath,
Or by that fair escape from fear and death
Can we forget the hope that erewhile led
Our little band to woe and drearihead?
But now are we grown old, Rolf; and to-day
Life is a little thing to cast away,
Nor can we suffer many years of it
If all goes wrong, so no more will I sit,
Praying for all the things that cannot be:
Tell thou our fellows what thou tellest me,
Nor fear that I will leave you in your need."
   Well, sirs, with all the rest I had such speed
That men enough of us resolved to go
The very bitterness of death to know
Or else to conquer him; some idle tale
With our kind hosts would plenteously avail,

For of our quest we durst not tell them aught,
Since something more than doubt was in our thought,
Though unconfessed, that we should fail at last,
Nor had we quite forgot our perils past.

  Alas! can weak men hide such thoughts as these?
I think the summer wind that bows the trees
Through which the dreamer wandereth muttering
Will bear abroad some knowledge of the thing
That so consumes him; howsoe'er that be,
We, born to drink the dregs of misery,
Found in the end that some one knew our aim.
  For while we weighed the chances of the game
That we must play, nor yet knew what to shun,
Or what to do, there came a certain one,
A young man strange within the place, to me,
Who, swearing me at first to secrecy,
Began to tell me of the hoped-for land.
The trap I saw not, with a shaking hand
And beating heart, unto the notes of years
I turned, long parchments blotted with my tears,
And tremulously read them out aloud;
But still, because the hurrying thoughts would crowd
My whirling brain, scarce heard the words I read.
Yet in the end it seemed that what he said
Tallied with that, heaped up so painfully.
  Now listen! this being done, he said to me,
"O godlike Eastern man, believest thou
That I who look so young and ruddy now
Am very old? because in sooth I come
To seek thee and to lead thee to our home
With all thy fellows. But if thou dost not,
Come now with me, for nigh unto this spot
My brother, left behind, an ancient man
Now dwelleth, but as grey-haired, weak and wan
As I am fresh; of me he doth not know,
So surely shall our speech together show,
The truth of this my message." "Yea," said I,
"I doubt thee not, yet would I certainly
Hear the old man talk if he liveth yet.
That I a clearer tale of this may set
Before my fellows; come then, lead me there."
  Thus easily I fell into the snare;
For as along the well-known streets we went,
An old hoar man there met us, weak and bent,
Who staying us, the while with age he shook,
My lusty fellow by the shoulder took,
And said, "Oh, stranger canst thou be the son,
Or but the younger double of such an one,
Who dwelt once in the weaver's street hereby?"
  But the young man looked on him lovingly,

And said, "O certes, thou art now grown old
That thou thy younger brother canst behold
And call him stranger." "Yea, yea, old enow,"
The other said, "what fables talkest thou?
My brother has but three years less than I,
Nor dealeth time with men so marvellously
That he should seem like twenty, I fourscore:
Thou art my nephew, let the jest pass o'er."

 "Nay," said he, "but it is not good to talk
Here in the crowded street, so let us walk
Unto thine habitation; dost thou mind,
When we were boys, how once we chanced to find
That crock of copper money hid away
Up in the loft, and how on that same day
We bought this toy and that, thou a short sword
And I a brazen boat."

   But at that word
The old man wildly on him 'gan to stare
And said no more, the while we three did fare
Unto his house, but there we being alone,
Many undoubted signs the younger one
Gave to his brother, saying withal, that he
Had gained the land of all felicity,
Where, after trials then too long to tell,
The slough of grisly eld from off him fell,
And left him strong, and fair, and young again;
Neither from that time had he suffered pain
Greater or less, or feared at all to die:
And though, he said, he knew not certainly
If he should live for ever, this he knew
His days should not be full of pain and few
As most men's lives were. Now when asked why he
Had left his home, a deadly land to see,
He said that people's chiefs had sent him there
Moved by report that tall men, white and fair,
Like to the Gods, had come across the sea
Of whom old seers had told that they should be
Lords of that land, therefore his charge was this,
To lead us forth to that abode of bliss,
But secretly, since for the other folk
They were as beasts to toil beneath the yoke,
"But," said he, "brother, thou shalt go with me,
If now at last no doubt be left in thee
Of who I am."

   At that, to end it all
The weak old man upon his neck did fall,
Rejoicing for his lot with many tears:
But I, rejoicing too, yet felt vague fears
Within my heart, for now almost too nigh
We seemed to that long sought felicity.
What should I do though? What could it avail

Unto these men, to make a feigned tale?
Besides in all no faltering could I find,
Nor did they go beyond, or fall behind,
What in such cases such-like men would do,
Therefore I needs must think their story true.
    So now unto my fellows did I go
And all things in due order straight did show,
And had the man who told the tale at hand;
Of whom some made great question of the land,
And where it was, and how he found it first;
And still he answered boldly to the worst
Of all their questions: then from out the place
He went, and we were left there face to face.
    And joy it was to see the dark cheeks, tanned
By many a summer of that fervent land,
Flush up with joy, and see the grey eyes gleam
Through the dull film of years, as that sweet dream
Flickered before them, now grown real and true.
    But when the certainty of all we knew,
Dreaming for sure our quest would not be vain,
We got us ready for the sea again.
But to the city's folk we told no more
Than that we needs must make for some far shore,
Whence we would come again to them, and bring
For them and us, full many a wished-for thing
To make them glad.

            Then answered they indeed
That our departing made their hearts to bleed,
But with no long words prayed us still to stay,
And I remembered me of that past day,
And somewhat grieved I felt, that so it was:
Not thinking how the deeds of men must pass,
And their remembrance as their bodies die,
Or, if their memories fade not utterly,
Like curious pictures shall they be at best,
For men to gaze at while they sit at rest,
Talking of alien things and feasting well.

    Ah me! I loiter, being right loth to tell
The things that happened to us in the end.
Down to the noble river did we wend
Where lay the ships we taught these folk to make,
And there the fairest of them did we take
And so began our voyage; thirty-three
Were left of us, who erst had crossed the sea,
Five of the forest people, and beside
None but the fair young man, our new-found guide,
And his old brother; setting sail with these
We left astern our gilded palaces
And all the good things God had given us there

With small regret, however good they were.
   Well, in twelve days our vessel reached the sea,
When turning round we ran on northerly
In sight of land at whiles; what need to say
How the time past from hopeful day to day?
Suffice it that the wind was fair and good,
And we most joyful, as still north we stood;
Until when we a month at sea had been,
And for six days no land at all had seen,
We sighted it once more, whereon our guide
Shouted, "O fellows, lay all fear aside,
This is the land whereof I spake to you."
But when the happy tidings all men knew,
Trembling and pale we watched the land grow great,
And when above the waves the noontide heat
Had raised a vapour 'twixt us and the land
That afternoon, we saw a high ness stand
Out in the sea, and nigher when we came,
And all the sky with sunset was a-flame,
'Neath the dark hill we saw a city lie,
Washed by the waves, girt round with ramparts high.
   A little nigher yet, and then our guide
Bade us to anchor, lowering from our side
The sailless keel wherein he erst had come,
Through many risks, to bring us to his home.
But when our eager hands this thing had done,
He and his brother gat therein alone.
But first he said, "Abide here till the morn,
And when ye hear the sound of harp and horn,
And varied music, run out every oar,
Up anchor, and make boldly for the shore.
O happy men! well-nigh do I regret
That I am not as you, to whom as yet
That moment past all moments is unknown,
When first unending life to you is shown.
But now I go, that all in readiness
May be, your souls with this delight to bless."
   He waved farewell to us and went, but we,
As the night grew, beheld across the sea
Lights moving on the quays, and now and then
We heard the chanting of the outland men.
How can I tell of that strange troublous night,
Troublous and strange, though 'neath the moonshine white,
Peace seemed upon the sea, the glimmering town,
The shadows of the tree-besprinkled down,
The moveless dewy folds of our loose sail?
But how could these for peace to us avail?
   Weary with longing, blind with great amaze,
We struggled now with past and future days;
And not in vain our former joy we thought,
Since thirty years our wandering feet had brought

To this at last—and yet, what will you have?
Can man be made content? We wished to save
The bygone years; our hope, our painted toy,
We feared to miss, drowned in that sea of joy.
Old faces still reproached us: "We are gone,
And ye are entering into bliss alone;
And can ye now forget? Year passes year,
And still ye live on joyous, free from fear;
But where are we? where is the memory
Of us, to whom ye once were drawn so nigh?
Forgetting and alone ye enter in;
Remembering all, alone we wail our sin,
And cannot touch you."—Ah, the blessed pain!
When heaven just gained was scarcely all a gain.
How could we weigh that boundless treasure then,
Or count the sorrows of the sons of men?
Ah, woe is me to think upon that night!

   Day came, and with the dawning of the light
We were astir, and from our deck espied
The people clustering by the water-side,
As if to meet us; then across the sea
We heard great horns strike up triumphantly,
And then scarce knowing what we did, we weighed
And running out the oars for shore we made,
With banners fluttering out from yard and mast.
   We reached the well-built marble quays at last,
Crowded with folk, and in the front of these
There stood our guide, decked out with braveries,
Holding his feeble brother by the hand,
Then speechless, trembling, did we now take land,
Leaving all woes behind, but when our feet
The happy soil of that blest land did meet,
Fast fell our tears, as on a July day
The thunder-shower falls pattering on the way,
And certes some one we desired to bless,
But scarce knew whom midst all our thankfulness.
   Now the crowd opened, and an ordered band
Of youths and damsels, flowering boughs in hand
Came forth to meet us, just as long ago,
When first we won some rest from pain and woe,
Except that now eld chained not anyone,
No man was wrinkled but ourselves alone,
But smooth and beautiful, bright-eyed and glad,
Were all we saw, in fair thin raiment clad
Fit for the sunny place.

         But now our friend,
Our guide, who brought us to this glorious end,
Led us amidst that band, who 'gan to sing
Some hymn of welcome, midst whose carolling

Faint-hearted men we must have been indeed
To doubt that all was won; nor did we heed
That, when we well were gotten from the quay,
Armed men went past us, by the very way
That we had come, nor thought of their intent,
For armour unto us was ornament,
And had been now, for many peaceful years,
Since bow and axe had dried the people's tears.

   Let all that pass—with song and minstrelsy
Through many streets they led us, fair to see,
For nowhere did we meet maimed, poor, or old,
But all were young and clad in silk and gold.
Like a king's court the common ways did seem
On that fair morn of our accomplished dream.

   Far did we go, through market-place and square,
Past fane and palace, till a temple fair
We came to, set aback midst towering trees,
But raised above the tallest of all these.
So there we entered through a brazen gate,
And all the thronging folk without did wait,
Except the golden-clad melodious band.
But when within the precinct we did stand,
Another rampart girdled round the fane,
And that being past another one again,
And small space was betwixt them, all these three
Of white stones laid in wondrous masonry
Were builded, but the fourth we now passed through
Was half of white and half of ruddy hue;
Nor did we reach the temple through this one,
For now a fifth wall came, of dark red stone
With golden coping and wide doors of gold;
And this being past, our eyes could then behold
The marvellous temple, foursquare, rising high
In stage on stage up toward the summer sky,
Like the unfinished tower that Nimrod built
Before the concord of the world was spilt.

   So now we came into the lowest hall,
A mighty way across from wall to wall,
Where carven pillars held a gold roof up,
And silver walls fine as an Indian cup,
With figures monstrous as a dream were wrought,
And under foot the floor beyond all thought
Was wonderful, for like the tumbling sea
Beset with monsters did it seem to be;
But in the midst a pool of ruddy gold
Caught in its waves a glittering fountain cold,
And through the bright shower of its silver spray
Dimly we saw the high raised dais, gay
With wondrous hangings, for high up and small
The windows were within the dreamlike hall;
Betwixt the pillars wandered damsels fair

Crooning low songs, or filling all the air
With incense wafted to strange images
That made us tremble, since we saw in these
The devils unto whom we now must cry
Ere we began our new felicity:
Nathless no altars did we see but one
Which dimly from before the dais shone
Built of green stone, with horns of copper bright.
  Now when we entered from the outer light
And all the scents of the fresh day were past,
With its sweet breezes, a dull shade seemed cast
Over our joy; what then? not if we would
Could we turn back—and surely all was good,
  But now they brought us vestments rich and fair,
And bade us our own raiment put off there,
Which straight we did, and with a hollow sound
Like mournful bells our armour smote the ground,
And damsels took the weapons from our hands
That might have gleamed with death in other lands,
And won us praise; at last when all was done,
And brighter than the Kaiser each man shone,
Us unarmed helpless men the music led
Up to the dais, and there our old guide said
"Rest, happy men, the time will not be long
Ere they will bring with incense, dance, and song
The sacred cup, your life and happiness,
And many a time this fair hour shall ye bless."

  Alas, sirs! words are weak to tell of it,
I seemed to see a smile of mockery flit
Across his face as from our thrones he turned,
And in my heart a sudden fear there burned,
The last, I said, for ever and a day;
But even then with harsh and ominous bray
A trumpet through the monstrous pillars rung,
And to our feet with sudden fear we sprung
Too late, too late! for through all doors did stream
Armed men, that filled the place with clash and gleam,
And when the dull sound of their moving feet
Was still, a fearful sight our eyes did meet,
A fearful sight to us—old men and grey
Betwixt the bands of soldiers took their way,
And at their head in wonderful attire,
Holding within his hand a pot of fire,
Moved the false brother of the traitrous guide,
Who with bowed head walked ever by his side;
But as anigh the elders 'gan to draw,
We, almost turned to stone by what we saw,
Heard the old man say to the younger one,
"Speak to them that thou knowest, O fair Son!"
  Then the wretch said, "O ye, who sought to find

Unending life against the law of kind,
Within this land, fear ye not now too much,
For no man's hand your bodies here shall touch,
But rather with all reverence folk shall tend
Your daily lives, until at last they end
By slow decay: and ye shall pardon us
The trap whereby beings made so glorious
As ye are made, we drew unto this place.
Rest ye content then! for although your race
Comes from the gods, yet are ye conquered here,
As we would conquer them, if we knew where
They dwell from day to day, and with what arms
We, overcoming them, might win such charms
That we might make the world what ye desire.
    "Rest then at ease, and if ye ere shall tire
Of this abode, remember at the worst
Life flitteth, whether it be blessed or cursed.
But will ye tire? ye are our gods on earth
Whiles that ye live, nor shall your lives lack mirth,
For song, fair women, and heart-cheering wine
The chain of solemn days shall here entwine
With odorous flowers; ah, surely ye are come,
When all is said, unto an envied home."

    Like an old dream, dreamed in another dream,
I hear his voice now, see the hopeless gleam,
Through the dark place of that thick wood of spears.
That fountain's splash rings yet within mine ears
I thought the fountain of eternal youth—
Yet I can scarce remember in good truth
What then I felt: I should have felt as he,
Who, waking after some festivity
Sees a dim land, and things unspeakable,
And comes to know at last that it is hell—
I cannot tell you, nor can tell you why
Driven by what hope, I cried my battle cry
And rushed upon him; this I know indeed
My naked hands were good to me at need,
That sent the traitor to his due reward,
Ere I was dragged off by the hurrying guard,
Who spite of all used neither sword nor spear,
Nay as it seemed, touched us with awe and fear.
Though at the last grown all to weak to strive
They brought us to the dais scarce alive,
And changed our tattered robes again, and there
Bound did we sit, each in his golden chair,
Beholding many mummeries that they wrought
About the altar; till at last they brought,
Crowned with fair flowers, and clad in robes of gold,
The folk that from the wood we won of old—
Why make long words? before our very eyes

Our friends they slew, a fitting sacrifice
To us their new gained gods, who sought to find
Within that land, a people just and kind
Who could not die, or take away the breath
From living men.
          What thing but that same death
Had we left now to hope for? death must come
And find us somewhere an enduring home.
Will grief kill men, as some folk think it will?
Then are we of all men most hard to kill.
The time went past, the dreary days went by
In dull unvarying round of misery,
Nor can I tell if it went fast or slow,
What would it profit you the time to know
That we spent there; all I can say to you
Is, that no hope our prison wall shone through,
That ever we were guarded carefully,
While day and dark and dark and day went by
Like such a dream, as in the early night
The sleeper wakes from in such sore afright,
Such panting horror, that to sleep again
He will not turn, to meet such shameful pain.

  Lo such were we, but as we hoped before
Where no hope was, so now, when all seemed o'er
But sorrow for our lives so cast away,
Again the bright sun brought about the day.
  At last the temple's dull monotony
Was broke by noise of armed men hurrying by
Within the precinct, and we seemed to hear
Shouts from without of anger and of fear,
And noises as of battle; and red blaze
The night sky showed; this lasted through two days.
But on the third our guards were whispering
Pale faced, as though they feared some coming thing,
And when the din increased about noontide,
No longer there with us would they abide,
But left us free; judge then if our hearts beat,
When any pain or death itself was sweet
To hideous life within that wicked place,
Where every day brought on its own disgrace.
  Few words betwixt us passed, we knew indeed
Where our old armour once so good at need
Hung up as relics nigh the altar-stead,
Thither we hurried, and from heel to head
Soon were we armed, and our old spears and swords
Clashing 'gainst steel and stone, spoke hopeful words
To us, the children of a warrior race.
But round unto the hubbub did we face
And through the precinct strove to make our way
Set close together; in besmirked array

Some met us, and some wounded very sore,
And some who wounded men to harbour bore;
But these too busy with their pain or woe
To note us much, unchallenged let us go:
Then here and there we passed some shrinking maid
In a dark corner trembling and afraid,
But eager for the news about the fight.
Through trodden gardens then we came in sight
Of the third rampart that begirt the fane,
Which now the foemen seemed at point to gain,
For o'er the wall the ladders 'gan to show,
And huge confusion was there down below
'Twixt wall and wall; but as the gate we passed
A man from out the crowd came hurrying fast,
But, drawing nigh us, stopped short suddenly,
And cried, "O, masters, help us or we die!
This impious people 'gainst their ancient lords
Have turned, and in their madness drawn their swords.
Yea, and they now prevail, and fearing not
The dreadful gods still grows their wrath more hot.
Wherefore to bring you here was my intent,
But the kind gods themselves your hands have sent
To save us all, and this fair holy house
With your strange arms, and hearts most valorous."
   No word we said, for even as he spoke
A frightful clamour from the wall outbroke,
As the thin line of soldiers thereupon
Crushed back, and broken, left the rampart won,
And leapt and tumbled therefrom as they could,
While in their place the conquering foemen stood:
Then the weak, wavering, huddled crowd below
Their weight upon the inner wall 'gan throw,
And at the narrow gates by hundreds died;
For not long did the enemy abide
On the gained rampart, but by every way
Got to the ground and 'gan all round to slay,
Till great and grim the slaughter grew to be.
But we well pleased our tyrants' end to see
Still firm against the inner wall did stand,
While round us surged the press on either hand.
Nor did we fear, for what was left of life
For us to fear for? so at last the strife
Drawn inward, in that place did much abate,
And we began to move unto the gate
Betwixt the dead and living, and these last
Ever with fearful glances by us passed
Nor hindered aught; but mindful of the lore
Our fathers gained on many a bloody shore,
We, when unto the street we made our way,
Moved as in fight nor broke our close array,
Though no man harmed us of the troubled crowd

That thronged the streets with shouts and curses loud,
But rather when our clashing arms they heard
Their hubbub lulled, and they as men afeard
Drew back before us.

          Well, as nigh we drew
Unto the sea, the men showed sparse and few,
Though frightened women standing in the street
Before their doors we did not fail to meet,
And passed by folk who at their doors laid down
Men wounded in the fight; so through the town
We reached the unguarded water-gate at last,
And there, nigh weeping, saw the green waves cast
Against the quays, whereby five tall ships lay:
For in that devil's house, right many a day
Had passed with all its dull obscenity
We counted not, and while we longed to die,
And by all men were now forgotten quite
Except those priests, the people as they might
Made ships like ours; in whose new handiwork
Few mariners and fearful now did lurk,
And these soon fled before us, therefore we
Stayed not to think, but running hastily
Down the lone quay, seized on the nighest ship,
Nor yet till we had let the hawser slip
Dared we be glad, and then indeed once more,
Though we no longer hoped for our fair shore,
Our past disgrace, worse than the very hell,
Though hope was dead, made things seem more than well,
For if we died that night, yet were we free.
   Ah! with what joy we sniffed the fresh salt sea
After the musky odours of that place;
With what delight each felt upon his face
The careless wind, our master and our slave,
As through the green seas fast from shore we drave,
Scarce witting where we went.
            But now when we
Beheld that city, far across the sea,
A thing gone past, nor any more could hear
The mingled shouts of victory and of fear,
From out the midst thereof shot up a fire
'In a long, wavering, murky, smoke-capped spire
That still with every minute wider grew,
So that the ending of the place we knew
Where we had passed such days of misery,
And still more glad turned round unto the sea.

   My tale grows near its ending, for we stood
Southward to our kind folk e'en as we could,
But made slow way, for ever heavily
Our ship sailed, and she often needs must lie

At anchor in some bay, the while with fear
Ourselves, we followed up the fearful deer,
Or filled our water-vessels, for indeed,
Of meat and drink were we in bitter need,
As well might be, for scarcely could we choose
What ships from off that harbour to cast loose.
   Midst this there died the captain, Nicholas,
Whom, though he brought us even to this pass,
I loved the most of all men; even now
When that seems long past, I can scarce tell how
I bear to live, since he could live no more.
Certes he took our failure very sore,
And often do I think he fain had died,
But yet for very love must needs abide
A little while, and yet awhile again,
As though to share the utmost of our pain,
And miss the ray of comfort and sweet rest
Wherewith ye end our long disastrous quest—
A drearier place than ever heretofore
The world seemed, as from that far nameless shore
We turned and left him 'neath the trees to bide;
For midst our rest worn out at last he died.
   And such seemed like to hap to us as well,
If any harder thing to us befell
Than was our common life; and still we talked
How our old friends would meet men foiled, and balked
Of all the things that were to make them glad;
Ah, sirs! no sight of them henceforth we had;
A wind arose, which blowing furiously
Drove us out helpless to the open sea;
Eight days it blew, and when it fell, we lay
Leaky, dismasted, a most helpless prey
To winds and waves, and with but little food;
Then with hard toil a feeble sail and rude
We rigged up somehow, and nigh hopelessly,
Expecting death, we staggered o'er the sea
For ten days more, but when all food and drink
Were gone for three days, and we needs must think
That in mid ocean we were doomed to die,
One morn again did land before us lie:
And we rejoiced, as much at least as he,
Who tossing on his bed deliriously,
Tortured with pain, hears the physician say
That he shall have one quiet painless day
Before he dies—What more? we soon did stand
In this your peaceful and delicious land
Amongst the simple kindly country folk,
But when I heard the language that they spoke,
From out my heart a joyous cry there burst,
So sore for friendly words was I athirst,
And I must fall a-weeping, to have come

To such a place that seemed a blissful home,
After the tossing from rough sea to sea;
So weak at last, so beaten down were we.
  What shall I say in these kind people's praise
Who treated us like brothers for ten days,
Till with their tending we grew strong again,
And then withal in country cart and wain
Brought us unto this city where we are;
May God be good to them for all their care.
  And now, sirs, all our wanderings have ye heard,
And all our story to the utmost word;
And here hath ending all our foolish quest,
Not at the worst if hardly at the best,
Since ye are good—Sirs, we are old and grey
Before our time; in what coin shall we pay
For this your goodness; take it not amiss
That we, poor souls, must pay you back for this
As good men pay back God Who, raised above
The heavens and earth, yet needeth earthly love.

THE ELDER OF THE CITY
  Oh, friends, content you! this is much indeed,
And we are paid, thus garnering for our need
Your blessings only, bringing in their train
God's blessings as the south wind brings the rain.
And for the rest, no little thing shall be
(Since ye through all yet keep your memory)
The gentle music of the bygone years,
Long past to us with all their hopes and fears.
Think, if the gods, who mayhap love us well,
Sent to our gates some ancient chronicle
Of that sweet unforgotten land long left,
Of all the lands wherefrom we now are reft—
Think, with what joyous hearts, what reverence,
What songs, what sweet flowers we should bring it thence,
What images would guard it, what a shrine
Above its well-loved black and white should shine!
How should it pay our labour day by day
To look upon the fair place where it lay;
With what rejoicings even should we take
Each well-writ copy that the scribes might make,
And bear them forth to hear the people's shout,
E'en as good rulers' children are borne out
To take the people's blessing on their birth,
When all the city falls to joy and mirth.

Such, sirs, are ye, our living chronicle,
And scarce can we be grieved at what befell
Your lives in that too hopeless quest of yours,
Since it shall bring us wealth of happy hours
Whiles that we live, and to our sons, delight,

And their sons' sons.

> But now, sirs, let us go,
> That we your new abodes with us may show,
> And tell you what your life henceforth may be,
> But poor, alas, to that ye hoped to see.

To The Reader

Think, listener, that I had the luck to stand,
Awhile ago within a flowery land,
Fair beyond words; that thence I brought away
Some blossoms that before my footsteps lay,
Not plucked by me, not over fresh or bright;
Yet, since they minded me of that delight,
Within the pages of this book I laid
Their tender petals, there in peace to fade.
Dry are they now, and void of all their scent
And lovely colour, yet what once was meant
By these dull stains, some men may yet descry
As dead upon the quivering leaves they lie.
  Behold them here, and mock me if you will,
But yet believe no scorn of men can kill
My love of that fair land wherefrom they came,
Where midst the grass their petals once did flame.

  Moreover, since that land as ye should know,
Bears not alone the gems for summer's show,
Or gold and pearls for fresh green-coated spring,
Or rich adornment for the flickering wing
Of fleeting autumn, but path little fear
For the white conqueror of the fruitful year,
So in these pages month by month I show
Some portion of the flowers that erst did blow
In lovely meadows of the varying land,
Wherein erewhile I had the luck to stand.

MARCH

Slayer of the winter, art thou here again?
O welcome, thou that bring'st the summer nigh!
The bitter wind makes not thy victory vain,
Nor will we mock thee for thy faint blue sky.
Welcome, O March! whose kindly days and dry
Make April ready for the throstle's song,
Thou first redresser of the winter's wrong!

Yea, welcome March! and though I die ere June,
Yet for the hope of life I give thee praise,
Striving to swell the burden of the tune
That even now I hear thy brown birds raise,
Unmindful of the past or coming days;
Who sing: 'O joy! a new year is begun:
What happiness to look upon the sun!'

Ah, what begetteth all this storm of bliss
But Death himself, who crying solemnly,
E'en from the heart of sweet Forgetfulness,
Bids us 'Rejoice, lest pleasureless ye die.
Within a little time must ye go by.
Stretch forth your open hands, and while ye live
Take all the gifts that Death and Life may give.'

Behold once more within a quiet land
The remnant of that once aspiring band,
With all hopes fallen away, but such as light
The sons of men to that unfailing night,
That death they needs must look on face to face.
   Time passed, and ever fell the days apace
From off the new-strung chaplet of their life;
Yet though the time with no bright deeds was rife,
Though no fulfilled desire now made them glad,
They were not quite unhappy, rest they had,
And with their hope their fear had passed away;
New things and strange they saw from day to day;
Honoured they were, and had no lack of things
For which men crouch before the feet of kings,
And, stripped of honour, yet may fail to have.
   Therefore their latter journey to the grave
Was like those days of later autumn-tide,
When he who in some town may chance to bide
Opens the window for the balmy air,
And seeing the golden hazy sky so fair,
And from some city garden hearing still
The wheeling rooks the air with music fill,
Sweet hopeful music, thinketh, Is this spring,
Surely the year can scarce be perishing?
But then he leaves the clamour of the town,
And sees the withered scanty leaves fall down,
The half-ploughed field, the flowerless garden-plot,
The dark full stream by summer long forgot,
The tangled hedges where, relaxed and dead,
The twining plants their withered berries shed,
And feels therewith the treachery of the sun,
And knows the pleasant time is well-nigh done.
   In such St. Luke's short summer lived these men,
Nearing the goal of threescore years and ten;
The elders of the town their comrades were,

And they to them were waxen now as dear
As ancient men to ancient men can be;
Grave matters of belief and polity
They spoke of oft, but not alone of these;
For in their times of idleness and ease
They told of poets' vain imaginings,
And memories vague of half-forgotten things,
Not true or false, but sweet to think upon.

  For nigh the time when first that land they won,
When new-born March made fresh the hopeful air,
The wanderers sat within a chamber fair,
Guests of that city's rulers, when the day
Far from the sunny noon had fallen away;
The sky grew dark, and on the window-pane
They heard the beating of the sudden rain.
Then, all being satisfied with plenteous feast,
There spoke an ancient man, the land's chief priest,
Who said, "Dear guests, the year begins to-day,
And fain are we, before it pass away,
To hear some tales of that now altered world,
Wherefrom our fathers in old time were hurled
By the hard hands of fate and destiny.
Nor would ye hear perchance unwillingly
How we have dealt with stories of the land
Wherein the tombs of our forefathers stand:
Wherefore henceforth two solemn feasts shall be
In every month, at which some history
Shall crown our joyance; and this day, indeed,
I have a story ready for our need,
If ye will hear it, though perchance it is
That many things therein are writ amiss,
This part forgotten, that part grown too great,
For these things, too, are in the hands of fate."
  They cried aloud for joy to hear him speak,
And as again the sinking sun did break
Through the dark clouds and blazed adown the hall,
His clear thin voice upon their ears did fall,
Telling a tale of times long passed away,
When men might cross a kingdom in a day,
And kings remembered they should one day die,
And all folk dwelt in great simplicity.

ATALANTA'S RACE

ARGUMENT

Atalanta, daughter of King Schœneus, not willing to lose her virgin's estate, made it a law to all suitors that they should run a race with her in the public place, and if they failed to overcome her

should die unrevenged; and thus many brave men perished. At last came Milanion, the son of Amphidamas, who, outrunning her with the help of Venus, gained the virgin and wedded her.

Through thick Arcadian woods a hunter went,
Following the beasts up, on a fresh spring day;
But since his horn-tipped bow but seldom bent,
Now at the noontide nought had happed to slay,
Within a vale he called his hounds away,
Hearkening the echoes of his lone voice cling
About the cliffs and through the beech-trees ring.

  But when they ended, still awhile he stood,
And but the sweet familiar thrush could hear,
And all the day-long noises of the wood,
And o'er the dry leaves of the vanished year
His hounds' feet pattering as they drew anear,
And heavy breathing from their heads low hung,
To see the mighty cornel bow unstrung.

  Then smiling did he turn to leave the place,
But with his first step some new fleeting thought
A shadow cast across his sun-burnt face;
I think the golden net that April brought
From some warm world his wavering soul had caught;
For, sunk in vague sweet longing, did he go   .
Betwixt the trees with doubtful steps and slow.

  Yet howsoever slow he went, at last
The trees grew sparser, and the wood was done;
Whereon one farewell, backward look he cast,
Then, turning round to see what place was won,
With shaded eyes looked underneath the sun,
And o'er green meads and new-turned furrows brown
Beheld the gleaming of King Schœneus' town.

  So thitherward he turned, and on each side
The folk were busy on the teeming land,
And man and maid from the brown furrows cried,
Or midst the newly-blossomed vines did stand,
And as the rustic weapon pressed the hand
Thought of the nodding of the well-filled ear,
Or how the knife the heavy bunch should shear.

  Merry it was: about him sung the birds,
The spring flowers bloomed along the firm dry road,
The sleek-skinned mothers of the sharp-horned herds
Now for the barefoot milking-maidens lowed;
While from the freshness of his blue abode,
Glad his death-bearing arrows to forget,
The broad sun blazed, nor scattered plagues as yet.

Through such fair things unto the gates he came,
And found them open, as though peace were there;
Wherethrough, unquestioned of his race or name,
He entered, and along the streets 'gan fare,
Which at the first of folk were well-nigh bare;
But pressing on, and going more hastily,
Men hurrying too he 'gan at last to see.

Following the last of these, he still pressed on,
Until an open space he came unto,
Where wreaths of fame had oft been lost and won,
For feats of strength folk there were wont to do.
And now our hunter looked for something new,
Because the whole wide space was bare, and stilled
The high seats were, with eager people filled.

There with the others to a seat he gat,
Whence he beheld a broidered canopy,
Neath which in fair array King Schœneus sat
Upon his throne with councillors thereby;
And underneath this well-wrought seat and high,
He saw a golden image of the sun,
A silver image of the Fleet-foot One.

A brazen altar stood beneath their feet
Whereon a thin flame flickered in the wind;
Nigh this a herald clad in raiment meet
Made ready even now his horn to wind,
By whom a huge man held a sword, entwined
With yellow flowers; these stood a little space
From off the altar, nigh the starting place.

And there two runners did the sign abide
Foot set to foot,—a young man slim and fair,
Crisp-haired, well knit, with firm limbs often tried
In places where no man his strength may spare;
Dainty his thin coat was, and on his hair
A golden circlet of renown he wore,
And in his hand an olive garland bore.

But on this day with whom shall he contend?
A maid stood by him like Diana clad
When in the woods she lists her bow to bend,
Too fair for one to look on and be glad,
Who scarcely yet has thirty summers had,
If he must still behold her from afar;
Too fair to let the world live free from war.

She seemed all earthly matters to forget;
Of all tormenting lines her face was clear,
Her wide grey eyes upon the goal were set

Calm and unmoved as though no soul were near,
But her foe trembled as a man in fear,
Nor from her loveliness one moment turned
His anxious face with fierce desire that burned.

  Now through the hush there broke the trumpet's clang
Just as the setting sun made eventide.
Then from light feet a spurt of dust there sprang,
And swiftly were they running side by side;
But silent did the thronging folk abide
Until the turning-post was reached at last,
And round about it still abreast they passed.

  But when the people saw how close they ran,
When halfway to the starting-point they were,
A cry of joy broke forth, whereat the man
Headed the white-foot runner, and drew near
Unto the very end of all his fear;
And scarce his straining feet the ground could feel,
And bliss unhoped for o'er his heart 'gan steal.

  But midst the loud victorious shouts he heard
Her footsteps drawing nearer, and the sound
Of fluttering raiment, and thereat afeard
His flushed and eager face he turned around,
And even then he felt her past him bound
Fleet as the wind, but scarcely saw her there
Till on the goal she laid her fingers fair.

  There stood she breathing like a little child
Amid some warlike clamour laid asleep,
For no victorious joy her red lips smiled,
Her cheek its wonted freshness did but keep;
No glance lit up her clear grey eyes and deep,
Though some divine thought softened all her face
As once more rang the trumpet through the place.

  But her late foe stopped short amidst his course,
One moment gazed upon her piteously,
Then with a groan his lingering feet did force
To leave the spot whence he her eyes could see;
And, changed like one who knows his time must be
But short and bitter, without any word
He knelt before the bearer of the sword;

  Then high rose up the gleaming deadly blade,
Bared of its flowers, and through the crowded place
Was silence now, and midst of it the maid
Went by the poor wretch at a gentle pace,
And he to hers upturned his sad white face;
Nor did his eyes behold another sight

Ere on his soul there fell eternal night.

 So was the pageant ended, and all folk
Talking of this and that familiar thing
In little groups from that sad concourse broke,
For now the shrill bats were upon the wing,
And soon dark night would slay the evening,
And in dark gardens sang the nightingale
Her little-heeded, oft-repeated tale.

 And with the last of all the hunter went,
Who, wondering at the strange sight he had seen,
Prayed an old man to tell him what it meant,
Both why the vanquished man so slain had been,
And if the maiden were an earthly queen,
Or rather what much more she seemed to be,
No sharer in the world's mortality.

 "Stranger," said he, "I pray she soon may die
Whose lovely youth has slain so many an one!
King Schœneus' daughter is she verily,
Who when her eyes first looked upon the sun
Was fain to end her life but new begun,
For he had vowed to leave but men alone
Sprung from his loins when he from earth was gone.

 "Therefore he bade one leave her in the wood,
And let wild things deal with her as they might,
But this being done, some cruel god thought good
To save her beauty in the world's despite:
Folk say that her, so delicate and white
As now she is, a rough root-grubbing bear
Amidst her shapeless cubs at first did rear.

 "In course of time the woodfolk slew her nurse,
And to their rude abode the youngling brought,
And reared her up to be a kingdom's curse,
Who grown a woman, of no kingdom thought,
But armed and swift, 'mid beasts destruction wrought,
Nor spared two shaggy centaur kings to slay
To whom her body seemed an easy prey.

 "So to this city, led by fate, she came
Whom known by signs, whereof I cannot tell,
King Schœneus for his child at last did claim,
Nor otherwise since that day doth she dwell
Sending too many a noble soul to hell—
What! thine eyes glisten! what then, thinkest thou
Her shining head unto the yoke to bow?

 "Listen, my son, and love some other maid

For she the saffron gown will never wear,
And on no flower-strewn couch shall she be laid,
Nor shall her voice make glad a lover's ear:
Yet if of Death thou hast not any fear,
Yea, rather, if thou lovest him utterly,
Thou still may'st woo her ere thou comest to die,

  "Like him that on this day thou sawest lie dead;
For, fearing as I deem the sea-born one,
The maid has vowed e'en such a man to wed
As in the course her swift feet can outrun,
But whoso fails herein, his days are done:
He came the nighest that was slain to-day,
Although with him I deem she did but play.

  "Behold, such mercy Atalanta gives
To those that long to win her loveliness;
Be wise! be sure that many a maid there lives
Gentler than she, of beauty little less,
Whose swimming eyes thy loving words shall bless,
When in some garden, knee set close to knee,
Thou sing'st the song that love may teach to thee."

  So to the hunter spake that ancient man,
And left him for his own home presently:
But he turned round, and through the moonlight wan
Reached the thick wood, and there 'twixt tree and tree
Distraught he passed the long night feverishly,
'Twixt sleep and waking, and at dawn arose
To wage hot war against his speechless foes.

  There to the hart's flank seemed his shaft to grow,
As panting down the broad green glades he flew,
There by his horn the Dryads well might know
His thrust against the bear's heart had been true,
And there Adonis' bane his javelin slew,
But still in vain through rough and smooth he went,.
For none the more his restlessness was spent.

  So wandering, he to Argive cities came,
And in the lists with valiant men he stood,
And by great deeds he won him praise and fame,
And heaps of wealth for little-valued blood;
But none of all these things, or life, seemed good
Unto his heart, where still unsatisfied
A ravenous longing warred with fear and pride.

  Therefore it happed when but a month had gone
Since he had left King Schœneus' city old,
In hunting-gear again, again alone
The forest-bordered meads did he behold,

Where still mid thoughts of August's quivering gold
Folk hoed the wheat, and clipped the vine in trust
Of faint October's purple-foaming must.

And once again he passed the peaceful gate,
While to his beating heart his lips did lie,
That owning not victorious love and fate,
Said, half aloud, "And here too must I try,
To win of alien men the mastery,
And gather for my head fresh meed of fame
And cast new glory on my father's name."

In spite of that, how beat his heart, when first
Folk said to him, "And art thou come to see
That which still makes our city's name accurst
Among all mothers for its cruelty?
Then know indeed that fate is good to thee
Because to-morrow a new luckless one
Against the whitefoot maid is pledged to run."

So on the morrow with no curious eyes
As once he did, that piteous sight he saw,
Nor did that wonder in his heart arise
As toward the goal the conquering maid 'gan draw,
Nor did he gaze upon her eyes with awe,
Too full the pain of longing filled his heart
For fear or wonder there to have a part.

But O, how long the night was ere it went!
How long it was before the dawn begun
Showed to the wakening birds the sun's intent
That not in darkness should the world be done!
And then, and then, how long before the sun
Bade silently the toilers of the earth
Get forth to fruitless cares or empty mirth!

And long it seemed that in the market-place
He stood and saw the chaffering folk go by,
Ere from the ivory throne King Schœneus' face
Looked down upon the murmur royally,
But then came trembling that the time was nigh
When he midst pitying looks his love must claim,
And jeering voices must salute his name.

But as the throng he pierced to gain the throne,
His alien face distraught and anxious told
What hopeless errand he was bound upon,
And, each to each, folk whispered to behold
His godlike limbs; nay, and one woman old
As he went by must pluck him by the sleeve
And pray him yet that wretched love to leave.

For sidling up she said, "Canst thou live twice,
Fair son? canst thou have joyful youth again,
That thus thou goest to the sacrifice
Thyself the victim? nay then, all in vain
Thy mother bore her longing and her pain,
And one more maiden on the earth must dwell
Hopeless of joy, nor fearing death and hell.

"O, fool, thou knowest not the compact then
That with the threeformed goddess she has made
To keep her from the loving lips of men,
And in no saffron gown to be arrayed,
And therewithal with glory to be paid,
And love of her the moonlit river sees
White 'gainst the shadow of the formless trees.

"Come back, and I myself will pray for thee
Unto the sea-born framer of delights,
To give thee her who on the earth may be
The fairest stirrer up to death and fights,
To quench with hopeful days and joyous nights
The flame that doth thy youthful heart consume:
Come back, nor give thy beauty to the tomb."

How should he listen to her earnest speech?
Words, such as he not once or twice had said
Unto himself, whose meaning scarce could reach
The firm abode of that sad hardihead—
He turned about, and through the marketstead
Swiftly he passed, until before the throne
In the cleared space he stood at last alone.

Then said the King, "Stranger, what dost thou here?
Have any of my folk done ill to thee?
Or art thou of the forest men in fear?
Or art thou of the sad fraternity
Who still will strive my daughter's mates to be,
Staking their lives to win to earthly bliss
The lonely maid, the friend of Artemis?"

"O King," he said, "thou sayest the word indeed;
Nor will I quit the strife till I have won
My sweet delight, or death to end my need.
And know that I am called Milanion,
Of King Amphidamas the well-loved son
So fear not that to thy old name, O King,
Much loss or shame my victory will bring."

"Nay, Prince," said Schœneus, "welcome to this land
Thou wert indeed, if thou wert here to try

Thy strength 'gainst some one mighty of his hand;
Nor would we grudge thee well-won mastery.
But now, why wilt thou come to me to die,
And at my door lay down thy luckless head,
Swelling the band of the unhappy dead,

"Whose curses even now my heart doth fear?
Lo, I am old, and know what life can be,
And what a bitter thing is death anear.
O Son! be wise, and hearken unto me,
And if no other can be dear to thee,
At least as now, yet is the world full wide,
And bliss in seeming hopeless hearts may hide:

"But if thou losest life, then all is lost."
"Nay, King," Milanion said, "thy words are vain.
Doubt not that I have counted well the cost.
But say, on what day wilt thou that I gain
Fulfilled delight, or death to end my pain?
Right glad were I if it could be to-day,
And all my doubts at rest for ever lay."

"Nay," said King Schœneus, "thus it shall not be,
But rather shalt thou let a month go by,
And weary with thy prayers for victory
What god thou know'st the kindest and most nigh.
So doing, still perchance thou shalt not die:
And with my goodwill wouldst thou have the maid,
For of the equal gods I grow afraid.

"And until then, O Prince, be thou my guest,
And all these troublous things awhile forget."
"Nay," said he, "couldst thou give my soul good rest,
And on mine head a sleepy garland set,
Then had I 'scaped the meshes of the net,
Nor shouldst thou hear from me another word;
But now, make sharp thy fearful heading sword.

"Yet will I do what son of man may do,
And promise all the gods may most desire,
That to myself I may at least be true;
And on that day my heart and limbs so tire,
With utmost strain and measureless desire,
That, at the worst, I may but fall asleep
When in the sunlight round that sword shall sweep."

He went with that, nor anywhere would bide,
But unto Argos restlessly did wend;
And there, as one who lays all hope aside,
Because the leech has said his life must end,
Silent farewell he bade to foe and friend,

And took his way unto the restless sea,
For there he deemed his rest and help might be.

Upon the shore of Argolis there stands
A temple to the goddess that he sought,
That, turned unto the lion-bearing lands,
Fenced from the east, of cold winds hath no thought,
Though to no homestead there the sheaves are brought,
No groaning press torments the close-clipped murk,
Lonely the fane stands, far from all men's work.

Pass through a close, set thick with myrtle trees,
Through the brass doors that guard the holy place,
And entering, hear the washing of the seas
That twice a-day rise high above the base,
And with the south-west urging them, embrace
The marble feet of her that standeth there
That shrink not, naked though they be and fair.

Small is the fane through which the seawind sings
About Queen Venus' well-wrought image white,
But hung around are many precious things,
The gifts of those who, longing for delight,
Have hung them there within the goddess' sight,
And in return have taken at her hands
The living treasures of the Grecian lands.

And thither now has come Milanion,
And showed unto the priests' wide open eyes
Gifts fairer than all those that there have shone,
Silk cloths, inwrought with Indian fantasies,
And bowls inscribed with sayings of the wise
Above the deeds of foolish living things,
And mirrors fit to be the gifts of kings.

And now before the Sea-born One he stands,
By the sweet veiling smoke made dim and soft,
And while the incense trickles from his hands,
And while the odorous smoke-wreaths hang aloft,
Thus Both he pray to her: "O Thou, who oft
Hast holpen man and maid in their distress,
Despise me not for this my wretchedness!

"O goddess, among us who dwell below,
Kings and great men, great for a little while,
Have pity on the lowly heads that bow,
Nor hate the hearts that love them without guile;
Wilt thou be worse than these, and is thy smile
A vain device of him who set thee here,
An empty dream of some artificer?

"O, great one, some men love, and are ashamed;
Some men are weary of the bonds of love;
Yea, and by some men lightly art thou blamed,
That from thy toils their lives they cannot move,
And 'mid the ranks of men their manhood prove.
Alas! O goddess, if thou slayest me
What new immortal can I serve but thee?

"Think then, will it bring honour to thy head
If folk say, 'Everything aside he cast
And to all fame and honour was he dead,
And to his one hope now is dead at last,
Since all unholpen he is gone and past:
Ah, the gods love not man, for certainly,
He to his helper did not cease to cry.'

"Nay, but thou wilt help; they who died before
Not single-hearted as I deem came here,
Therefore unthanked they laid their gifts before
Thy stainless feet, still shivering with their fear,
Lest in their eyes their true thought might appear,
Who sought to be the lords of that fair town,
Dreaded of men and winners of renown.

"O Queen, thou knowest I pray not for this:
O set us down together in some place
Where not a voice can break our heaven of bliss,
Where nought but rocks and I can see her face,
Softening beneath the marvel of thy grace,
Where not a foot our vanished steps can track—
The golden age, the golden age come back!

"O fairest, hear me now who do thy will,
Plead for thy rebel that he be not slain,
But live and love and be thy servant still;
Ah, give her joy and take away my pain,
And thus two long enduring servants gain.
An easy thing this is to do for me,
What need of my vain words to weary thee!

"But none the less, this place will I not leave
Until I needs must go my death to meet,
Or at thy hands some happy sign receive
That in great joy we twain may one day greet
Thy presence here and kiss thy silver feet,
Such as we deem thee, fair beyond all words,
Victorious o'er our servants and our lords."

Then from the altar back a space he drew,
But from the Queen turned not his face away,
But 'gainst a pillar leaned, until the blue

That arched the sky, at ending of the day,
Was turned to ruddy gold and changing grey,
And clear, but low, the nigh-ebbed windless sea
In the still evening murmured ceaselessly.

  And there he stood when all the sun was down,
Nor had he moved, when the dim golden light,
Like the far lustre of a godlike town,
Had left the world to seeming hopeless night,
Nor would he move the more when wan moonlight
Streamed through the pillars for a little while,
And lighted up the white Queen's changeless smile.

  Nought noted he the shallow flowing sea
As step by step it set the wrack a-swim,
The yellow torchlight nothing noted he
Wherein with fluttering gown and half-bared limb
The temple damsels sung their midnight hymn,
And nought the doubled stillness of the fane
When they were gone and all was hushed again.

  But when the waves had touched the marble base,
And steps the fish swim over twice a-day,
The dawn beheld him sunken in his place
Upon the floor; and sleeping there he lay,
Not heeding aught the little jets of spray
The roughened sea brought nigh, across him cast,
For as one dead all thought from him had passed.

  Yet long before the sun had showed his head,
Long ere the varied hangings on the wall
Had gained once more their blue and green and red,
He rose as one some well-known sign doth call
When war upon the city's gates doth fall,
And scarce like one fresh risen out of sleep,
He 'gan again his broken watch to keep.

  Then he turned round; not for the sea-gull's cry
That wheeled above the temple in his flight,
Not for the fresh south wind that lovingly
Breathed on the new-born day and dying night,
But some strange hope 'twixt fear and great delight
Drew round his face, now flushed, now pale and wan,
And still constrained his eyes the sea to scan.

  Now a faint light lit up the southern sky,
Not sun or moon, for all the world was grey,
But this a bright cloud seemed, that drew anigh,
Lighting the dull waves that beneath it lay
As toward the temple still it took its way,
And still grew greater, till Milanion

Saw nought for dazzling light that round him shone.

But as he staggered with his arms outspread,
Delicious unnamed odours breathed around,
For languid happiness he bowed his head,
And with wet eyes sank down upon the ground,
Nor wished for aught, nor any dream he found
To give him reason for that happiness,
Or make him ask more knowledge of his bliss.

At last his eyes were cleared, and he could see
Through happy tears the goddess face to face
With that faint image of Divinity,
Whose well-wrought smile and dainty changeless grace
Until that morn so gladdened all the place;
Then he, unwitting cried aloud her name
And covered up his eyes for fear and shame.

But through the stillness he her voice could hear
Piercing his heart with joy scarce bearable,
That said, "Milanion, wherefore dost thou fear,
I am not hard to those who love me well;
List to what I a second time will tell,
And thou mayest hear perchance, and live to save
The cruel maiden from a loveless grave.

"See, by my feet three golden apples lie—
Such fruit among the heavy roses falls,
Such fruit my watchful damsels carefully
Store up within the best loved of my walls,
Ancient Damascus, where the lover calls
Above my unseen head, and faint and light
The rose-leaves flutter round me in the night.

"And note, that these are not alone most fair
With heavenly gold, but longing strange they bring
Unto the hearts of men, who will not care
Beholding these, for any once-loved thing
Till round the shining sides their fingers cling.
And thou shalt see thy well-girt swiftfoot maid
By sight of these amid her glory stayed.

"For bearing these within a scrip with thee,
When first she heads thee from the starting-place
Cast down the first one for her eyes to see,
And when she turns aside make on apace,
And if again she heads thee in the race
Spare not the other two to cast aside
If she not long enough behind will bide.

"Farewell, and when has come the happy time

That she Diana's raiment must unbind
And all the world seems blessed with Saturn's clime,
And thou with eager arms about her twined
Beholdest first her grey eyes growing kind,
Surely, O trembler, thou shalt scarcely then
Forget the Helper of unhappy men."

   Milanion raised his head at this last word
For now so soft and kind she seemed to be
No longer of her Godhead was he feared;
Too late he looked, for nothing could he see
But the white image glimmering doubtfully
In the departing twilight cold and grey,
And those three apples on the steps that lay.

   These then he caught up quivering with delight,
Yet fearful lest it all might be a dream,
And though aweary with the watchful night,
And sleepless nights of longing, still did deem
He could not sleep; but yet the first sun-beam
That smote the fane across the heaving deep
Shone on him laid in calm untroubled sleep.

   But little ere the noontide did he rise,
And why he felt so happy scarce could tell
Until the gleaming apples met his eyes.
Then leaving the fair place where this befell
Oft he looked back as one who loved it well,
Then homeward to the haunts of men 'gan wend
To bring all things unto a happy end.

Now has the lingering month at last gone by,
Again are all folk round the running place,
Nor other seems the dismal pageantry
Than heretofore, but that another face
Looks o'er the smooth course ready for the race,
For now, beheld of all, Milanion
Stands on the spot he twice has looked upon.

   But yet—what change is this that holds the maid?
Does she indeed see in his glittering eye
More than disdain of the sharp shearing blade,
Some happy hope of help and victory?
The others seemed to say, "We come to die,
Look down upon us for a little while,
That dead, we may bethink us of thy smile."

   But he—what look of mastery was this
He cast on her? why were his lips so red?
Why was his face so flushed with happiness?
So looks not one who deems himself but dead,

E'en if to death he bows a willing head;
So rather looks a god well pleased to find
Some earthly damsel fashioned to his mind.

   Why must she drop her lids before his gaze,
And even as she casts adown her eyes
Redden to note his eager glance of praise,
And wish that she were clad in other guise?
Why must the memory to her heart arise
Of things unnoticed when they first were heard,
Some lover's song, some answering maiden's word?

   What makes these longings, vague, without a name,
And this vain pity never felt before,
This sudden languor, this contempt of fame,
This tender sorrow for the time past o'er,
These doubts that grow each minute more and more?
Why does she tremble as the time grows near,
And weak defeat and woeful victory fear?

   But while she seemed to hear her beating heart,
Above their heads the trumpet blast rang out
And forth they sprang; and she must play her part;
Then flew her white feet, knowing not a doubt,
Though slackening once, she turned her head about,
But then she cried aloud and faster fled
Than e'er before, and all men deemed him dead.

   But with no sound he raised aloft his hand,
And thence what seemed a ray of light there flew
And past the maid rolled on along the sand;
Then trembling she her feet together drew
And in her heart a strong desire there grew
To have the toy; some god she thought had given
That gift to her, to make of earth a heaven.

   Then from the course with eager steps she ran,
And in her odorous bosom laid the gold.
But when she turned again, the great-limbed man,
Now well ahead she failed not to behold,
And mindful of her glory waxing cold,
Sprang up and followed him in hot pursuit,
Though with one hand she touched the golden fruit.

   Note too, the bow that she was wont to bear
She laid aside to grasp the glittering prize,
And o'er her shoulder from the quiver fair
Three arrows fell and lay before her eyes
Unnoticed, as amidst the people's cries
She sprang to head the strong Milanion,
Who now the turning-post had well nigh won.

But as he set his mighty hand on it
White fingers underneath his own were laid,
And white limbs from his dazzled eyes did flit,
Then he the second fruit cast by the maid,
But she ran on awhile, then as afraid
Wavered and stopped, and turned and made no stay,
Until the globe with its bright fellow lay.

Then, as a troubled glance she cast around
Now far ahead the Argive could she see,
And in her garment's hem one hand she wound
To keep the double prize, and strenuously
Sped o'er the course, and little doubt had she
To win the day, though now but scanty space
Was left betwixt him and the winning place.

Short was the way unto such winged feet,
Quickly she gained upon him till at last
He turned about her eager eyes to meet
And from his hand the third fair apple cast.
She wavered not, but turned and ran so fast
After the prize that should her bliss fulfil,
That in her hand it lay ere it was still.

Nor did she rest, but turned about to win
Once more, an unblest woeful victory
And yet—and yet—why does her breath begin
To fail her, and her feet drag heavily?
Why fails she now to see if far or nigh
The goal is? why do her grey eyes grow dim?
Why do these tremors run through every limb?

She spreads her arms abroad some stay to find
Else must she fall, indeed, and findeth this,
A strong man's arms about her body twined.
Nor may she shudder now to feel his kiss,
So wrapped she is in new unbroken bliss:
Made happy that the foe the prize hath won.
She weeps glad tears for all her glory done.

Shatter the trumpet, hew adown the posts!
Upon the brazen altar break the sword,
And scatter incense to appease the ghosts
Of those who died here by their own award.
Bring forth the image of the mighty Lord,
And her who unseen o'er the runners hung,
And did a deed for ever to be sung.

Here are the gathered folk, make no delay,
Open King Schœneus' well-filled treasury,

Bring out the gifts long hid from light of day,
The golden bowls o'erwrought with imagery,
Gold chains, and unguents brought from over sea,
The saffron gown the old Phœnician brought,
Within the temple of the Goddess wrought.

  O ye, O damsels, who shall never see
Her, that Love's servant bringeth now to you,
Returning from another victory,
In some cool bower do all that now is due!
Since she in token of her service new
Shall give to Venus offerings rich enow,
Her maiden zone, her arrows, and her bow.

So when his last word's echo died away,
The growing wind at end of that wild day
Alone they heard, for silence bound them all;
Yea, on their hearts a weight had seemed to fall,
As unto the scarce-hoped felicity
The tale drew round—the end of life so nigh,
The aim so little, and the joy so vain—
For as a child's unmeasured joy brings pain
Unto a grown man holding grief at bay,
So the old fervent story of that day
Brought pain half-sweet, to these: till now the fire
Upon the hearth sent up a flickering spire
Of ruddy flame, as fell the burned-through logs,
And, waked by sudden silence, grey old dogs,
The friends of this or that man, rose and fawned
On hands they knew; withal once more there dawned
The light of common day on those old hearts,
And all were ready now to play their parts,
And take what feeble joy might yet remain
In place of all they once had hoped to gain.

Now on the second day that these did meet
March was a-dying through soft days and sweet,
Too hopeful for the wild days yet to be;
But in the hall that ancient company,
Not lacking younger folk that day at least,
Softened by spring were gathered at the feast,
And as the time drew on, throughout the hall
A horn was sounded, giving note to all
That they at last the looked-for tale should hear.

  Then spake a Wanderer, "O kind hosts and dear,
Hearken a little unto such a tale
As folk with us will tell in every vale
About the yule-tide fire, when the snow
Deep in the passes, letteth men to go
From place to place: now there few great folk be,

Although we upland men have memory
Of ills kings did us; yet as now indeed
Few have much wealth, few are in utter need.
Like the wise ants a kingless, happy folk
We long have been, not galled by any yoke,
But the white leaguer of the winter tide
Whereby all men at home are bound to bide.
—Alas, my folly! how I talk of it,
As though from this place where to-day we sit
The way thereto was short—Ah, would to God
Upon the snow-freed herbage now I trod!
But pardon, sirs; the time goes swiftly by,
Hearken a tale of conquering destiny.

THE MAN BORN TO BE KING

ARGUMENT

It was foretold to a great king, that he who should reign after him should be low-born and poor; which thing came to pass in the end, for all that the king could do?

A King there was in days of old
Who ruled wide lands, nor lacked for gold,
Nor honour, nor much longed-for praise,
And his days were called happy days,
So peaceable his kingdoms were,
While others wrapt in war and fear
Fell ever unto worse and worse.
  Therefore his city was the nurse
Of all that men then had of lore,
And none were driven from his door
That seemed well-skilled in anything;
So of the sages was he king;
And from this learned man and that,
Little by little, lore he gat,
And many a lordless, troubled land
Fell scarce loth to his dreaded hand.
  Midst this it chanced that, on a day,
Clad in his glittering gold array,
He held a royal festival;
And nigh him in his glorious hall
Beheld his sages most and least,
Sitting much honoured at the feast.
But mid the faces so well-known,
Of men he well might call his own,
He saw a little wizened man
With face grown rather grey than wan
From lapse of years, beardless was he,
And bald as is the winter tree;

But his two deep-set, glittering eyes
Gleamed at the sight of mysteries
None knew but he; few words he said,
And unto those small heed was paid;
But the king, young, yet old in guile,
Failed not to note a flickering smile
Upon his face, as now and then
He turned him from the learned men
Toward the king's seat, so thought to know
What new thing he might have to show;
And presently, the meat being done,
He bade them bring him to his throne,
And when before him he was come,
He said, "Be welcome to my home;
What is thine art, canst thou in rhyme
Tell stories of the ancient time?
Or dost thou chronicle old wars?
Or know'st thou of the change of stars?
Or seek'st thou the transmuting stone?
Or canst thou make the shattered bone
Grow whole, and dying men live on
Till years like thine at last are won?
Or what thing bring'st thou to me here,
Where nought but men of lore are dear
To me and mine?"

       "O King," said he,
"But few things know I certainly,
Though I have toiled for many a day
Along the hard and doubtful way
That bringeth wise men to the grave:
And now for all the years I gave,
To know all things that man can learn,
A few months learned life I earn,
Nor feel much liker to a god
Than when beside my sheep I trod
Upon the thymy, wind-swept down.
Yet am I come unto thy town
To tell thee somewhat that I learned
As on the stars I gazed, and yearned
To cast this weary body off,
With all its chains of mock and scoff
And creeping death—for as I read
The sure decrees with joy and dread,
Somewhat I saw writ down of thee,
And who shall have the sovereignty
When thou art gone."

       "Nay," said the King,
"Speak quick and tell me of the thing."
  "Sire," said the sage, "thine ancient line
Thou holdest as a thing divine,
So long and undisturbed it is,

But now shall there be end to this,
For surely in my glittering text
I read that he who shall sit next,
On this thine ancient throne and high,
Shall he no better born than I
Whose grandsire none remembereth,
Nor where my father first drew breath."
  "Yea," said the King, "and this may be;
Yet, O Sage, ere I credit thee,
Some token certes must thou show,
Or tell me what I think to know,
Alone, among all folk alive;
Then surely great gifts will I give
To thee, and make thee head of all
Who watch the planets rise and fall."
  "Bid these stand backward from thy throne,"
The sage said, "then to thee alone
Long hidden matters will I tell;
And then, if thou believest, well—
And if thou dost not—well also;
No gift I ask, but leave to go,
For strange to me is this thy state,
And for thyself, thou well may'st hate
My crabbed age and misery."
  "Well," said the King, "let this thing be;
And ye, my masters, stand aback!
For of the fresh air have I lack,
And in my pleasance would I walk
To hearken this grave elder's talk
And gain new lore."
             Therewith he rose
And led the way unto a close,
Shaded with grey-leaved olive-trees;
And when they were amidst of these
He turned about and said, "Speak, friend,
And of thy folly make an end,
And take this golden chain therefore."
  "Rightly thou namest my weak lore,"
The sage said, "therefore to the end
Be wise, and what the fates may send
Take thou, nor struggle in the net
Wherein thine helpless feet are set!
Hearken! a year is well-nigh done
Since, at the hottest of the sun,
Stood Antony beneath this tree,
And took a jewelled cup of thee,
And drank swift death in guise of wine;
Since he, most trusted of all thine,
At last too full of knowledge grew,
And chiefly, he of all men knew
How the Earl Marshal Hugh had died,

Since he had drawn him on to ride
Into a bushment of his foes,
To meet death from unnumbered blows."
  "Thou knowest that by me he died,"
The King said, "How if now I cried
Help! the magician slayeth me?"
Swiftly should twenty sword-blades be
Clashing within thy ribs, and thou
Nearer to death than even now."
  "Not thus, O King, I fear to die,"
The Sage said; "Death shall pass me by
Many a year yet, because perchance,
I fear not aught his clattering dance,
And have enough of weary days.
—But thou—farewell, and win the praise
Of sages, by thy hearkening
With heed to this most certain thing.
Fear not because this thing I know,
For to my grey tower back I go
High raised above the heathy hills
Where the great erne the swift hare kills,
Or stoops upon the new-yeaned lamb;
There almost as a god I am
Unto few folk, who hear thy name
Indeed, but know nought of thy fame,
Nay, scarce if thou be man or beast."
So saying, back unto the feast
He turned, and went adown the hall,
Not heeding any gibe or call;
And left the palace and the town
With face turned toward his windy down.
Back to the hall, too, the King went,
With eyes upon the pavement bent
In pensive thought, delighting not
In riches and his kingly lot;
But thinking how his days began,
And of the lonely souls of man.

  But time past, and midst this and that,
The wise man's message he forgat;
And as a king he lived his life,
And took to him a noble wife
Of the kings' daughters, rich and fair.
And they being wed for nigh a year,
And she now growing great with child,
It happed unto the forest wild
This king with many folk must ride
At ending of the summer-tide;
There boar and hart they brought to bay,
And had right noble prize that day;
But when the noon was now long past,,

And the thick woods grew overcast,
They roused the mightiest hart of all.
Then loudly 'gan the king to call
Unto his huntsmen, not to leave
That mighty beast for dusk nor eve
Till they had won him; with which word
His horn he blew, and forth he spurred,
Taking no thought of most or least,
But only of that royal beast.
And over rough and smooth he rode,
Nor yet for anything abode,
Till dark night swallowing up the day
With blindness his swift course must stay.
Nor was there with him any one,
So far his fair steed had outrun
The best of all his hunting-folk.
  So, glancing at the stars that broke
'Twixt the thick branches here and there,
Backward he turned, and peered with care
Into the darkness, but saw nought,
Nor heard his folk, and therewith thought
His bed must be the brake leaves brown.
Then in a while he lighted down,
And felt about a little space,
If he might find a softer place;
But as he groped from tree to tree
Some glimmering light he seemed to see
'Twixt the dark stems, and thither turned,
If yet perchance some wood-fire burned
Within a peasant's hut, where he
Might find, amidst their misery,
Rough food, or shelter at the least.
  So, leading on his wearied beast,
Blindly he crept from tree to tree,
Till slowly grew that light to be
The thing he looked for, and he found
A hut on a cleared space of ground,
From whose half-opened door there streamed
The light that erst far off had gleamed.
Then of that shelter was he fain,
But just as he made shift to gain
The open space in front of it,
A shadow o'er the grass did flit,
And on the wretched threshold stood
A big man, with a bar of wood
In his right hand, who seemed as though
He got him ready for a blow;
But ere he spoke the King cried, "Friend,
May God good hap upon thee send,
If thou wilt give me rest this night,
And food according to thy might."

"Nay," said the carle, "my wife lieth
In labour, and is nigh her death:
Nor canst thou enter here at all;
But nearby is my asses' stall,
Who on this night bide in the town;
There, if thou wilt, mayst thou lie down,
And sleep until the dawn of day,
And I will bring thee what I may
Of food and drink."
                    Then said the King,
"Thanked be thou; neither for nothing
Shalt thou this good deed do to me."
"Nay," said the carle, "let these things be,
Surely I think before the morn,
To be too weary and forlorn
For gold much heart in me to put."
With that he turned, and from the hut
Brought out a lantern, and rye-bread,
And wine, and showed the king a shed,
Strewed with a litter of dry brake:
Withal he muttered, for his sake,
Unto Our Lady some rude prayer,
And turned about and left him there.
  So when the rye-bread, nowise fine,
The king had munched, and with green wine
Had quenched his thirst, his horse he tied
Unto a post, and there beside
He fell asleep upon the brake.

  But in an hour did he awake,
Astonied with an unnamed fear,
For words were ringing in his ear
Like the last echo of a scream,
"Take! take!" but of the vanished dream
No image was there left to him.
Then, trembling sore in every limb,
Did he arise, and drew his sword,
And passed forth on the forest sward,
And cautiously about he crept;
But he heard nought at all, except
Some groaning of the woodman's wife,
And forest sounds well known, but rife
With terror to the lonely soul.
  Then he lay down again, to roll
His limbs within his huntsman's cloak;
And slept again, and once more woke
To tremble with that unknown fear,
And other echoing words to hear—
"Give up! give up!" nor anything
Showed more why these strange words should ring
About him. Then he sat upright,

Bewildered, gazing through the night,
Until his weary eyes, grown dim,
Showed not the starlit tree-trunks slim
Against the black wood, grey and plain;
And into sleep he sank again,
And woke not soon: but sleeping dreamed
That he awoke, nor other seemed
The place he woke in but that shed,
And there beside his bracken bed
He seemed to see the ancient sage
Shrivelled yet more with untold age,
Who bending down his head to him
Said, with a mocking smile and grim,
"Take, or give up; what matters it?
This child new-born shall surely sit
Upon thy seat when thou art gone,
And dwelling 'twixt straight walls of stone."
    Again the King woke at that word
And sat up, panting and afeard,
And staring out into the night,
Where yet the woods thought not of light;
And fain he was to cast off sleep,
Such visions from his eyes to keep.
Heavy his head grew none the less,
'Twixt 'wildering thoughts and weariness,
And soon he fell asleep once more,
Nor dreamed, nor woke again, before
The sun shone through the forest trees;
And, shivering in the morning breeze,
He blinked with just-awakened eyes,
And pondering on those mysteries,
Unto the woodman's hut he went.

    Him he found kneeling down, and bent
In moody grief above a bed,
Whereon his wife lay, stark and dead,
Whose soul near morn had passed away;
And 'twixt the dead and living lay
A new-born man-child, fair and great.
So in the door the King did wait
To watch the man, who had no heed
Of this or that, so sore did bleed
The new-made wound within his heart.
But as the King gazed, for his part
He did but see his threatened foe,
And ever hard his heart did grow
With deadly hate and wilfulness:
And sight of that poor man's distress
Made it the harder, as of nought
But that unbroken line he thought
Of which he was the last: withal

His scornful troubled eyes did fall
Upon that nest of poverty,
Where nought of joy he seemed to see.
    On straw the poor dead woman lay;
The door alone let in the day,
Showing the trodden earthen floor,
A board on trestles weak and poor,
Three stumps of tree for stool or chair,
A half-glazed pipkin, nothing fair,
A bowl of porridge by the wife
Untouched by lips that lacked for life,
A platter and a bowl of wood;
And in the further corner stood
A bow cut from the wych-elm tree,
A holly club, and arrows three
Ill pointed, heavy, spliced with thread.

    Ah! soothly, well remembered
Was that unblissful wretched home,
Those four bare walls, in days to come;
And often in the coming years
He called to mind the pattering tears
That, on the rent old sackcloth cast
About the body, fell full fast,
'Twixt half-meant prayers and curses wild,
And that weak wailing of the child,
His threatened dreaded enemy,
The mighty king that was to be.
    But as he gazed unsoftened there,
With hate begot of scorn and care,
Loudly he heard a great horn blow,
And his own hunting call did know,
And soon began the shouts to hear
Of his own people drawing near.
Then lifting up his horn, he blew
A long shrill point, but as he threw
His head aback, beheld his folk,
Who from the close-set thicket broke
And o'er the cleared space swiftly passed,
With shouts that he was found at last.
    Then turned the carle his doleful face,
And slowly rising in his place,
Drew thwart his eyes his fingers strong,
And on that gay-dressed glittering throng
Gazed stupidly, as still he heard
The name of King; but said no word.
    But his guest spoke, "Sirs, well be ye!
This luckless woodman, whom ye see,
Gave me good harbour through the night
And such poor victual as he might;
Therefore shall he have more than gold

For his reward; since dead and cold
His helpmate lies who last night died.
See now the youngling by her side;
Him will I take and rear him so
That he shall no more lie alow
In straw, or from the beech-tree dine.
But rather use white linen fine
And silver plate; and with the sword
Shall learn to serve some King or Lord.
How say'st thou, good man?"
                                        "Sire," he said,
Weeping, but shamefaced,—"Since here dead
She lies, that erst kept house for me,
E'en as thou willest let it be;
Though I had hoped to have a son
To help me get the day's work done.
And now, indeed, forth must he go
If unto manhood he should grow,
And lonely I must wander forth,
To whom east, west, and south, and north
Are all alike: forgive it me
If little thanks I give to thee
Who scarce can thank great God in heaven
For what is left of what was given."
   Small heed unto him the King gave,
But trembling in his haste to have
The body of his enemy,
Said to an old squire, "Bring to me
The babe, and give the good man this
Wherewith to gain a little bliss,
In place of all his troubles gone,
Nor need he now be long alone."
   The carle's rough face, at clink of gold,
Lit up, though still did he behold
The wasted body lying there;
But stooping, a rough box, foursquare,
Made of old wood and lined with hay,
Wherein the helpless infant lay,
He raised, and gave it to the squire
Who on the floor cast down his hire,
Nor sooth dared murmur aught the while,
But turning smiled a grim hard smile
To see the carle his pieces count
Still weeping: so did all men mount
And turning round into the wood
Forgat him and his drearihood,
And soon were far off from the hut.

   Then coming out, the door he shut
Behind him, and adown a glade,
Towards a rude hermitage he made

To fetch the priest unto his need,
To bury her and say her bede—
So when all things that he might do
Were done aright, heavy with woe,
He left the woodland hut behind
To take such chance as he might find
In other lands, forgetting all
That in that forest did befall.

   But through the wild wood rode the King,
Moody and thinking on the thing,
Nor free from that unreasoning fear;
Till now, when they had drawn anear
The open country, and could see
The road run on from close to lea,
And lastly by a wooden bridge
A long way from that heathy ridge
Cross over a deep lowland stream—
Then in his eyes there came a gleam,
And his hand fell upon his sword,
And turning round to squire and lord
He said, "Ride sirs, the way is clear,
Nor of my people have I fear,
Nor do my foes range over wide;
And for myself fain would I ride
Right slowly homewards through the fields
Noting what this and that one yields;
While by my squire who bears the child
Lightly my way shall be beguiled.
For some nurse now he needs must have
This tender life of his to save;
And doubtless by the stream there is
Some house where he may dwell in bliss,
Till he grow old enough to learn
How gold and glory he may earn;
And grow, perchance, to be a lord."
   With downcast eyes he spoke that word;
But forth they galloped speedily,
And he drew rein and stood to see
Their green coats lessening as they went.
This man unto the other bent,
Until mid dust and haze at last
Into a wavering mass they passed;
Then 'twixt the hedgerows vanished quite
Just told of by the dust-cloud white
Rolled upwards 'twixt the elm-trunks slim.

   Then turned the king about to him,
Who held the child, noting again
The thing wherein he had been lain,
And on one side of it could see

A lion painted hastily
In red upon a ground of white,
As though of old it had been dight
For some lord's rough-wrought palisade;
But naked 'mid the hay was laid
The child, and had no mark or sign.
  Then said the king, "My ancient line
Thou and thy sires through good and ill
Have served, and unto thee my will
Is law enough from day to day;
Ride nigh me hearkening what I say."
  He shook his rein and side by side
Down through the meadows did they ride,
And opening all his heart, the king
Told to the old man everything
Both of the sage, and of his dream;
Withal drawn nigh unto the stream,
He said, "Yet this shall never be,
For surely as thou lovest me,
Adown this water shall he float
With this rough box for ark and boat,
Then if mine old line he must spill
There let God save him if he will,
While I in no case shed his blood."
  "Yea," said the squire, "thy words are good,
For the whole sin shall lie on me,
Who greater things would do for thee
If need there were; yet note, I pray,
It may be he will 'scape this day
And live; and what wouldst thou do then
If thou shouldst meet him among men?
I counsel thee to let him go
Since sure to nought thy will shall grow."
  "Yea, yea," the king said, "let all be
That may be, if I once but see
This ark whirl in the eddies swift
Or tangled in the autumn drift
And wrong side up:" but with that word
Their horse-hoofs on the plank he heard,
And swift across the bridge he rode,
And nigh the end of it abode,
Then turned to watch the old squire stop,
And leaning o'er the bridge-rail drop
The luckless child; he heard withal
A muttered word and splashing fall
And from the wakened child a cry,
And saw the cradle hurrying by,
Whirled round and sinking, but as yet
Holding the child, nor overset.
  Now somewhat, soothly at the sight
Did the king doubt if he outright

Had rid him of his feeble foe,
But frowning did he turn to go
Unto his home, nor knew indeed
How better he might help his need;
And as unto his house he rode
Full little care for all he showed,
Still bidding Samuel the squire
Unto his bridle-hand ride nigher,
To whom he talked of careless things,
As unto such will talk great kings.
  But when unto his palace gate
He came at last, thereby did wait
The chamberlain with eager eyes
Above his lips grown grave with lies,
In haste to tell him that the queen,
While in the wild-wood he had been,
Had borne a daughter unto him
Strong, fair of face, and straight of limb.
So well at ease and glad thereat
His troubled dream he nigh forgat,
His troubled waking, and the ride
Unto the fateful river-side;
Or thought of all as little things
Unmeet to trouble souls of kings.

So passed the days, so passed the years
In such-like hopes, and such-like fears,
And such-like deeds in field and hall
As unto royal men befall,
And fourteen years have passed away
Since on the huddled brake he lay
And dreamed that dream, remembered now
Once and again, when slow and slow
The minutes of some sleepless night
Crawl toward the dawning of the light.

  Remembered not on this sweet morn
When to the ringing of the horn,
Jingle of bits and mingled shout
Toward that same stream he rideth out
To see his grey-winged falcons fly.
  So long he rode he drew anigh
A mill upon the river's brim,
That seemed a goodly place to him,
For o'er the oily smooth millhead
There hung the apples growing red,
And many an ancient apple-tree
Within the orchard could he see,
While the smooth millwalls white and black
Shook to the great wheel's measured clack,
And grumble of the gear within;

While o'er the roof that dulled that din
The doves sat crooning half the day,
And round the half-cut stack of hay
The sparrows fluttered twittering.
   There smiling stayed the joyous king,
And since the autumn noon was hot
Thought good anigh that pleasant spot
To dine that day, and therewith sent
To tell the miller his intent:
Who held the stirrup of the king,
Bareheaded, joyful at the thing,
While from his horse he lit adown,
Then lead him o'er an elm-beam brown,
New cut in February tide
That crossed the stream from side to side,
So underneath the apple trees
The king sat careless, well at ease
And ate and drank right merrily.
   To whom the miller drew anigh
Among the courtiers, bringing there
Such as he could of country fare,
Green yellowing plums from off his wall,
Wasp-bitten pears, the first to fall
From off the wavering spire-like tree,
Junkets, and cream and fresh honey.
   Smiling the king regarded him,
For he was round-paunched, short of limb,
Red-faced, with long, lank flaxen hair;
But with him was a boy, right fair,
Grey-eyed, and yellow-haired, most like
Unto some Michael who doth strike
The dragon on a minster wall,
So sweet-eyed was he, and withal
So fearless of all things he seemed.
But when he saw him the king deemed
He scarce could be the miller's kin,
And laughing said, "Hast thou within
Thy dusty mill the dame who bore
This stripling in the days of yore,
For fain were I to see her now,
If she be liker him than thou?"
   "Sire," said the miller, "that may be
And thou my dame shall surely see;
But for the stripling, neither I
Begat him, nor my wife did lie
In labour when the lad was born,
But as an outcast and forlorn
We found him fourteen years to-day,
So quick the time has passed away."

   Then the king, hearkening what he said,

A vanished day remembered,
And troubled grew his face thereat;
But while he thought of this and that
The man turned from him and was gone
And by him stood the lad alone;
At whom he gazed, and as their eyes
Met, a great horror 'gan arise
Within his heart, and back he shrank
And shuddering a deep draught he drank,
Scarce knowing if his royal wine
He touched, or juice of some hedge-vine.
   But as his eyes he lifted up
From off his jewelled golden cup,
Once more the miller drew anigh,
By whom his wife went timidly
Bearing some burden in her hand;
So when before him she did stand
And he beheld her worn and old,
And black-haired, then that hair of gold,
Grey eyes, firm lips, and round cleft chin,
Brought stronger memory of his sin.
   But the carle spake, "Dame, tell the King
How this befell, a little thing
The thoughts of such great folk to hold,
Speak out, and fear not to be bold."
   "My tale," she said, "is short enow,
For this day fourteen years ago
Along this river-side I rode
From market to our poor abode,
Where we dwelt far from other men,
Since thinner was the country then
Than now it is; so as I went
And wearied o'er my panniers bent,
From out the stream a feeble cry
I heard, and therewith presently,
From off my mule's back could I see
This boy who standeth here by thee,
A naked, new-born infant, laid
In a rough ark that had been stayed
By a thick tangled bed of weed;
So pitying the youngling's need,
Dismounting, did I wade for him
Waist deep, whose ark now scarce did swim;
And he, with cold, and misery,
And hunger, was at point to die.
   "Withal, I bare him to the mill
And cherished him, and had good will
To bring the babe up as mine own;
Since childless were we and alone,
And no one came to father it.
So oft have I rejoiced to sit

Beside the fire and watch him play.
And now, behold him!—but some day
I look to lose him, for, indeed,
I deem he comes of royal seed,
Unmeet for us: and now, my lord,
Have you heard every foolish word
About my son—this boy—whose name
Is Michael soothly, since he came
To us this day nigh Michaelmas.
—See, sire, the ark wherein he was!
Which I have kept."
                    Therewith she drew
A cloth away; but the King knew,
Long ere she moved, what he should see,
Nor looked, but seeming carelessly
Leaned on the board and hid his eyes.
But at the last did he arise
And saw the painted lion red,
Not faded, well remembered;
Withal he thought, "And who of these
Were with me then amongst the trees
To see this box;" but presently
He thought again that none but he
And the grey squire, old Samuel,
That painting could have noted well.
Since Samuel his cloak had cast
About it, and therewith had past
Throughout the forest on that day,
And not till all were well away
Had drawn it off before the King.
But changed and downcast at the thing
He left the lovely autumn place,
Still haunted by the new-found face
Of his old foe, and back he rode
Unto his ancient rich abode,
Forcing but dismal merriment
As midst his smiling lords he went;
Who yet failed not to note his mood,
So changed: and some men of the wood
Remembered them, but said not aught,
Yea, trembled lest their hidden thought
Some bird should learn, and carry it.

  The morrow come, the King did sit
Alone, to talk with Samuel,
Who yet lived, gathering wage for hell.
He from the presence in a while
Came forth, and with his ugly smile
He muttered, "Well betide me, then,
St. Peter! they are lucky men
Who serve no kings, since they indeed

May damn themselves each for his need.
And will not he outlive this day
Whom the deep water could not slay,
Ere yet his lips had tasted food?
—With that a horse, both strong and good,
He gat of the king's equerry,
And toward the mill rode speedily.

  There Michael by the mill-tail lay,
Watching the swift stream snatch away
His float from midst the careless dace;
But thinking of the thin, dark face,
That yesterday all men he saw
Gaze at with seeming love and awe;
Nor had he, wondering at the lords,
Lost one word of the housewife's words;
And still he noted that the King
Beheld him as a wondrous thing,
Strange to find there: so in his heart
He thought to play some royal part
In this wild play of life, and made
Stories, wherein great words he said,
And did great deeds in desperate fight.
But midst these thoughts there came in sight
He who had carried him of yore,
From out the woodman's broken door,
Dressed like a king's man, with fine gold
Touching his hard brown hands and old,
So was his sleeve embroidered;
A plumed hat had he on his head,
And by his side a cutting sword
Fit for the girdle of a lord;
And round his neck a knife he bore,
Whose hilt was well enamelled o'er,
With green leaves on a golden ground,
Whose stem a silver scroll enwound;
Charged with those letters, writ in black,
Strike! for no dead man cometh back!
  The boy gazed at him earnestly,
With beating heart, as he drew nigh.
And when at last he drew his rein
Beside him, thought that not in vain
His dream might be. But Samuel
Below his breath said; "Surely well
Shalt thou fulfil thy destiny;
And, spite of all, thou wilt not die
Till thou hast won the arched crown?
  But with that word he lighted down,
And said aloud, "Lad, tell to me
Where the good miller I may see,
For from the King I come to-day,

And have a word to him to say;
I think, indeed, concerning thee;
For surely thou his lad must be."
   Then Michael leapt up, nor took heed
Of how the nibbling dace might feed
Upon the loose ends of his bait;
"Fair sir," he said, "my sire doth wait
Until men bring his mare from grass,
For to the good town will he pass,
Since he has need of household gear;
Follow, my lord, the place is here."
   Withal, the good steed being made fast,
Unto the other side they passed,
And by the door the miller found,
Who bowed before him to the ground,
And asked what he would have him do
Then from his bosom Samuel drew
A scroll, and said, "Good friend, read here,
And do my bidding without fear
Of doing ill."
         "Sir," said the man,
"But little lettered skill I can;
Let my dame come, for she can read
Well written letters at good need."
   "Nay, friend," he said, "suffice it thee
This seal at the scroll's end to see,
My Lord the King's; and hear my word,
That I come hither from my lord
Thy foundling lad to have away
To serve the King from this same day."
   Downcast the miller looked thereat,
And twisting round his dusty hat,
Said, "Well, my lord, so must it be,
Nor is he aught akin to me,
Nor seems so: none the less would I
Have left him, when I came to die,
All things I have, with this my mill,
Wherein he hath no 'prentice skill,
Young as he is: and surely here
Might he have lived, with little fear,
A life of plenty and of bliss—
Near by, too, a fair maid there is,
I looked should be good wife to him."

   Meanwhile young Michael's head 'gan swim
With thoughts of noble life and praise;
And he forgat the happy days
Wherein the happy dreams he dreamed
That now so near fulfilment seemed;
And, looking through the open mill,
Stared at the grey and windy hill

And saw it not, but some fair place
Made strange with many a changing face.
And all his life that was to be.
  But Samuel, laughing scornfully,
Said, "O good soul, thou thinkest then
This is a life for well-born men,
As our lord deems this youngling is—
Tell me good lad, where lies thy bliss?
  But Michael turned shamefaced and red,
Waked from his dream, and stammering said,
"Fair sir, my life is sweet and good,
And John, the ranger of the wood,
Saith that I draw so good a bow,
That I shall have full skill enow
Ere many months have passed me by
To join the muster, and to try
To win the bag of florins white,
That folk, on Barnaby the bright,
Shoot for within the market town.
Sir, please you to look up and down
The weedy reaches of our stream,
And note the bubbles of the bream,
And see the great chub take the fly,
And watch the long pike basking lie
Outside the shadow of the weed.
Withal there come unto our need
Woodcock and snipe when swallows go;
And now the water-hen flies low
With feet that well nigh touch the reeds,
And plovers cry about the meads,
And the stares chatter; certes, sir,
It is a fair place all the year."
  Eyeing him grimly, Samuel said,
"Thou show'st churl's breeding, by my head,
In foul despite of thy fair face!
Take heart, for to a better place
Thou goest now.—Miller, farewell,
Nor need'st thou to the neighbours tell
The noble fortunes of the lad;
For, certes, he shall not be glad
To know them in a year or twain.
Yet shall thy finding not be vain,
And thou mayst bless it; for behold
This bag wherein is store of gold;
Take it and let thy hinds go play,
And grind no corn for many a day,
For it would buy thy mill and thee."
  He turned to go, but pensively
Stood Michael, for his broken dream
Doubtful and far away did seem
Amid the squire's rough mockeries;

And tears were gathering in his eyes.
But the kind miller's rough farewell
Rang in his ears; and Samuel
Stamped with his foot and plucked his sleeve;
So therewithal he turned to leave
His old abode, the quiet place,
Trembling, with wet and tearful face.
    But even as he turned there came
From out the house the simple dame
And cast rough arms about the lad,
Saying, "For that I have been glad
By means of thee this many a day,
My mourning heart this hour doth pay.
But fair son, may'st thou live in bliss,
And die in peace; remembering this,
When thou art come to high estate,
That in our house, early and late,
The happy house that shall be sad,
Thou hadst the best of all we had
And love unfeigned from us twain,
Whose hearts thou madest young again,
Hearts that the quicker old shall grow
Now thou art gone."
                    "Good dame, enow,"
Quoth Samuel, "the day grows late,
And sure the king for meat shall wait
Until he see this new-found lord."
He strode away upon that word;
And half ashamed, and half afeard,
Yet eager as his dream he neared,
Shyly the lad went after him.
They crossed the stream and by its brim
Both mounted the great warhorse grey,
And without word they rode away.

    But as along the river's edge
They went, and brown birds in the sedge
Twittered their sweet and formless tune
In the fair autumn afternoon,
And reach by reach the well-known stream
They passed, again the hopeful dream
Of one too young to think death near,
Who scarce had learned the name of fear
Remorseful memories put to flight;
Lovely the whole world showed and bright.
Nor did the harsh voice rouse again
The thought of mockery or of pain,
For other thoughts held Samuel.
    So, riding silently and well,
They reached at last the dusty road
That led unto the King's abode.

But Samuel turned away his face
Therefrom, and at a steady pace
The great horse thundered o'er the bridge,
And made on toward the heathy ridge,
Wherefrom they rode that other day.
But Michael, noting well the way,
Why thus they went, fell wondering,
And said aloud, "Dwells then the King,
Fair sir, as now within the wood?"

  "Young fool, where that it seems him good
He dwelleth," quoth old Samuel,
"And now it pleaseth him to dwell
With the black monks across the wood."

  Withal he muttered in his hood,
"Curst be the King, and thee also,
Who thrust me out such deeds to do;
When I should bide at home to pray,
Who draw so nigh my ending day."
So saying forth his horse he spurred
And to himself said yet this word,
"Yea, yea, and of all days forlorn
God curse the day when I was born."

  Therewith he groaned; yet saying thus
His case seemed hard and piteous,
When he remembered how of old
Another tale he might have told.

  So as each thought his own thoughts still,
The horse began to breast the hill,
And still they went on higher ground,
Until as Michael turned him round
He saw the sunny country-side
Spread out before him far and wide,
Golden amidst its waning green,
Joyous with varied life unseen.
Meanwhile from side to side of them
The trees began their way to hem,
As still he gazed from tree to tree,
And when he turned back presently
He saw before him like a wall
Uncounted tree trunks dim and tall.
Then with their melancholy sound
The odorous spruce woods met around
Those wayfarers, and when he turned
Once more, far off the sunlight burned
In star-like spots, while from o'erhead,
Dim twilight through the boughs was shed.

  Not there as yet had Michael been,
Nor had he left the meadows green
Dotted about with spreading trees,
And fresh with sun and rain and breeze,
For those mirk woods, and still his eyes

Gazed round about for mysteries.
Since many an old wife's tale he knew;
Huge woodcutters in raiment blue,
The remnant of a mighty race,
The ancient masters of the place,
And hammering trolls he looked to see,
And dancers of the faërie,
Who, as the ancient stories told,
In front were lovely to behold,
But empty shells seen from behind.

  So on they rode until the wind
Had died out, stifled by the trees,
And Michael 'mid those images
Of strange things made alive by fear,
Grew drowsy in the forest drear;
Nor noted how the time went past
Until they nigh had reached at last
The borders of the spruce-tree wood;
And with a tingling of the blood
Samuel bethought him of the day
When turned about the other way
He carried him he rode with now.
For the firs ended on the brow
Of a rough gravelly hill, and there
Lay a small valley nowise fair
Beneath them, clear at first of all
But brake, till amid rushes tall
Down in the bottom alders grew
Crabbed and rough; and winding through
The clayey mounds a brook there was
Oozy and foul, half choked with grass.
  There now the Squire awhile drew rein,
And noted how the ground again
Rose up upon the other side,
And saw a green glade opening wide
'Twixt oaks and hollies, and he knew
Full well what place it led unto;
Withal he heard the bittern's boom,
And though without the fir-wood's gloom
They now were come, yet red and low
The sun above the trees did show,
And in despite of hardihead,
The old squire had a mortal dread
Of lying in the wood alone
When that was done that should be done.
  Now Michael, wakened by the wind,
Clutched tighter at the belt behind,
And with wide eyes was staring round,
When Samuel said, "Get to the ground,
My horse shall e'en sink deep enow,

Without thy body, in this slough;
And haste thee, or we both shall lie
Beneath the trees, and be as dry
As autumn dew can make us. Haste!
The time is short for thee to waste."
   Then from the horse the boy did glide,
And slowly down the valley side
They went, and Michael, wakened now,
Sang such rude songs as he might know,
Grown fresh and joyous of his life;
While Samuel, clutching at the knife
About his neck that hung, again
Down in the bottom tightened rein,
And turning, in a hoarse voice said,
"My girths are loosening, by my head!
Come nigh and draw them tighter, lad."
   Then Michael stayed his carol glad,
And noting little in his mirth
The other's voice, unto the girth
Without a word straight set his hand:
But as with bent head he did stand,
Straining to tighten what was tight,
In Samuel's hand the steel flashed bright,
And fell, deep smitten in his side,
Then, leaping back, the poor lad cried,
As if for help, and staggering fell,
With wide eyes fixed on Samuel;
Who none the less grown deadly pale,
Lit down, lest that should not avail
To slay him, and beside him knelt,
And since his eyes were closed now, felt
His heart that beat yet: therewithal
His hand upon the knife did fall.
But, ere his fingers clutched it well,
Far off he seemed to hear a bell,
And trembling knelt upright again,
And listening, listened not in vain,
For clear he heard a tinkling sound.
Then to his horse from off the ground
He leapt, nor reasoned with his dread,
But thought the angel of the dead
Was drawing nigh the slayer to slay,
Ere scarce the soul had passed away.
One dreadful moment yet he heard
That bell, then like a madman spurred
His noble horse; that maddened too,
The close-set fir-wood galloped through,
Not stayed by any stock or stone,
Until the furious race being done,
Anigh the bridge he fell down dead;
And Samuel, mazed with guilt and dread,

Wandered afoot throughout the night,
But came, at dawning of the light,
Half-dead unto the palace gate.
   There till the opening did he wait;
Then, by the King's own signet-ring,
He gained the chamber of the king,
And painfully what he had done
He told, and how the thing had gone.
And said withal: "Yet is he dead,
And surely that which made my dread
Shall give thee joy: for doubt not aught
That bell the angels to him brought,
That he in Abraham's breast might lie—
So ends, O King, the prophecy."
   Nathless the King scowled, ill content,
And said, "I deemed that I had sent
A man of war to do my will,
Who lacked for neither force nor skill,
And thou com'st with a woman's face,
Bewildered with thy desperate race,
And made an idiot with thy fear,
Nor bring'st me any token here!"
   Therewith he rose and gat away,
But brooding on it through that day,
Thought that all things went not so ill
As first he deemed, and that he still
Might leave his old line flourishing.
Therewith both gold and many a thing
Unto old Samuel he gave,
But thereby failed his life to save;
Who, not so old in years as sin,
Died ere the winter, and within
The minster choir was laid asleep,
With carven saints his head to keep.

   And so the days and years went by,
And still in great felicity
The King dwelt, wanting only this—
A son wherewith to share his bliss,
And reign when he was dead and gone.
Nor had he daughter, save that one
Born on the night when Michael first,
Forlorn, alone, and doubly cursed,
Felt on him this world's bitter air.
   This daughter, midst fair maids most fair,
Was not yet wed, though at this time,
Being come unto her maiden's prime,
She looked upon her eighteenth May.
   Midst this her mother passed away,
Not much lamented of the King,
Who had the thought of marrying

Some dame more fertile, and who sent
A wily man with this intent
To spy the countries out and find
Some great king's daughter, wise and kind,
And fresh, and fair, in face and limb,
In all things a fit mate for him.
  So in short time it came to pass
Again the King well wedded was,
And hoped once more to have a son.
  And when this fair dame he had won,
A year in peace he dwelt with her,
Until the time was drawing near
When first his eyes beheld that foe
He deemed was dead these years ago.
Now at that time, as custom was,
His daughter was about to pass
Unto a distant house of his,
Some king had built for worldly bliss
In ancient days: there, far removed
From courts or towns, the dame he loved
The dead king had been wont to see
Play mid the summer greenery,
Or like Erigone of old
Stand in the vineyards girt with gold,
To queen it o'er the vintagers,
Half worshipping that face of hers.
Long years agone these folk were passed,
Their crimes forgotten, or else cast
Into the glowing crucible
Of time, that tempers all things well,
That maketh pleasure out of pain,
And out of ruin golden gain;
Nathless, unshaken still, there stood
The towers and ramparts red as blood;
Wherein their lives had passed away;
And still the lovely gardens lay
About them, changed, but smiling still,
As in past time, on good or ill.
  Thither the Princess Cecily
Must go awhile in peace to be;
For now, midst care, and doubt, and toil,
Proud words drawn back, and half-healed broil,
The King had found one meet to wed
His daughter, of great godlihead,
Wealth, and unbroken royalty.
And now he said to her, when she
Was setting out for that fair place,
"O daughter, thou shalt see my face
Before a month is fully gone,
Nor wilt thou see me then alone;
For that man shall be with me then,

Whom I have chosen from all men
To give my dearest treasure to.
Most fain he is to look on you,
Nor needst thou fear him for thy part,
Who holdeth many a woman's heart
As the net holds the silvery fish.
Farewell—and all things thou mayst wish
I pray God grant thee."
                Therewithal
He kissed her, and from out the hall
She passed, not shamefaced, or afraid
Of what might happen; though, indeed,
Her heart of no man's heart had need
To make her happy as she thought.

   Ever the new sun daily brought
Fresh joy of life to her bedside,
The world before her open wide
Was spread, a place for joy and bliss.
Her lips had trembled with no kiss,
Wherewith love slayeth fear and shame;
Her grey eyes conscious of no blame,
Beheld unmoved the eyes of men;
Her hearing grew no dimmer when
Some unused footstep she might hear;
And unto no man was she dear,
But as some goddess might have been
When Greek men worshipped many a queen.

   Now with her armed folk forth she rode
Unto that ancient fair abode,
And while the lark sung o'er the corn,
Love gilded not the waning morn;
And when the sun rose high above,
High thoughts she thought, but not of love;
And when that sun the world did leave,
He left no love to light the eve.
The moon no melancholy brought,
The dawn no vain, remorseful thought.
But all untroubled her sweet face
Passed 'neath the gate of that old place,
And there her bridegroom she abode.

   But scarce was she upon the road
Ere news unto the King was brought
That Peter, the old abbot, sought
To see him, having newly come
From the wild place that was his home
Across the forest; so the King
Bade him to enter, well willing
To hear what he might have to say;

Who, entering the hall straightway,
Had with him an old, reverend man,
The Sub-prior, father Adrian,
And five monks more, and therewithal
Ten of his folk, stout men and tall,
Who bore armed staves and coats of fence.
　So, when he came to audience,
He prayed the King of this or that,
Whereof my tale-teller forgat,
And graciously the King heard all,
And said at last, "Well, what may fall,
Thou go'st not hence, fair lord, to-day;
Unless in vain a king must pray,
Thou and thy monks shall eat with me;
While feast thine axe-men merrily."
　Withal, he eyed the abbot's folk
In careless mood, then once more spoke,
"Tall men thou feedest, by the rood!
Lord Abbot, come they from the wood?
Dwell many more such thereabout?
Fain were I such should swell the shout
When I am armed, and rank meets rank."
　But as he spoke his loud voice sank
Wavering, nor heard he aught at all
Of the faint noises of the hall,
Or what the monk in answer said;
For, looking from a steel-clad head,
Those eyes again did he behold,
That erst from 'neath the locks of gold
Kindly and bold, but soft with awe,
Beneath the apple-boughs he saw.
　But when for sure this thing he knew
Pale to the very lips he grew.
Till gathering heart within a while
With the faint semblance of a smile,
He seemed to note the Abbot's words
That he heard not; then from the lords
He turned, and facing Michael said,
"Raise up the steel cap from thine head,
That I may see if thou look'st bold;
Methinks, I know thy face of old,
Whence com'st thou?

　　　　　　　Michael lifted straight
From off his brow the steel cap's weight,
And showed the bright locks curling round
His fresh and ruddy face, sun-browned,
And in a voice clear as a bell,
Told all his story, till he fell
Sore wounded in that dismal vale;
And said withal, "My lord, the tale

Of what came after, none knoweth
Better than he, who, from ill death
Saved me that tide, and made me man,
My lord, the sub-prior Adrian."
    "Speak on then, father," quoth the King,
Making as he was still hearkening.
"My lord," said Adrian, "I, who then
Was but a server of poor men,
Outside our Abbey walls, one day
Was called by one in poor array,
A charcoal-burner's lad, who said.
That soon his father would be dead,
And that of all things he would have
His rights, that he his soul might save.
I made no tarrying at that word,
But took between mine hands the Lord,
And bade the boy bear forth the bell
For though few folk there were to tell.
Who passed that way, nathless, I trow
The beasts were glad that news to know.
    "Well, by the pinewood's skirts we went
While through its twilight the bell sent
A heavenly tinkling; but the lad
'Gan telling me of fears he had
Of elves who dwell within the wood.
I chid him thereat, as was good,
Bidding him note Whom in mine hands
I held, The Ransom of all Lands.
But as the firwood's dim twilight
Waxed into day, and fair and bright
The evening sun showed through the trees,
Our ears fanned by the evening breeze,
The galloping of horse-hoofs heard,
Wherewith my page hung back afeard
Of elves and such-like; but I said,
'Wilt thou thy father shouldst be dead
Ere we can reach him? Oh my son,
Fear not that aught can stay This One.'
    "Therewith I smote my mule, and he
Ran forward with me hastily
As fearing to be left behind.
Well, as we went, what should we find
Down by the stream, but this my son,
Who seemed as though his days were done;
For in his side a knife there stood
Wherefrom ran out a stream of blood,
Soaking the grass and water-mint;
Then, I dismounting, we by dint
Of all our strength, the poor youth laid
Upon my mule, and down a glade
Of oaks and hollies then we passed,

And reached the woodman's home at last;
A poor hut, built of wattled wood,
And by its crooked gable stood
A ruinous shed, unroofed and old
That beasts of burden once did hold.
Thyself; my lord, mayst know it well,
Since thereabout the wild swine dwell;
And hart, and hind, and roe are there—
So the lad's wounds I staunched with care
Forthwith, and then the man I shrived,
Who none the less got well and lived
For many a day: then back I went
And the next day our leech I sent
With drugs to tend upon the lad.
Who soon was as he ne'er had had
A hurt at all: and he being well
We took him in our house to dwell,
And taught him letters, and, indeed,
Before long, Latin could he read
As well as I; but hath no will
To turn unto religion still.
Yet is he good and doth no wrong;
And being thereto both hale and strong,
My lord, the Abbot, sayeth of him,
'He shall serve God with heart and limb,
Not heart and voice.' Therefore, my lord,
Thou seest him armed with spear and sword
For their defence who feed him still,
Teach him, and guard his soul from ill.
Ho, Michael! hast thou there with thee
The fair-wrought knife I first did see
Deep in thy side?—there, show it now
Unto the King, that he may know
Our tale is not a fabled thing."
   Withal the King, as one listening,
With his thin, anxious face and pale,
Sat leaning forward through this tale,
Scarce noting here and there a word.
But all being told, at last he heard
His own voice changed, and harsh, and low,
That said, "Fair lord, I fain would know,
Since this your man at arms seems true,
What thing will he be worth to you;
For better had he wear my rose
Than loiter in your Abbey-close,
Poring o'er books no man can read."
   "O sire!" the monk said, "if your need
Be great of such men, let him go;
My men-at-arms need make no show
Of fairness, nor should ladies miss,
E'en as thou say'st, such men as this."

Laughing he spoke; the King the while,
His pale face puckering to a smile;
Then, as in some confused dream,
In Michael's hand he saw the gleam
Of that same steel remembered well,
The gift he gave to Samuel;
Drawn from his father's ancient chest
To do that morn his own behest.
And as he now beheld its sheen,
The twining stem of gold and green,
The white scroll with the letters black,—
Strike! for no dead man cometh back!
He hardened yet his heart once more,
And grown unhappy as before,
When last he had that face in sight,
Brought now the third time to the light,
Once more grew treacherous, fierce, and fell.
    Now was the Abbot feasted well
With all his folk, then went away,
But Michael clad in rich array
Became the king's man, and was thought.
By all most happy to be brought
Unto such hopeful fair estate.

    For ten days yet the King did wait,
Which past, for Michael did he send,
And he being come, said to him, "Friend,
Take now this letter from my hand
And go unto our southern land;
My captain Hugh shall go with thee
For one day's journey, then shall he
Tell thee which way thou hast to ride;
The third day thence about noontide
If thou dost well, thou shouldst be close
Unto my Castle of the Rose
Where dwells my daughter; needs it is
That no man living should see this
Until that thou within my wall
Hast given it to the seneschal;
Be wise and wary then, that thou
Mayst think of this that happeneth now
As birthday to thine high estate."
    So said he, knowing not that fate
Was dealing otherwise than he.
    But Michael going, presently
Met Hugh, a big man rough and black,
And who of nought but words had lack,
With him he mounted, and set forth
And daylong rode on from the north.
    Now if the King had hope that Hugh
Some deed like Samuel's might do

I know not, certes nought he said
To that hard heart and narrow head,
Who knew no wiles but wiles of war,
And was as true as such men are;
Yet had there been a tale to tell
If Michael had not held him well,
And backward still the wrath had turned
Wherewith his heart not seldom burned
At scornful words his fellow said.
   At last they reached cross ways that led
One west, one southward still, whereat
Hugh, taking off his feathered hat,
Bowed low in scorn, and said, "Fair sir,
Unto the westward must I spur,
While you go southward, soon to get
I doubt not, an earl's coronet;
Farewell, my lord, and yet beware
Thou dost not at my lady stare
Too hard, lest thou shouldst plumb the moat,
Or have a halter round thy throat."
   But Michael to his scoff said nought,
But upon high things set his thought
As his departing hooves he heard.
And still betwixt the hedgerows spurred,
And when, the twilight was o'erpast
At a small inn drew rein at last,
And slept that night as such folk can;
And while next morn the thrushes ran
Their first course through the autumn dew
The gossamers did he dash through,
And on his way rode steadily
The live-long day, nor yet was he
Alone, as well might be that day
Since a fair town was in his way,
Stout hinds he passed, and yeomen good,
Some friar in his heavy hood,
And well-coifed housewives mounted high
Above their maunds, while merrily
The well-shod damsel trudged along
Beside them, sending forth some song
As little taught as is a bird's;
And good men, good wives, priests, and herds,
And merry maids failed not to send
Good wishes for his journey's end
Unto him as still on he sped,
Free from all evil thoughts or dread.

   Withal again the day went by,
And in that city's hostelry
He slept, and by the dawn of day
Next morn again was on his way,

And leaving the scarce wakened street
The newly risen sun did greet
With cheerful heart. His way wound on
Still up and up till he had won
Up to a great hill's chalky brow,
Whence looking back he saw below
The town spread out, church, square, and street,
And baily, crawling up the feet
Of the long yew-besprinkled hill;
And in the fragrant air and still,
Seeming to gain new life from it,
The doves from roof to roof did flit:
The early fires sent up their smoke
That seemed to him to tell of folk
New wakened unto great delight:
For he upon that morning bright,
So joyous felt, so free from pain,
He seemed as he were born again
Into some new immortal state
That knew no envy, fear, or hate.
   Now the road turned to his left hand
And led him through a table-land,
Windy and barren of all grain;
But where a hollow specked the plain
The yew-trees hugged the sides of it,
And 'mid them did the woodlark flit
Or sang well-sheltered from the wind,
And all about the sheep did find
Sweet grass, the while the shepherd's song
Rang clear as Michael sped along.
   Long time he rode, till suddenly,
When now the sun was broad and high,
From out a hollow where the yew
Still guarded patches of the dew,
He found at last that he had won
That highland's edge, and gazed upon
A valley that beneath the haze
Of that most fair of autumn days,
Showed glorious; fair with golden sheaves,
Rich with the darkened autumn-leaves,
Gay with the water-meadows green,
The bright blue streams that lay between,
The miles of beauty stretched away
From that bleak hill-side bare and grey,
Till white cliffs over slopes of vine,
Drew 'gainst the sky a broken line.
And twixt the vineyards and the stream
Michael saw gilded spirelets gleam;
For, hedged with many a flowery close,
There lay the Castle of the Rose,
His hurried journey's aim and end.

Then downward he began to wend,
And 'twixt the flowery hedges sweet
He heard the hook smite down the wheat,
And murmur of the unseen folk;
But when he reached the stream that broke
The golden plain, but leisurely
He passed the bridge, for he could see
The masters of that ripening realm,
Cast down beneath an ancient elm
Upon a little strip of grass,
From hand to hand the pitcher pass,
While on the turf beside them lay
The ashen-handled sickles grey,
The matters of their cheer between:
Slices of white cheese, specked with green,
And greenstriped onions and ryebread,
And summer apples faintly red,
Even beneath the crimson skin;
And yellow grapes, well ripe and thin,
Plucked from the cottage gable-end.

    And certes Michael felt their friend
Hearing their voices, nor forgot
His boyhood and the pleasant spot
Beside the well-remembered stream;
And friendly did this water seem
As through its white-flowered weeds it ran
Bearing good things to beast and man.
    Yea, as the parapet he passed,
And they a greeting toward him cast,
Once more he felt a boy again;
As though beneath the harvest wain
He was asleep, by that old stream,
And all these things were but a dream—
The King, the squire, the hurrying ride
Unto the lonely quagmire side;
The sudden pain, the deadly swoon,
The feverish life from noon to noon;
The tending of the kind old man,
The black and white Dominican,
The hour before the abbot's throne,
The poring o'er old books alone,
In summer morn; the King again,
The envious greetings of strange men,
This mighty horse and rich array,
This journey on an unknown way.
    Surely he thought to wake from it,
And once more by the waggon sit,
Blinking upon the sunny mill.
    But not for either good or ill

Shall he see one of all those days;
On through the quivering noontide haze
He rode, and now on either hand
Heavy with fruit the trees did stand;
Nor had he ridden long, ere he
The red towers of the house could see
Grey on the wind-beat southern side:
And soon the gates thrown open wide
He saw, the long-fixed drawbridge down,
The moat, with lilies overgrown,
Midst which the gold-scaled fishes lay:
Such peace was there for many a day.
   And deep within the archway's shade
The warder on his cloak was laid,
Dozing, one hand upon a harp.
And nigh him a great golden carp
Lay stiff with all his troubles done,
Drawn from the moat ere yet the sun
Was high, and nigh him was his bane,
An angling rod of Indian cane.
   Now hearing Michael's horse-hooves smite
The causeway, shading from the light
His eyes, as one scarce yet awake,
He made a shift his spear to take,
And, eyeing Michael's badge the while,
Rose up, and with a lazy smile,
Said, "Ho! fair sir, abide, abide,
And show why hitherward ye ride
Unto my lady's royal home."
Said Michael, "From the king I come,
As by my badge ye well may see;
And letters have I here with me
To give my lord the Seneschal."
   "Yea," said the man, "But in the hall
He feasteth now; what haste is there,
Certes full quickly cometh care;
And sure I am he will not read
Thy letters, or to aught give heed
Till he has played out all the play,
And every guest has gone away;
So thou, O damoiseau, must wait;
Tie up thine horse anigh the gate,
And sit with me, and thou shalt hear
The Kaiser lieth on his bier.
Thou laughest—hast thou never heard
Of this same valorous Red Beard,
And how he died? well, I can sing
Of many another dainty thing,
Thou wilt not a long while forget,
The budget is not empty yet.
Peter! I think thou mockest me,

But thou art young and fair perdie,
I wish thee luck—well, thou mayest go
And feel the afternoon wind blow
Within Dame Bertha's pleasance here;
She who was held so lief and dear,
All this was built but for her sake,
Who made the hearts of men to ache;
And dying full of years and shame
Yet left an unforgotten name—
God rest her soul!"
        Michael the while
Hearkened his talking with a smile,
Then said, "O friend, I think to hear
Both 'The King lieth on his bier'
And many another song of thee,
Ere I depart; but now show me
The pleasance of the ancient queen,
For these red towers above the green
Show like the gates of paradise,
That surely somewhere through them lies."
  Then said the warder, "That may be
If thou knows't what may come to thee—
When past the drawbridge thou hast gone,
Upon the left three steps of stone
Lead to a path beneath the wall
Of the great court, that folk now call
The falconer's path, nor canst thou miss
Going thereby, to find the bliss
Thou look'st for, since the path ends there,
And through a wicket gilded fair
The garden lies where thou wouldst be
Nor will I fail to come to thee
Whene'er my Lord the Seneschal
Shall pass well fed from out the hall."
  Then Michael, thanking him, passed on,
And soon the gilded wicket won,
And entered that pleasance sweet,
And wandered there with wary feet
And open mouth, as though he deemed
That in some lovely dream he dreamed,
And feared to wake to common day,
So fair was all; and e'en decay
Brought there but pensive loveliness,
Where autumn those old walls did bless
With wealth of fruit, and through the grass
Unscared the spring-born thrush did pass,
Who yet knew nought of winter-tide.
  So wandering, to a fountain's side
He came, and o'er the basin hung,
Watching the fishes, as he sung
Some song remembered from of old,

Ere yet the miller won that gold.
But soon made drowsy with his ride,
And the warm hazy autumn-tide,
And many a musical sweet sound,
He cast him down upon the ground,
And watched the glittering water leap,
Still singing low, nor thought to sleep.
  But scarce three minutes had gone by
Before, as if in mockery,
The starling chattered o'er his head,
And nothing he remembered,
Nor dreamed of aught that he had seen.

  Meanwhile unto that garden green
Had come the Princess, and with her
A maiden that she held right dear,
Who knew the inmost of her mind.
Now those twain, as the scented wind
Played with their raiment or their hair,
Had late been running here and there,
Chasing each other merrily,
As maids do, thinking no one by;
But now, well wearied therewithal,
Had let their gathered garments fall
About their feet, and slowly went:
And through the leaves a murmur sent,
As of two happy doves that sing
The soft returning of the spring.
  Now of these twain the Princess spoke
The less, but into laughter broke
Not seldom, and would redden oft,
As on her lips her fingers soft
She laid, as still the other maid,
Half grave, half smiling, follies said.
  So in their walk they drew anigh
That fountain in the midst, whereby
Lay Michael sleeping, dreaming nought
Of such fair things so nigh him brought;
They, when the fountain shaft was past,
Beheld him on the ground down-cast,
And stopped at first, until the maid
Stepped lightly forward to the shade,
And when she had gazed there awhile
Came running back again, a smile
Parting her lips, and her bright eyes
Afire with many fantasies;
And ere the Lady Cecily
Could speak a word, "Hush! hush!" said she;
"Did I not say that he would come
To woo thee in thy peaceful home
Before thy father brought him here?

Come, and behold him, have no fear!
The great bell would not wake him now,
Right in his ears."
            "Nay, what dost thou?"
The Princess said; "Let us go hence;
Thou know'st I give obedience
To what my father bids; but I
A maid full fain would live and die,
Since I am born to be a queen."

  "Yea, yea, for such as thou hast seen,
That may be well," the other said.
"But come now, come; for by my head
This one must be from Paradise;
Come swiftly then, if thou art wise
Ere aught can snatch him back again."
  She caught her hand, and not in vain
She prayed; for now some kindly thought
To Cecily's brow fair colour brought,
And quickly 'gan her heart to beat
As love drew near those eyes to greet,
Who knew him not till that sweet hour.

  So over the fair, pink-edged flower,
Softly she stepped; but when she came
Anigh the sleeper, lovely shame
Cast a soft mist before her eyes
Full filled of many fantasies.
But when she saw him lying there
She smiled to see her mate so fair;
And in her heart did Love begin
To tell his tale, nor thought she sin
To gaze on him that was her own,
Not doubting he was come alone
To woo her, whom midst arms and gold
She deemed she should at first behold;
And with that thought love grew again
Until departing was a pain,
Though fear grew with that growing love;
And with her lingering footsteps strove
As from the place she turned to go,
Sighing and murmuring words full low.
But as her raiment's hem she raised,
And for her merry fellow gazed
Shamefaced and changed, she met her eyes
Turned grave and sad with ill surprise;
Who while the princess mazed did stand
Had drawn from Michael's loosened band
The king's scroll, which she held out now
To Cecily, and whispered low,
"Read, and do quickly what thou wilt,
Sad, sad! such fair life to be spilt:

Come further first."
                    With that they stepped
A pace or two from where he slept,
And then she read,
                    "Lord Seneschal,
On thee and thine may all good fall;
Greeting hereby the king sendeth,
And biddeth thee to put to death
His enemy who beareth this;
And as thou lovest life and bliss,
And all thy goods thou holdest dear,
Set thou his head upon a spear
A good half furlong from the gate,
Our coming hitherward to wait—
So perish the King's enemies!"
   She read, and scarcely had her eyes
Seen clear her father's name and seal,
Ere all love's power her heart did feel,
That drew her back in spite of shame,
To him who was not e'en a name
Unto her a short hour agone.
Panting she said, "Wait thou alone
Beside him, watch him carefully
And let him sleep if none draw nigh:
If of himself he waketh, then
Hide him until I come again,
When thou hast told him of the snare—
If thou betrayest me beware!
For death shall be the least of all
The ills that on thine head shall fall—
What say I, thou art dear to me,
And doubly dear now shalt thou be,
Thou shalt have power and majesty,
And be more queen in all than I—
Few words are best, be wise, be wise!"

   Withal she turned about her eyes
Once more, and swiftly as a man
Betwixt the garden trees she ran,
Until, her own bower reached at last,
She made good haste, and quickly passed
Unto her secret treasury.
There, hurrying since the time was nigh
For folk to come from meat, she took
From 'twixt the leaves of a great book
A royal scroll, signed, sealed, but blank,
Then, with a hand that never shrank
Or trembled, she the scroll did fill
With these words, writ with clerkly skill,—
"Unto the Seneschal, Sir Rafe,
Who holdeth our fair castle safe,

Greeting and health! O well-beloved,
Know that at this time we are moved
To wed our daughter, so we send
Him who bears this, our perfect friend,
To be her bridegroom; so do thou
Ask nought of him, since well we know
His race and great nobility,
And how he is most fit to be
Our son; therefore snake no delay,
But wed the twain upon the day
Thou readest this: and see that all
Take oath to him, whate'er shall fall
To do his bidding as our heir;
So doing still be lief and dear
As I have held thee yet to be."
   She cast the pen down hastily
At that last letter, for she heard
How even now the people stirred
Within the hall: nor dared she think
What bitter potion she must drink
If now she failed, so falsely bold
That life or death did she enfold
Within its cover, making shift
To seal it with her father's gift,
A signet of cornelian.

   Then swiftly down the stairs she ran
And reached the garden; but her fears
Brought shouts and thunder to her ears,
That were but lazy words of men
Full-fed, far off; nay, even when
Her limbs caught up her flying gown
The noise seemed loud enough to drown
The twitter of the autumn birds,
And her own muttered breathless words
That to her heart seemed loud indeed.
   Yet therewithal she made good speed
And reached the fountain seen of none
Where yet abode her friend alone,
Watching the sleeper, who just now
Turned in his sleep and muttered low.
Therewith fair Agnes saying nought
From out her hand the letter caught;
And while she leaned against the stone
Stole up to Michael's side alone,
And with a cool, unshrinking hand
Thrust the new scroll deep in his band,
And turned about unto her friend;
Who having come unto the end
Of all her courage, trembled there
With face upturned for fresher air,

And parted lips grown grey and pale,
And limbs that now began to fail,
And hands wherefrom all strength had gone,
Scarce fresher than the blue-veined stone
That feeble still she strove to clutch.
  But when she felt her lady's touch,
Feebly she said, "Go! let me die
And end this sudden misery
That in such wise has wrapped my life,
I am too weak for such a strife,
So sick I am with shame and fear;
Would thou hadst never brought me here!"
  But Agnes took her hand and said,
"Nay, queen, and must we three be dead
Because thou fearest; all is safe
If boldly thou wilt face Sir Rafe."
  So saying, did she draw her hence,
Past tree and bower, and high pleached fence
Unto the garden's further end,
And left her there and back did wend,
And from the house made haste to get
A gilded maund wherein she set
A flask of ancient island wine,
Ripe fruits and wheaten manchets fine,
And many such a delicate
As goddesses in old time ate,
Ere Helen was a Trojan queen;
So passing through the garden green
She cast her eager eyes again
Upon the spot where he had lain,
But found it empty, so sped on
Till she at last the place had won
Where Cecily lay weak and white
Within that fair bower of delight.
  Her straight she made to eat and drink,
And said, "See now thou dost not shrink
From this thy deed; let love slay fear
Now, when thy life shall grow so dear,
Each minute should seem loss to thee
If thou for thy felicity
Couldst stay to count them; for I say,
This day shall be thy happy day."
  Therewith she smiled to see the wine
Embraced by her fingers fine;
And her sweet face grow bright again
With sudden pleasure after pain.
  Again she spoke, "What is this word
That dreaming, I perchance, have heard,
But certainly remember well;
That some old soothsayer did tell
Strange things unto my lord, the King,

That on thy hand the spousal ring
No Kaiser's son, no King should set,
But one a peasant did beget—
What sayst thou?"
                   But the Queen flushed red;
"Such fables I have heard," she said;
"And thou—is it such scathe to me,
The bride of such a man to be?"
  "Nay," said she, "God will have him King;
How shall we do a better thing
With this or that one than He can;
God's friend must be a goodly man."
  But with that word she heard the sound
Of folk who through the mazes wound
Bearing the message; then she said,
"Be strong, pluck up thine hardihead,
Speak little, so shall all be well,
For now our own tale will they tell."

  And even as she spoke they came
And all the green place was aflame
With golden raiment of the lords;
While Cecily, noting not their words,
Rose up to go; and for her part
By this had fate so steeled her heart,
Scarce otherwise she seemed, than when
She passed before the eyes of men
At Tourney or high festival.
But when they now had reached the hall,
And up its very steps they went,
Her head a little down she bent;
Nor raised it till the dais was gained
For fear that love some monster feigned
To be a god, and she should be
Smit by her own bolt wretchedly.
But at the rustling, crowded dais
She gathered heart her eyes to raise,
And there beheld her love, indeed,
Clad in her father's serving weed,
But proud, and flushed, and calm withal,
Fearless of aught that might befal,
Nor too astonied, for he thought,
"From point to point my life is brought
Through wonders till it comes to this;
And trouble cometh after bliss,
And I will bear all as I may,
And ever as day passeth day,
My life will hammer from the twain,
Forging a long enduring chain."
  But midst these thoughts their young eyes met,
And every word did he forget

Wherewith men name unhappiness,
As read again those words did bless
With double blessings his glad ears,
And if she trembled with her fears,
And if with doubt, and love, and shame,
The rosy colour went and came
In her sweet cheeks and smooth bright brow,
Little did folk think of it now,
But as of maiden modesty,
Shamefaced to see the bridegroom nigh.

   And now when Rafe the Seneschal
Had read the message down the Hall,
And turned to her, quite calm again,
Her face had grown, and with no pain
She raised her serious eyes to his
Grown soft and pensive with his bliss,
And said,

          "Prince, thou art welcome here,
Where all my father loves is dear,
And full trust do I put in thee,
For that so great nobility
He knoweth in thee; be as kind
As I would be to thee, and find
A happy life from day to day,
Till all our days are past away."

   What more than found the bystanders
He found within this speech of hers,
I know not; some faint quivering
In the last words; some little thing
That checked the cold words' even flow.
But yet they set his heart aglow,
And he in turn said eagerly:—

   "Surely I count it nought to die
For him who brought me unto this;
For thee, who givest me this bliss;
Yea, even dost me such a grace
To look with kind eyes in my face,
And send sweet music to my ears."

   But at his words she, mazed with tears,
Seemed faint, and failing quickly, when
Above the low hum of the men
Uprose the sweet bells' sudden clang,
As men unto the chapel rang;
While just outside the singing folk
Into most heavenly carols broke.
And going softly up the hall
Boys bore aloft the verges tall
Before the bishop's gold-clad head.

   Then forth his bride young Michael led,
And nought to him seemed good or bad
Except the lovely hand he had;

But she the while was murmuring low,
"If he could know, if he could know,
What love, what love, his love should be!"

   But while mid mirth and minstrelsy
The ancient Castle of the Rose
Such pageant to the autumn shows
The King sits ill at ease at home,
For in these days the news is come
That he who in his line should wed,
Lies in his own town stark and dead,
Slain in a tumult in the street.
   Brooding on this he deemed it meet,
Since nigh the day was come, when she
Her bridegroom's visage looked to see,
To hold the settled day with her.
And bid her at the least to wear
Dull mourning guise for gold and white.
So on another morning bright,
When the whole promised month was past,
He drew anigh the place at last
Where Michael's dead head, looking down
Upon the highway with a frown,
He doubted not at last to see.
So 'twixt the fruitful greenery
He rode, scarce touched by care the while,
Humming a roundel with a smile.
   Withal, ere yet he drew anigh,
He heard their watch-horn sound from high
Nor wondered, for their wont was so,
And well his banner they might know
Amidst the stubble lands afar:
But now a distant point of war
He seemed to hear, and bade draw rein,
But listening cried, "Push on again!
They do but send forth minstrelsy
Because my daughter thinks to see
The man who lieth on his bier."
So on they passed, till sharp and clear
They heard the pipe and shrill fife sound;
And restlessly the King glanced round
To see that he had striven for,
The crushing of that sage's lore,
The last confusion of that fate.
   But drawn still nigher to the gate
They turned a sharp bend of the road,
And saw the pageant that abode
The solemn coming of the King.

   For first on each side, maids did sing,
Dressed in gold raiment; then there came

The minstrels in their coats of flame;
And then the many-coloured lords,
The knights' spears, and the swordmen's swords,
Backed by the glittering wood of bills.
  So now, presaging many ills,
The King drew rein, yet none the less
He shrank not from his hardiness,
But thought, "Well, at the worst I die,
And yet perchance long life may lie
Before me—I will hold my peace;
The dumb man's borders still increase."
  But as he strengthened thus his heart
He saw the crowd before him part,
And down the long melodious lane,
Hand locked in hand there passed the twain,
As fair as any earth has found,
Clad as king's children are, and crowned.
Behind them went the chiefest lords,
And two old knights with sheathed swords
The banners of the kingdom bore.
  But now the King had pondered sore,
By when they reached him, though, indeed,
The time was short unto his need,
Betwixt his heart's first startled pang
And those old banner-bearers' clang
Anigh his saddle-bow: but he
Across their heads scowled heavily,
Not saying aught awhile: at last,
Ere any glance at them he cast,
He said, "Whence come ye? what are ye?
What play is this ye play to me?"
  None answered,—Cecily, faint and white,
The rather Michael's hand clutched tight,
And seemed to speak, but not one word
The nearest to her could have heard.
Then the King spoke again,—"Sir Rafe,
Meseems this youngling came here safe
A week agone?"
        "Yea, sir," he said;
"Therefore the twain I straight did wed,
E'en as thy letters bound me to."
"And thus thou diddest well to do,"
The King said. "Tell me on what day
Her old life she did put away."
  "Sire, the eleventh day this is
Since that they gained their earthly bliss;"
Quoth old Sir Rafe. The King said nought,
But with his head bowed down in thought,
Stood a long while; but at the last
Upward a smiling face he cast,
And cried aloud above the folk,

"Shout for the joining of the yoke
Betwixt these twain; And thou, fair lord,
Who dost so well my every word,
Nor makest doubt of anything,
Wear thou the collar of thy King;
And a duke's banner, cut foursquare,
Henceforth shall men before thee bear
In tourney and in stricken field.

  "But this mine heir shall bear my shield,
Carry my banner, wear my crown,
Ride equal with me through my town,
Sit on the same step of the throne;
In nothing will I reign alone;
Nor be ye with him miscontent,
For that with little ornament
Of gold and folk to you he came;
For he is of an ancient name
That needeth not the clink of gold—
The ancientest the world doth hold;
For in the fertile Asian land,
Where great Damascus now doth stand,
Ages agone his line was born,
Ere yet men knew the gift of corn;
And there, anigh to Paradise,
His ancestors grew stout and wise;
And certes he from Asia bore
No little of their piercing lore.

  "Look then to have great happiness,
For every wrong shall he redress."

  Then did the people's shouting drown
His clatter as he leapt adown;
And taking in each hand a hand
Of the two lovers, now did stand
Betwixt them on the flower-strewn way,
And to himself meanwhile 'gan say,

  "How many an hour might I have been
Right merry in the gardens green;
How many a glorious day had I
Made happy with some victory;
What noble deeds I might have done,
What bright renown my deeds have won;
What blessings would have made me glad;
What little burdens had I had;
What calmness in the hope of praise;
What joy of well-accomplished days,
If I had let these things alone;
Nor sought to sit upon my throne
Like God between the cherubim.
But now—but now, my days wax dim, .

And all this fairness have I tost
Unto the winds, and all have lost
For nought, for nought! yet will I strive
My little end of life to live;
Nor will I look behind me more,
Nor forward to the doubtful shore."

  With that he made the sign to turn,
And straight the autumn air did burn
With many a point of steel and gold;
And through the trees the carol rolled
Once more, until the autumn thrush
Far off 'gan twittering on his bush,
Made mindful of the long-lived spring.

  So mid sweet song and tabouring,
And shouts amid the apple-grove,
And soft caressing of his love,
Began the new King Michael's reign.
Nor will the poor folk see again
A king like him on any throne,
Or such good deeds to all men done:
For then, as saith the chronicle,
It was the time, as all men tell,
When scarce a man would stop to gaze
At gold crowns hung above the ways.

He ended; and midst those who heard were some
Who, midst his tale, half dreamed they were at home,
Round the great fire upon the winter night;
And, with the memory of the fresh delight
Wherewith they first had heard that story told,
Forgetting not they were grown weak and old,
Yet felt as if they had at least grown grey
Within the land left for so many a day.
He, with the gestures they were wont to see,
So told his tale, so strange with eld was he,
Just so he stammered, and in just such wise
He sighed, beginning fresh, as their young eyes,
Their ears, in happy days passed long ago,
Had ever noted other old men do,
When they, full filled with their quick-coming joys,
Would gaze on old folk as on carven toys.

  But he being silent, silently awhile
They mused on these things, masking with a smile
The vain regrets that in their hearts arose,
The while with eager talk the young folk chose
The parts that pleased them; but their elder hosts
Falling to talk, yet noted well the ghosts
Of old desires within their wasted eyes,

Till one by one the fresh-stirred memories,
So bitter-sweet, flickered and died away;
And as old men may do, whose hopes grew grey
Before their beards, they made a little mirth
Until the great moon rose upon the earth.

APRIL

O fair midspring, besung so oft and oft,
How can I praise thy loveliness enow?
Thy sun that burns not, and thy breezes soft
That o'er the blossoms of the orchard blow,
The thousand things that 'neath the young leaves grow,
The hopes and chances of the growing year,
Winter forgotten long, and summer near.

  When Summer brings the lily and the rose,
She brings us fear; her very death she brings
Hid in her anxious heart, the forge of woes;
And, dull with fear, no more the mavis sings.
But thou! thou diest not, but thy fresh life clings
About the fainting autumn's sweet decay,
When in' the earth the hopeful seed they lay.

  Ah! life of all the year, why yet do I
Amid thy snowy blossoms' fragrant drift,
Still long for that which never draweth nigh,
Striving my pleasure from my pain to sift,
Some weight from off my fluttering mirth to lift?
Now, when far bells are ringing, "Come again,
Come back, past years! why will ye pass in vain?"

And now the watery April sun lit up
Upon the fair board golden ewer and cup,
And over the bright silken tapestry
The fresh young boughs were gladdening every eye,
And round the board old faces you might see
Amidst the blossoms and their greenery.
  So when the flutes were silent, and the birds,
Rejoicing in their flood of unknown words,
Were heard again, a silken-fastened book
A certain elder from his raiment took,
And said, "O friends, few words are best to-day,
And no new thing I bring you; yet ye may
Be pleased to hear an ancient tale again,
That, told so long ago, doth yet remain
Fresh e'en 'mongst us, far from the Argive land:
Which tale this book, writ wholly by mine hand,
Holds gathered up as I have heard it told.

"Surely I fear me, midst the ancient gold
Base metal ye will light on here and there,
Though I have noted everything with care,
And with good will have set down nothing new:
Nor holds the land another book for you
That has the tale in full with nought beside,
So unto me let your good word betide;
Though, take it as ye may, no small delight
I had, herein this well-loved tale to write."

THE DOOM OF KING ACRISIUS

ARGUMENT

Acrisius, king of Argos, being warned by an oracle that the son of his daughter Danaë should slay
him, shut her up in a brazen tower built for that end beside the sea: there, though no man could
come nigh her, she nevertheless bore a son to Jove, and she and her new-born son, set adrift on
the sea, came to the island of Seriphos. Thence her son, grown to manhood, set out to win the
Gorgon's Head, and accomplished that end by the help of Minerva; and afterwards rescued
Andromeda, daughter of Cepheus, from a terrible doom, and wedded her. Coming back to
Seriphos he took his mother thence, and made for Argos, but by stress of weather came to
Thessaly, and there, at Larissa, accomplished the prophecy, by unwittingly slaying Acrisius. In the
end he founded the city of Mycenæ, and died there.

Now of the King Acrisius shall ye hear,
Who, thinking he could free his life from fear,
Did that which brought but death on him at last.
   In Argos did he reign in days long past,
And had one daughter, fair as man could see,
Who in old tales is callèd Danaë;
But as she grew up fairer day by day,
A wandering oracle to him did say,
That whatso else might happen, soon or late
He should be taken in the toils of fate,
And by the fruit of his own daughter's womb
Be slain at last, and set within his tomb;
And therefore heavy sorrow on him fell,
That she he thought to love so passing well
Must henceforth be his deadliest dread and woe.
   Long time he pondered what was best to do;
And whiles he thought that he would send her forth
To wed some king far in the snowy north,
And whiles that by great gifts of goods and gold
Some lying prophet might be bought and sold
To swear his daughter he must sacrifice,
If he would yet find favour in the eyes
Of the dread gods who govern everything;
And sometimes seemed it better to the King,
That he might 'scape the shedding of her blood

By leaving her in some far lonely wood,
Wherein the Dryads might the maiden find,
Or beasts might slay her, following but their kind.
  So passed his anxious days, until at last,
When many a plot through his vexed brain had passed,
He lacked the heart his flesh and blood to slay,
Yet neither would he she should go away
From out his sight, or be at large at all;
Therefore his wisest craftsmen did he call,
And bade them make for him a tower foursquare,
Such as no man had yet seen anywhere,
For therein neither stone nor wood should be,
But all be wrought of brass most cunningly.
  Now thither oft would maiden Danae stray,
And watch its strange walls growing day by day,
Because, poor soul! she knew not anything
Of these forebodings of the fearful King,
Nor how he meted out for her this doom,
Therein to dwell as in a living tomb.
But on a day, she, coming there alone,
Found it all finished and the workmen gone,
And no one nigh, so through the open door
She entered, and went up from floor to floor,
And through its chambers wandered without dread;
And, entering one, she found therein a bed,
Dight daintily, as though to serve a queen;
And all the walls adorned with hangings green,
Tables and benches in good order set,
And all things new, by no one used as yet.
  With that she murmured, "When again I see
My father, will I bid him tell to me
Who shall live here and die here, for, no doubt,
Whoever enters here shall ne'er go out:
Therefore the walls are made so high and great,
Therefore the bolts are measureless of weight,
The windows small, barred, turned towards the sea,
That none from land may tell who here may be.
No doubt some man the King my father fears
Above all other, here shall pass his years.
Alas, poor soul! scarce shall he see the sun,
Or care to know when the hot day is done,
Or ever see sweet flowers again, or grass,
Or take much note of how the seasons pass.
Truly we folk who dwell in rest and ease
But lightly think of such abodes as these;
And I, who live wrapped round about with bliss,
Shall go from hence and soon forget all this:
For in my garden many a sweet flower blooms,
Wide open are the doors of all my rooms,
And lightly folk come in and lightly go;
And I have known as yet but childish woe."

Therewith she turned about to leave the place,
But as unto the door she set her face
A bitter wailing from outside she heard,
And somewhat therewithal she waxed afeard,
And stopped awhile; yet listening, she but thought,
"This is the man who to his doom is brought
By weeping friends, who come to see the last
Of that dear face they know shall soon be past
From them for ever." Then she 'gan to go
Adown the brazen stairs with footsteps slow.

   But quick the shrieks and wailing drew anear,
Till in her ears it sounded sharp and clear,
And then she said, "Alas! and must I see
These weeping faces drawn with agony?
Would I had not come here to-day!" Withal
She started, as upon her ear did fall
The sound of shutting of the outer door,
And people coming up from floor to floor;
And paler then she grew, but moved to meet
The woful sounds and slow-ascending feet,
Shrinking with pity for that wretched one
Whose life of joy upon that day was done.

   Thus down the stairs with saddened heart she passed,
And to a lower chamber came at last;
But as she went beneath the archway wide
The door was opened from the other side,
And in poured many maidens, whom she knew
For her own fair companions, leal and true;
And after them two soldiers armed there came,
With knitted brows and eyes downcast for shame.

   But when those damsels saw her standing there,
Anew they wept, and tore their unbound hair;
But midst their wailing, still no word they said,
Until she spoke oppressed with sickening dread:

   "O tell me what has happened to me then!
For is my father slain of outland men?
Or have the gods sent death upon the land?
Or is it mine own death that they command?
Alas, alas! but slay me quick, I pray,
Nor let me linger on from day to day,
Maddened with fear like this, that sickens me,
And makes me seem the half-dead thing ye see."

   Then, like a man constrained, a soldier said
These cruel words unto the wretched maid:
"Lady, lose hope and fear now once for all;
Here must thou dwell betwixt brass wall and wall
Until the gods send gentle death to thee;
And these as erst thine handmaidens shall be:
And if thou askest why the thing is so,
Thus the King wills it, for a while ago
An oracle foretold that thou shouldst live

To have a son, who bitter death should give
Unto thy father; so, to save this shame
From falling on the glorious Argive name,
He deemed it well that thou shouldst live indeed,
But yet apart from man thy life shouldst lead.
So in this place thy days must pass away,
And we who are thy guards, from day to day
Will bring thee everything that thou mayst need.
But pardon us, constrained to do this deed
By the King's will, and oaths that we have sworn
Ere to this life of sorrow thou wert born."
  Therewith they turned and went, and soon the sound
Of shutting doors smote like a deadly wound
Into her heart; and yet no word she spoke,
But fell as one beneath a deadly stroke.

  Then they who there her fellows were to be
Bore up her body, groaning heavily,
Unto the upper chamber where that day
She came before, and on the bed did lay
The wretched maid, and then they sat around,
With heavy heads and hair that swept the ground,
To weep the passing of those happy days
When many an one their happy lot would praise.
But now and then, when bitterly would sting
The loss of some nigh-reached desired thing,
To a loud wail their weeping would arise.
  Then in a while did Danae ope her eyes,
And to her aching forehead raised her hand;
But when she saw that wan, dishevelled band,
She soon remembered this was no ill dream,
But that all things were e'en as they did seem,
Then she arose, but soon upon the bed
Sank down again, and hid her troubled head,
And moaned and moaned, and when a damsel came
And touched her hand, and called her by her name,
She knew her not, but turned her head away:
Nor did she know when dark night followed day.

  So passed by many a day in mourning sore,
And weariness oppressed her evermore
In that unhappy prison-house of brass;
And yet a little the first sting did pass
That smote her, and she ate and drank and slept,
And fair and bright her body Venus kept,
Yea, such a grace the sea-born goddess fair
Did to her, that the ripples of her hair
Grew brighter, and the colour in her face
And lovely lips waned not in that sad place;
And rounder grew her limbs from day to day;
Yea, as upon the golden bed she lay,

You would have thought the Queen herself had come
To meet some love far from her golden home.
    And once it happed at the first hour of day
In golden morn upon her bed she lay,
Newly awakened to her daily woe,
And heard the rough sea beat the rocks below,
The wheeling sea-gull screaming on the wing,
Sea-swallows swift, and many a happy thing,
Till bitterly the tears ran down her cheek,
And stretching forth her arms and fingers weak,
'Twixt moans these piteous helpless words she said:—
"O Queen Diana, make me now thy maid,
And take me from this place and set me down
By the boar-haunted hills, that oak-woods crown,
Amid thy crowd of trim-girt maidens fair.
    "And shall I not be safe from men-folk there,
Thou cruel King, when she is guarding me,
The mighty maid from whom the shepherds flee,
When in the gathering dusk 'twixt day and night,
The dead leaves tell them of her footsteps light,
Because they mind how dear Actæon bought
The lovely sight for which he never sought,
Diana naked in the water wan.
    "Yea, what fear should I have of any man
When through the woods I, wandering merrily,
With girt-up gown, sharp sword upon the thigh,
Full quiver on the back, stout bow in hand,
Should tread with firm feet many a grassy land,
And grow strong-limbed in following up the deer,
And meet the lions' eyes with little fear.
    "Alas! no doubt she hears not; many a maid
She has already, of no beast afraid,
Crisp-haired, with arms made meet for archery,
Whose limbs unclad no man shall ever see;
Though the birds see them, and the seeding grass
Harsh and unloving over them may pass,
When carelessly through rough and smooth they run,
And bough and briar catches many a one.
    "Alas! why on these free maids is my thought,
When to such misery my life is brought?
I, who so long a happy maid have been,
The daughter of a great King and a Queen;
And why these fresh things do I think upon,
Who now shall see but little of the sun?
    "Here every day shall have the same sad tale,
My weary damsels with their faces pale,
The dashing of the sea on this bleak rock,
Pipe of the wind through cranny and through lock,
The sea-bird's cry, like mine grown hoarse and shrill,
The far off sound of horn upon the hill,
The merry pipe about the shepherd's home,

And all the things whereto I ne'er may come.
  "O ye who rule below, I pray this boon,
I may not live here long, but perish soon,
Forgotten, but at peace, since I feel nought;
For even now it comes across my thought
That here my wretched body dwells alone,
And that my soul with all my hope is gone.

  "Father, thy blood upon thine own head be
If any solace Venus send to me
Within this wretched place which thou hast made,
Of thine own flesh and blood too much afraid."
  Truly Diana heard not, for that tide
Upon the green grass by a river side,
Wherein she had just bathed her body sweet,
She stooped to tie the sandals to her feet,
Her linen gown upon the herbage lay,
And round her was there standing many a may
Making her ready for the morning chase.
  But so it happed that Venus by the place
Was passing, just arisen from the sea,
And heard the maid complaining bitterly,
So to the window-bars she drew anigh,
And thence unseen, she saw the maiden lie,
As on the grass herself she might have lain
When in the thicket lay Adonis slain;
For power and joy she smiled thereat, and thought
"She shall not suffer all this pain for nought."
And slowly for Olympus sailed away,
And thither came at hottest of the day.
  Then through the heavenly courts she went, and when
She found the father both of gods and men,
She smiled upon him, and said, "Knowest thou
What deeds are wrought by men in Argos now?
Wherein a brazen tower well builded is,
That hides a maid away from all my bliss;
Since thereby thinks Acrisius to forego,
This doom that has been fated long ago,
That by his daughter's son he shall be slain;
Wherefore he puts the damsel to this pain
To see no man, and thinks to 'scape his doom
If she but live and die with barren womb;
And great dishonour is it unto me
That such a maiden lives so wretchedly;
And great dishonour is it to us all
That ill upon a guiltless head should fall
To save a King from what we have decreed.
Now, therefore, tell me, shall his impious deed
Save him alive, while she that might have borne
Great kings and glorious heroes, lives forlorn
Of love's delight, in solitude and woe?"

Then said the Thunderer, "Daughter, nowise so
Shall this be in the end; heed what shall fall,
And let none think that any brazen wall
Can let the Gods from doing what shall be."

Now therewithal went Venus to the sea
Glad of her father's words, and, as she went,
Unseen the gladness of the spring she sent
Across the happy lands o'er which she moved,
Until all men felt joyous and beloved.
But while to Paphos carelessly she fared,
All day upon the tower the hot sun glared,
And Danaë within that narrow space
Went to and fro, and sometimes hid her face
Between her hands, moaning in her despair,
Or sometimes tore the fillets from her hair,
And sometimes would begin a piteous tale
Unto her maids, and in the midst would fail
For sobs and tears; but mostly would she sit
Over against the window, watching it,
And feel the light wind blowing from the sea
Against her face, with hands laid listlessly
Together in her lap; so passed the day,
And to their sleep her damsels went away,
And through the dead of night she slept awhile,
But when the dawn came, woke up with a smile,
As though she had forgotten all her pain,
But soon the heavy burden felt again,
And on her bed lay tossing wretchedly,
Until the sun had nigh looked o'er the sea.
In that fresh morn was no one stirring yet,
And many a man his troubles did forget
Buried in sleep, but nothing she forgat,
She raised herself and up in bed she sat,
And towards the window turned round wearily
To watch the changing colours of the sky;
And many a time she sighed, and seemed as though
She would have told the story of her woe
To whatsoever god near by might be
Betwixt the grey sky and the cold grey sea,
But to her lips no sound at all would rise,
Except those oft repeated heavy sighs.
And yet, indeed, within a little while
Her face grew calm, the shadow of a smile
Stole o'er her parted lips and sweet grey eyes,
And slowly from the bed did she arise,
And towards the window drew, and yet did seem,
Although her eyes were open, still to dream.
There on the sill she laid her slender hand,
And looking seaward, pensive did she stand,

And seemed as though she waited for the sun
To bring her news her misery was done;
At last he came and over the green sea
His golden road shone out right gloriously,
And into Danae's face his glory came
And lit her softly waving hair like flame.
But in his light she held out both her hands,
As though he brought her from some far-off lands
Healing for all her great distress and woe.

But yellower now the sunbeams seemed to grow
Not whiter as their wont is, and she heard
A tinkling sound that made her, half afeard,
Draw back a little from the fresh green sea,
Then to a clang the noise rose suddenly,
And gently was she smitten on the breast,
And some bright thing within her palm did rest,
And trickled down her shoulder and her side,
And on her limbs a little did abide,
Or lay upon her feet a little while.

Then in her face increased the doubtful smile,
While o'er her eyes a drowsy film there came,
And in her cheeks a flush as if of shame,
And, looking round about, could she behold
The chamber scattered o'er with shining gold,
That grew, till ankle-deep she stood in it.

Then through her limbs a tremor did there flit
As through white water runs the summer wind,
And many a wild hope came into her mind,
But her knees bent and soft she sank down there,
And on the gold was spread her golden hair,
And like an ivory image still she lay,
Until the night again had hidden day.

But when again she lifted up her head,
She found herself laid soft within her bed,
While midmost of the room the taper shone,
And all her damsels from the place were gone,
And by her head a gold-robed man there stood,
At sight of whom the damsel's shamefast blood
Made all her face red to the golden hair,
And quick she covered up her bosom fair.

Then in a great voice said he, "Danaë,
Sweet child, be glad, and have no fear of me,
And have no shame, nor hide from thy new love
The breast that on this day has pillowed Jove.
Come now, come from that balmy nest of thine,
And stand with me beneath the taper's shine
That I may see thy beauty once again;
Then never shalt thou be in any pain,
But if thou liftest up thy face to Jove

I shall be kind to my sweet simple love;
I shall bethink me of thy body sweet,
From golden head to rosy little feet."
    Then, trembling sore, from out the bed she came
And hid away her face for dread and shame,
But soon she trembled more for very love,
To feel the loving hands of mighty Jove
Draw down her hands, and kisses on the head
And tender bosom, as again he said,
"Now must I go; and sweet love, Danae,
Fear nothing more that man can do to thee,
For soon shall come an ending to thy woe,
And thou shalt have a son whose name shall grow
Still greater, till the mountains melt away
And men no more can tell the night from day."

    Then forth he sprang and o'er the sea did fly
And loud it thundered from a cloudless sky.

So when her damsels came to her next day,
And thought to see her laid in her old way
Upon the bed, and looking out to sea
Moaning full oft, and sighing heavily,
They found her singing o'er a web of silk
Where through the even warp as white as milk
Quick flew the shuttle from her arm of snow,
And somewhat from her girded gown did show
On the black treadles both her rosy feet,
Moving a little as the tall green wheat
Moves in the June when Zephyr blows on it,
So, like a goddess weaving did she sit.
    But when she saw her maidens wondering stand
She ceased her song and stayed her busy hand,
And said, "Girls, if ye see me glad to-day
Be nought amazed, for all things pass away;
The good days die, but also die the bad.
    "See now, in sleep last night a dream I had
That in his claws an eagle lifted me
And bore me to a land across the sea:
Wherefore I think that here I shall not die
But live to feel dew falling from the sky,
And set my feet deep in the meadow grass
And underneath the scented pine-trees pass,
Or in the garden feel the western breeze,
The herald of the rain, sweep through the trees,
Or in the hottest of the summer day,.
Betwixt green banks within the mill-stream play.
    "For either shall my father soon relent,
Or for my sake some marvel shall be sent,
And either way these doors shall open wide;
And then doubt not to see me soon a bride

With some king's amorous son before my feet.
   "Ah! verily my life shall then be sweet;
Before these days I knew not life or death,
With little hope or fear I drew my breath,
But now when all this sorrow is o'erpast,
Then shall I feel how sweet life is at last,
And know how dear peace is from all these fears.
   "So no more will I waste my life in tears,
But pass the time as swiftly as may be,
Until ye step out on the turf with me."

   Then glad they were, when such-like words they heard,
And yet some doubted and were sore afeard
That she had grown light-headed with her woe,
Dreading the time might come when she would throw
Her body on the ground and perish there,
Slain by her own hand mighty with despair.
Nathless the days more merrily went by
And from that prison men heard minstrelsy,
When nought but mourning, fisher-folk afeard
Who passed that way, in other times had heard.

   Yet truly Danae said that all things pass
And are forgotten; in that house of brass
Forgotten was the stunning bitter pain
Wherewith she entered it, and yet again
In no long time, hope was forgotten too
When wringing torments moaning from her drew,
And to and fro the pale scared damsels went,
And those her guards unto Acrisius sent.
   But ere the messenger returned again
She had been eased of half her bitterest pain,
And on her breast a fair man-child was laid;
Then round the messenger her maids afraid
Drew weeping; but he charged them earnestly,
Ever to watch her in that chamber high,
Lest any man should steal the babe away,
And so to bide until there came a day
When on her feet she might arise and go,
Whereof by messengers the King must know;
So, threatening torments unendurable,
If any harm through treachery befell,
He left them, and no more to them he told,
But in his face the sooth they might behold.
   Now, therefore when some wretched days were past,
And trembling by the bed she stood at last,
She heard the opening of the outer door,
And footsteps came again from floor to floor,
And soon with all-armed men her chamber shone,
Who with few words now led her forth alone
Adown the stairs from out the brazen place;

And on her hot hands, and her tear-stained face
Half-fainting, the pine-scented air she felt,
And all about the salt sea savour smelt,
And in her ears the dashing of the sea
Rang ever; thus the God had set her free.
  But by the shore further they led her still
To where the sea beat on a barren hill,
And a long stage of timber met the sea,
At end whereof was tossing fearfully
A little boat that had no oars or sail,
Or aught that could the mariner avail.
Thither with her their steps the soldiers bent,
And as along the narrow way they went
The salt waves leapt aloft to kiss her feet
And in the wind streamed out her tresses sweet;
But little heed she took of feet or head
For nought she doubted she to death was led,
But ever did she hold against her breast
The little babe, and spoke not for the rest,
No, not when in the boat they bade her go,
And 'twixt its bulwarks thin she lay alow,
Nor when adrift they set her presently
And all about was but the angry sea.

  No word she said until the sun was down,
And she beheld the moon that on no town,
On no fair homestead, no green pasture shone,
But lit up the unwearied sea alone;
No word she said till she was far from shore
And on her breast the babe was wailing sore,
And then she lifted up her face to Jove,
And said, "O thou who once didst call me love,
Hast thou forgotten those fair words of thine,
When underneath the taper's glimmering shine
Thou bad'st me stand that thou mightst look on me,
And love thou call'dst me, and sweet Danae?
Now of thy promised help am I most fain
For on what day can I have greater pain
Than this wherein to-night my body is,
And brought thereto by what, but thy sweet kiss?"
  But neither did she pray the God in vain;
For straight he set himself to end her pain,
And while he cast on her a gentle sleep,
The winds within their houses did he keep
Except the west which soft on her did blow,
That swiftly through the sea the boat might go.

  Far out to sea a certain isle doth lie
Men call Seriphos, craggy, steep, and high:
It rises up on every side but one,
And mariners its ill-famed headlands shun;

But toward the south the meads slope soft adown,
Until they meet the yellow sands and brown,
That slope themselves so gently to the sea,
The nymphs are hidden only to the knee
When half a mile of rippling water is
Between the waves that their white limbs do kiss
And the last wave that washes shells ashore.
  To this fair place the west wind onward bore
The skiff that carried Danae and her son,
And on the morn, when scarce the dusk was done,
Upon the sands the shallop ran aground;
And still they slept, and for awhile around
Their wretched bed the waves sang lullaby,
But sank at last and left the long strand dry.
  Then uprose Danaë, and nothing knew
What land it was: about her sea-fowl flew;
Behind her back the yet retreating sea
Beat on the yellow sands unceasingly;
Landward she saw the low green meadows lie,
Dotted with homesteads, rich with elm-trees high;
And at her feet the little boat there lay
That happily had brought her on the way.
  But as it happed, the brother of the King
Had ridden forth to hear the sea-fowl sing,
With hawk on fist, right early on that morn,
Hard by the place whereunto she was borne.
He, seeing far away a white thing stand,
Deemed her at first some maiden of the sand,
Such as to fishers sings a honied strain,
And leaves them longing for her love in vain.
So, wishful to behold the sea-folk's bride,
He set the spurs into his horse's side.
But drawing nigher, he but saw her there,
Not moving much, her unbound yellow hair
Heavy with dew and washing of the sea;
And her wet raiment clinging amorously
About her body, in the wind's despite;
And in her arms her woe and her delight,
Spreading abroad the small hands helplessly
That on some day should still the battle's cry.
And furthermore he saw where by her lay
The boat that brought her o'er the watery way:
Then, though he knew not whence she might have come,
He doubted not the firm land was her home.

  But when he came anigh, beholding him,
She fell a trembling in her every limb,
And kneeling to him held the young babe out,
And said: "O Sir, if, as I have no doubt,
In this strange land thou art a king and lord,
Speak unto me some comfortable word.

"Born of a king who rules a lovely land,
I in my house that by the sea doth stand,
With all my girls, made merry on a day:
Now some of them upon the sands did play,
Dancing unto their fellows' minstrelsy;
And some it pleased upon sweet flowers to lie,
Ripe fruits around, and thence to look on them;
And some were fain to lift their kirtles' hem,
And through the shallows chase the fishes fleet;
But in this shallop would I have my seat
Alone, and holding this my little son,
And knowing not that my good days were done.
    "Now how it chanced, in sooth I cannot say,
But yet I think that one there was that day,
Who for some hidden cause did hate me sore,
Who cut the cord that bound me to the shore,
And soon amidst my helpless shrieks the boat,
Oarless and sailless, out to sea did float.
    "But now that many a danger has been passed,
The gods have sent me to your land at last,
Alive, indeed, but such-like as you see,
Cold and drenched through with washing of the sea,
Half-clad, and kneeling on an unknown land, .
And for a morsel holding out my hand."

    Then said he, "Lady, fear not any more,
For you are come unto no savage shore,
But here shall be a queen as erst at home:
And if thou askest whereto thou art come,
This is the isle Seriphos; and for me,
My name is Dictys, and right royally
My brother lives, the king of all the isle.
Him shalt thou see within a little while,
And doubtless he will give thee everything
That 'longs unto the daughter of a king.
    "Meanwhile I bid thee in mine house to rest,
And there thy wearied body shall be dressed
In seemly raiment by my women slaves,
And thou shalt wash thee from the bitter waves,
And eat and drink, and sleep full easily;
And on the morrow shalt thou come with me
And take King Polydectes by the hand,
Who in good peace rules o'er this quiet land."
    Then on his horse he set the Queen, while he
Walked by the side thereof right soberly,
And half asleep, as slow they went along,
She laid her hand upon the war-horse strong,
While Dictys by her side Jove's offspring bore,
And thus they left the sea-beat yellow shore.
And as one dreaming to the house she came,
Where in the sun the brazen doors did flame;

And there she ate and drank as in a dream;
Dreamlike to her the scented bath did seem
After the icy sprinkling of the waves,
And like a dream the fair, slim women-slaves,
Who laid her in the fair bed, where she slept
Dreamless, until the horned white moon had stept
Over the fresh pine-scented hills again.
   But when the sun next day drave forth his wain,
The damsel, clad in queen-like gold array,
With Dictys to the palace took her way;
And there by minstrels duly were they met,
Who brought them to the great hall, where was set
The King upon a royal throne of gold:
Black-bearded was he, thirty summers old,
Comely and strong, and seemed a king indeed;
Who, when he saw the minstrels thither lead
Fair Danaë, rose up to her, and said:
"Oh, welcome, lady! be no more afraid
That thou shalt lose thy state and dignity;
Yea, since a gem the gods have sent to me,
With plates of silver will I overlay
The casket that has brought it on the way,
And set it in King Neptune's house to stand
Until the sea shall wash away the land.

   "And for thyself a fair house shalt thou have
With all things needful, and right many a slave,
Both men and women; fair shall all things be
That thou mayst dwell here in felicity,
And that no care may wrinkle thy smooth brow.

   "And for the child, when he is old enow
The priests of Pallas shall of him have care,
And thou shalt dwell hard by her temple fair;
But on this good day in mine hall abide,
And do me grace in sitting by my side."

   Then mounted she the dais and sat, and then
Was she beheld of all the island-men
Who praised her much, and praised the sturdy child,
Who at their shouting made as if he smiled.

   So passed the feast, and at the end of day
Towards her own house did Danae go away,
That stood amid Minerva's olive-trees
Hidden away from moaning of the seas.

   And there began fair Danae's life again,
And quite forgotten was her ancient pain,
And peacefully did day succeed to clay,
While fairer grew the well-loved child alway,
And strong and wise beyond his scanty years,
And in the island all his little peers
Held him for lord whatso might be their worth,
And Perseus is his name from this time forth.

Lo, eighteen summers now have come and gone
Since on the beach fair Danae stood alone
Holding her little son, nor yet was she
Less fair than when the hoarse unwilling sea
Moaned loud that Neptune drew him from her feet,
And the wind sighed upon her bosom sweet.
For in that long past half-forgotten time,
While yet the world was young, and the sweet clime,
Golden and mild, no bitter storm-clouds bred,
Light lay the years upon the untroubled head,
And longer men lived then by many a year
Than in these days, when every week is dear.

  Now on a day was held a royal feast
Whereon there should be slain full many a beast
Unto Minerva; thereto the King came,
And in his heart love lit a greedy flame
At sight of Danae's arms stretched out in prayer
Unto the goddess, and her yellow hair,
Wreathed round with olive wreaths, that hung adown
Over the soft folds of her linen gown;
And when at last he took her by the hand
Speechless by her did Polydectes stand,
So much with fond desire bewildered
At sight of all that wondrous white and red,
That peaceful face wherein all past distress
Had melted into perfect loveliness.
  So when that night he lay upon his bed,
Full many a thought he turned within his head
Of how he best might unto that attain,
Whose lack now filled him with such burning pain.
And at the first it seemed a little thing
For him who was a rich man and a king,
Either by gifts to win her, or to send
And fetch her thither, and perforce to end
Her widowhood; but then there came the thought,
"By force or gifts hither she might be brought,
And here might I get that for which I long,
Yet has she here a son both brave and strong,
Nor will he think it much to end my days
If he may get thereby the people's praise,
E'en if therewith he shortly needs must die;
Ah, verily, a purblind fool was I,
That when I first beheld that matchless face
I had no eyes to see her heavenly grace;
Then with few words might I have held her here
And kept her for mine own with little fear;
But now I have no will the lad to slay,
For he would be revenged some evil day,
Who now Jove's offspring do I think to be,

So dowered he is with might and majesty.
   "Yet could I find perchance some fair pretence
Whereby with honour I might send him hence,
Nor have the youngling's blood upon my head,
Then might he be well nigh as good as dead."
   So pondering on his bed long time he lay,
Until the night began to mix with day,
And then he smiled and so to sleep turned round,
As though at last some sure way he had found.

   And now it chanced to come round to the day,
When all the lords clad in their rich array
Unto the King should come for royal feast;
And there the way was, that both most and least
Should thither bear some present for the King,
As horse or sword, gold chain, fair cup, or ring.
Unto which feast was Perseus bidden now
Who giftless came, bare as the winter bough,
For little was his wealth in that strange land.
   So there ashamed it was his lot to stand,
Before the guests were called to meat, and when
He sat amidst those royally-clad men
Little he spake for shame of his estate,
Not knowing yet his god-like birth and great.
   So passed the feast, and when the full time came
To show the gifts, he waxed all red for shame:
For through the hall white horses were brought up,
And well-clad slaves, and many a dainty cup,
And many a gem well set in brooch or ring,
And laid before the daïs of the King.
But all alone of great folk of the land
With eyes cast down for rage did Perseus stand,
Yet for his manhood thence he would not go.
   Now some that secretly were bidden so,
Beholding him began to gibe and jeer,
Yet not too loud, held back perchance by fear,
And thus a murmur spread about the hall
As, each to each, men cast about the ball,
Which the King heard, or seemed to hear at last,
And round the noisy hall a look he cast,
And then beholding Perseus with a smile
He said, "Good friends, fair lords, be still awhile,
And say no ill about this giftless guest,
For truly not the worst, if scarce the best,
I hold him, and forsooth so rich 1 live
Within this land, that I myself may give
Somewhat to him, nor yet take from him aught,
And when I bade him here this was my thought."
   Then stretching out his arm did he take up
From off the board, a jewelled golden cup
And said, "O Perseus, come and sit by me,

And from my hand take this, that thou dost see
And be my friend." Then Perseus drew anear,
And took the cup and said, "This shall be dear
Unto mine eyes while on the earth I live;
And yet a gift I in my turn may give,
When to this land comes bitter war, or when
Some enemy thou hast among great men;
Yea, sire, among these knights and lords I swear
To do whatso thou bidd'st me without fear."

   Then the King smiled and said, "Yea, verily,
Then wilt thou give a great gift unto me,
Nor yet, forsooth, too early by a day;
To-morrow may'st thou be upon thy way.
   "Far in the western sea a land there is
Desert and vast, and emptied of all bliss,
Where dwell the Gorgons wretchedly enow;
Two of them die not, one above her brow
And wretched head bears serpents, for the shame
That on an ill day fell upon her name,
When in Minerva's shrine great sin was wrought,
For thither by the Sea-god she was brought,
And in the maiden's house in love they mixed;
Who wrathful, in her once fair tresses fixed
'That snaky brood, and shut her evermore
Within a land west of the Lybian shore.
   "Now if a king could gain this snaky head
Full well for war were he apparelled,
Because no man may look thereon and live.
A great gift, therefore, Perseus, wouldst thou give
If thou shouldst bring this wonder unto me;
And for the place, far in the western sea
It lies, I say, but nothing more I know,
Therefore I bid thee, to some wise man go
Who has been used this many a day to pore
O'er ancient books of long-forgotten lore."

   Thus spoke the King, knowing the while full well
None but a god of that far land could tell.
   But Perseus answered, "O my Lord, the King,
Thou settest me to win a dreadful thing,
Yet for thy bounty this gift will I give
Unto thine hands, if I should chance to live."
   With that he turned, and silent, full of thought,
From out the hall he passed not noting aught,
And toward his home he went but soberly,
And thence went forth an ancient man to see
He hoped might tell him that he wished to know
And to what land it were the best to go.
But when he told the elder all the tale,
He shook his head, and said, "Nought will avail

My lore for this, nor dwells the man on earth
Whose wisdom for this thing will be of worth,
Yea, to this dreadful land no man shall win
Unless some god himself shall help therein;
Therefore, my son, I rede thee stay at home,
For thou shalt have full many a chance to roam
Seeking for something that all men love well,
Not for an unknown isle where monsters dwell."

    Then forth again went Perseus soberly
And walked along the border of the sea,
Upon the yellow sands where first he came
That time that he was deemed his mother's shame.
    And now was it the first hour of the night,
Therefore within the west a yellow light
Yet shone, though risen was the horned moon,
Whose lonely cold grey beams would quench it soon,
Though now her light was shining doubtfully
On the wet sands, for low down was the sea
But rising, and the salt-sea wind blew strong
And drave the hurrying breakers swift along.
So there walked Perseus thinking many a thing
About those last words of the wily king,
And as he went at last he came upon
An ancient woman, who said, "Fair, my son,
What dost thou wandering here in the cold night?
When in the King's hall glance from shade to light
The golden sandals of the dancing girls,
And in the gold cups set with gems and pearls
The wine shines fair that glads the heart of man;
What dost thou wandering 'neath the moonlight wan?"

    "This have I done," said he, "as one should swear
To make the vine bear bunches twice a year,
For I have sworn the Gorgon's head to bring
A worthy gift unto our island King,
When neither I, nor any man can tell
In what far land apart from men they dwell.
Some god alone can help me in my need;
And yet unless somehow I do the deed
An exile I must be from this fair land,
Nor with my peers shall I have heart to stand."
    Grim in the moonlight smiled the aged crone,
And said, "If living there thou com'st, alone
Of all men yet, what thinkest thou to do?
Then verily thy journey shalt thou rue,
For whoso looks upon that face meets death,
That in his sick heart freezes up his breath
Until he has the semblance of a stone."
    But Perseus answered straightly to the crone,
"O Mother, if the gods but give me grace

To come anigh that fair and dreadful face,
Well may they give me grace enough also
Their enemy and mine to lay alow."
    Now as he spake, the white moon risen high
Burst from a cloud, and shone out gloriously,
And down the sands her path of silver shone,
And lighted full upon that ancient crone;
And there a marvel Perseus saw indeed,
Because in face, in figure, and in weed,
She wholly changed before his wondering eyes.
    Now tall and straight her figure did arise,
That erst seemed bent with weight of many a year,
And on her head a helmet shone out clear
For the rent clout that held the grizzled head:
With a fair breastplate was she furnished,
From whence a hauberk to her knees fell down;
And underneath, a perfumed linen gown,
O'erwrought with many-coloured Indian silk,
Fell to her sandall'd feet, as white as milk.
Grey-eyed she was, like amber shone her hair,
Aloft she held her right arm round and bare,
Whose long white fingers closed upon a spear.

    Then trembled Perseus with unwonted fear
When he beheld before him Pallas stand,
And with bowed head he stood and outstretched hand:
But she smiled on him softly, and she said,
"Hold up again, O Perseus, thy fair head,
Because thou art indeed my father's son,
And in this quest that now thou goest upon
Thou shalt not fail: I swear it by my head,
And that black water all immortals dread.
    "Look now before my feet, and thou shalt see
Four helpful things the high gods lend to thee,
Not willing thou shouldst journey forth in vain:
Hermes himself, the many-eyed one's bane,
Gives these two-winged shoes, to carry thee
Tireless high over every land and sea;
This cap is his whose chariot caught away
The maid of Enna from her gentle play;
And if thou art hard-pressed of any one
Set this on thee, and so be seen of none:
The halting god was craftsman of this blade,
No better shone, when, making heaven afraid,
The giants round our golden houses cried,
For neither brass nor steel its edge can bide,
Or flinty rocks or gleaming adamant:
With these, indeed, but one thing dost thou want,
And that I give thee; little need'st thou reck
Of those grey hopeless eyes, if round thy neck
Thou hang'st this shield, that, hanging once on mine,

In the grim giant's hopeless eyes did shine.
  "And now be strong, and fly forth with good heart
Far northward, till thou seest the ice-walls part
The weary sea from snow-clad lands and wan:
There dwell the Gorgons' ancient sisters three
Men call the Graiæ, who make shift to see
With one eye, which they pass from hand to hand.
Now make thyself unseen in this white land
And snatch the eye, while crooning songs they sit,
From hand to withered hand still passing it;
And let them buy it back by telling thee
How thou shalt find within the western sea
The unknown country where their sisters dwell.
  "Which thing unto thee I myself would tell,
But when with many a curse I set them there,
I in my wrath by a great oath did swear
I would not name again the country grey
Wherein they dwell, with little light of day.
  "Good speed, O Perseus; make no tarrying,
But straightly set thyself to do this thing."

  Now as his ears yet rung with words like these,
And on the sand he sank upon his knees
Before the goddess, there he knelt alone
As in a dream; but still the white moon shone
Upon the sword, the shield, and cap and shoes,
Which half adrad he was at first to use,
Until the goddess gave him heart at last,
And his own gear in haste aside he cast,
And armed himself in that wild, lonely place:
Then turning round, northward he set his face,
And rose aloft and o'er the lands 'gan fly,
Betwixt the green earth and the windy sky.
  Young was the night when first he left the sands
Of small Seriphos, but right many lands
Before the moon was down his winged feet
Had borne him over, tireless, strong, and fleet.
Then in the starlight black beneath him lay
The German forests, where the wild swine play,
Fearless of what Diana's maids may do,
Who ever have more will to wander through
The warm and grassy woods of Thessaly,
Or in Sicilian orange-gardens lie.
  But ere the hot sun on his arms 'gan shine
He had passed o'er the Danube and the Rhine,
And heard the faint sound of the northern sea;
But ever northward flew untiringly,
Till Thule lay beneath his feet at last.
Then o'er its desert icy hills he passed,
And on beneath a feeble sun he flew,
Till, rising like a wall, the cliffs he knew

That Pallas told him of: the sun was high,
But on the pale ice shone but wretchedly;
Pale blue the great mass was, and cold enow;
Grey tattered moss hung from its jagged brow,
No wind was there at all, though ever beat
The leaden tideless sea against its feet.

   Then lighted Perseus on that dreary land,
And when on the white plain his feet did stand
He saw no sign of either beast or man,
Except that near by rose a palace wan,
Built of some metal that he could not name.
Thither he went, and to a great door came
That stood wide open, so without a word
He entered in, and drew his deadly sword,
Though neither sword or man could you behold
More than folk see their death ere they grow old.
   So having entered, through a cloïster grey
With cautious steps and slow he took his way,
At end whereof he found a mighty hall;
Where, bare of hangings, a white marble wall
And milk-white pillars held the roof aloft,
And nothing was therein of fair or soft;
And at one end, upon a dais high,
There sat the crones that had the single eye,
Clad in blue sweeping cloak and snow-white gown;
While o'er their backs their straight white hair hung down
In long thin locks; dreadful their faces were
Carved all about with wrinkles of despair;
And as they sat they crooned a dreary song,
Complaining that their lives should last so long,
In that sad place that no one came anear,
In that wan place desert of hope and fear;
And singing, still they rocked their bodies bent,
And ever each to each the eye they sent.

   Awhile stood Perseus gazing on the three
Then sheathed his sword, and toward them warily
He went, and from the last one snatched the eye,
Who, feeling it gone from her, with a cry
Sprung up and said, "O sisters, he is here
That we were warned so long ago to fear,
And verily he has the eye of me."
   Then those three, thinking they no more should see
What feeble light the sun could show them there,
And that of all joys now their life was bare,
Began a wailing and lamenting sore
That they were worse than ever heretofore.
   Then Perseus cried, "Unseen am I indeed,
But yet a mortal man, who have a need
Your wisdom can make good, if so ye will;

Now neither do I wish you any ill,
Nor this your treasure will I keep from you
If ye will tell me what I needs must do
To gain, upon the earth or under it,
The dreary country where your sisters sit:
Of whom, as wise men say, the one is fair
As any goddess, but with snaky hair
And body that shall perish on some day,
While the two others ancient are, and grey
As ye be, but shall see the whole world die."

  Then said they, "Rash man, give us back the eye
Or rue this day, for wretched as we are,
Beholding not fair peace or godlike war,
Or any of the deeds of men at all,
Yet are we strong, and on thy head shall fall
Our heavy curses, and but dismally
Thy life shall pass until thou com'st to die."

  "Make no delay," he said, "to do this thing,
Or this your cherished sight I soon shall fling
Into the sea, or burn it up with fire."

  "What else, what else, but this wilt thou desire?"
They said, "Wilt thou have long youth at our hands?
Or wilt thou be the king of lovely lands?
Or store up wealth to lead thy life in mirth?
Or wilt thou have the beauty of the earth
With all her kindness for thy very own?
Choose what thou wilt except this thing alone."

  "Nay," said he, "for nought else I left my home,
For this sole knowledge hither am I come,
Not all unholpen of the gods above;
Nor yet shall words my stedfast purpose move."

  Then with that last word did he hold his peace,
And they no less from wailing words did cease,
Hoping that in that silence he might think
Of their dread words and from the evils shrink
Wherewith they threatened him; but in his heart
Most godlike courage fit for such a part
The white-armed goddess of the loom had set,
Nor in that land her help did he forget.

  Withal, when many an hour had now gone by,
Together did the awesome sisters cry,
"O man! O man! hear that which thou would'st know,
And with thy knowledge let the dread curse go,
We, least of all, have 'scaped, of those who dwell
Upon this wretched fire-concealing shell.
Slave of the cruel gods! go, get ye hence,
And storing deeds for fruitless penitence,
Go east, as though in Scythia was your home,
But when unto the wind-beat seas ye come
Stop short, and turn round to the south again

Until ye reach the western land of Spain;
There take your way unto the narrow seas
That wash the pillars of great Hercules,
And thenceforth go thou westward as thou mayst
Until ye find a dark land long laid waste,
Where green cliffs rise from out an inky sea,
But no green leaf may grow on bush or tree.
No sun makes day there, no moon lighteth night,
The long years there must pass in grey twilight;
There dwell our sisters, walking dismally,
Between the dull-brown caverns and the sea.

"Tool in the hands of gods! do there thy might!
Nor fall like us, nor strive for peace and right;
But give our own unto us and be gone,
And leave us to our misery alone."

Then straight he put the eye into the hand
Of her that spoke, and turned from that white land,
Leaving them singing their grim song again.
But flying forth he came at last to Spain,
And so unto the southern end of it,
And then with restless wings due west did flit.
For many a day across the sea he flew,
That lay beneath him clear enough and blue,
Until at last rose such a thick grey mist,
That of what lay beneath him nought he wist;
But still through this he flew a night and day
Hearkening the washing of the watery way,
Unseen: but when, at ending of the night,
The mist was gone and grey sea came in sight,
He thought that he had reached another world;
This way and that the leaden seas were hurled,
Moved by no wind, but by some unseen power;
Twilight it was and still his feet dropped lower,
As through the thickening, dim hot air he passed,
Until he feared to reach the sea at last.
But even as his feet dragged in the sea,
He, praying to the goddess fervently,
Felt her good help, for soon he rose again
Three fathoms up, and flew with lessened pain;
And looking through the dimness could behold
The wretched land whereof the sisters told.
And soon could see how down the green cliffs fell
A yellow stream, that from some inland well
Arose, and through the land ran sluggishly,
Until it poured with dull plash in the sea
Like molten lead; and nigher as he came
He saw great birds, whose kind he could not name,
That whirling noiselessly about did seem
To seek a prey within that leaden stream;

And drawing nigher yet, at last he saw
That many of them held, with beak or claw,
Great snakes they tore still flying through the air.
Then making for the cliff and lighting there
He saw, indeed, that tawny stream and dull
Of intertwining writhen snakes was full,
So, with a shudder, thence he turned away,
And through the untrodden land he took his way.
   Now cave-pierced rocks there rose up everywhere,
And gaunt old trees, of leaves and fruit all bare;
And midst this wretchedness a mighty hall,
Whose great stones made a black and shining wall;
The doors were open, and thence came a cry
Of one in anguish wailing bitterly;
Then o'er its threshold passed the son of Jove,
Well shielded by the grey-eyed Maiden's love.
   Now there he saw two women bent and old,
Like to those three that erst he did behold
Far northward, sitting well-nigh motionless,
Their eyes grown stony with their long distress,
Stared out at nought, and still no sound they made,
And on their knees their wrinkled hands were laid.
   But a third woman paced about the hall,
And ever turned her head from wall to wall
And moaned aloud, and shrieked in her despair;
Because the golden tresses of her hair
Were moved by writhing snakes from side to side,
That in their writhing oftentimes would glide
On to her breast, or shuddering shoulders white;
Or, falling down, the hideous things would light
Upon her feet, and crawling thence would twine
Their slimy folds about her ankles fine.
But in a thin red garment was she clad,
And round her waist a jewelled band she had,
The gift of Neptune on the fatal day
When fate her happiness first put away.
   So there awhile unseen did Perseus stand,
With softening heart, and doubtful trembling hand
Laid on his sword hilt, muttering, "Would that she
Had never turned her woeful face to me."
But therewith Pallas smote him with this thought,
"Does she desire to live, who has been brought
Into such utter woe and misery,
Wherefrom no god or man can set her free,
Since Pallas' dreadful vow shall bind her fast,
Till earth and heaven are gone, and all is past?
And yet, would God the thing were at an end."
   Then with that word, he saw her stop and rend
The raiment from her tender breast and soft,
And with a great cry lift her arms aloft;
Then on her breast her head sank, as she said,

"O ye, be merciful, and strike me dead!
How many an one cries unto you to live,
Which gift ye find no little thing to give,
O give it now to such, and unto me
That other gift from which all people flee!
   "O was it not enough to take away
The flowery meadows and the light of day?
Or not enough to take away from me
The once-loved faces that I used to see;
To take away sweet sounds and melodies,
The song of birds, the rustle of the trees;
To make the prattle of the children cease,
And wrap my soul in shadowy hollow peace,
Devoid of longing? Ah, no, not for me!
For those who die your friends this rest shall be;
For me no rest from shame and sore distress,
For me no moment of forgetfulness;
For me a soul that still might love and hate,
Shut in this fearful land and desolate,
Changed by mine eyes to horror and to stone;
For me perpetual anguish all alone,
Midst many a tormenting misery,
Because I know not if I e'er shall die.
   "And yet, and yet, thee will I pray unto,
Thou dweller in the varying halls of blue,
Fathoms beneath the treacherous bridge of lands.
Call now to mind that day upon the sands,
Hard by the house of Pallas white and cold,
Where hidden in some wave thou didst behold
This body, fearless of the cold grey sea,
And dowered as yet with fresh virginity.
   "How many things thou promisedst me then!
Who among all the daughters of great men
Should be like me? what sweet and happy life!
What peace, if all the world should be at strife,
Thou promisedst me then! Lay all aside,
And give unto the great Earth-Shaker's bride
That which the wretch shut up in prison drear,
Deprived of all, yet ceases not to fear;
That which all men fear more than all distress,
Irrevocable dull forgetfulness."

   Her constant woeful prayer was heard at last,
For now behind her unseen Perseus passed,
And silently whirled the great sword around;
And when it fell, she fell upon the ground,
And felt no more of all her bitter pain.
   But from their seats rose up with curses vain
The two immortals when they saw her fall
Headless upon the floor, and loud 'gan call
On those that came not, because far away

Their friends and kindred were upon that day.
Then to and fro about the hall they ran
To find the slayer, were he god or man,
And when unseen from out the place he drew,
Upon the unhappy corpse, with wails, they threw
Their wretched and immortal bodies old:
But when the one the other did behold,
Alive and hideous there before her eyes,
Such anguish for the past time would arise
Within their hearts, that the lone hall would ring
With dreadful shrieks of many an impious thing.
   Yet of their woe but little Perseus knew,
As with a stout heart south-east still he flew.

Now at his side a wallet Perseus bore,
With threads of yellow gold embroidered o'er
Shuddering, therein he laid the fearful head,
Lest he unwitting yet might join the dead,
Or those he loved by sight of it be slain.
   But strong fate led him to the Lybian plain,
Where, at the ending of a sultry day,
A palace huge and fair beneath him lay,
Whose roofs with silver plates were covered o'er;
Then lighting down by its enormous door,
He heard unmeasured sounds of revelry,
And thought, 'A fair place this will be for me,
Who lack both food and drink, and rest this night.'
So turning to the ruddy flood of light,
Up the huge steps he toiled unto the hall;
But even as his eager foot did fall
Upon the threshold, such a mocking shout
Rang in his ears as Etna sendeth out
When, at the day's end, round the stithy cold
The Cyclops some unmeasured banquet hold.
And monstrous men could he see sitting there,
Burnt by the sun, with length of straight back hair,
And taller far than men are wont to be;
And at a gold-strewn daïs could he see
A mighty King, a fearful man to face,
Brown-skinned and black-haired, of the giants' race,
Who seeing him, with thundering voice 'gan call,
"O Stranger, come forthwith into the hall,
Atlas would see thee!" Forth stood Perseus then,
And going 'twixt the rows of uncouth men
Seemed but a pigmy; but his heart was great,
And vain is might against the stroke of fate.
   Then the King cried, "Who art thou, little one?
Surely in thy land weak must be the sun
If there are bred such tender folk as thou:
May the gods grant such men are few enow!
Art thou a king's son?" Loud he laughed withal,

And shouts of laughter rang throughout the hall,
Like clattering thunder on a July night.
But Perseus quailed not. "Little were my might,"
He said, "if helpless on the earth I were;
But to the equal gods my life is dear,
And certes victory over Jove's own son
By earthly men shall not be lightly won."

So spake he, moving inward from the door,
But louder laughed the black king than before,
And all his people shouted at his beck;
Therewith he cried, "Break now this Prince's neck,
And take him forth and hang him up straightway
Before my door, that henceforth from this day
Pigmies and jesters may take better heed,
Lest at our hands they gain a liar's meed."

Then started up two huge men from the board,
And Perseus, seeing them come, half drew his sword,
Looking this way and that; but in a while,
Upon his wallet with a deadly smile
He set his hand, and forth the head he drew,
Dead, white midst golden hair, where serpents blue
Yet dangled dead; and ere they stooped to take
His outstretched arms, before them he did shake
The dreadful thing: then stopped they suddenly,
Stone dead, without a wound or any cry.

Then toward the King he held aloft the head,
And as he stiffened cried at him, and said,
"O King! when such a gift I bring to thee,
Wilt thou be dumb and neither hear nor see?
Listen how sing thy men, and in thy hall
How swift the merry dancers' feet do fall!"

For now these, thinking him some god to be,
Cried in their fear, and made great haste to flee,
Crowding about the great doors of the hall,
Until not one was left of great or small,
But the dead king, and those that there had died.—
Lo, in such way Medusa's head was tried!

But when the living giant-folk were gone,
And with the dead men there he stood alone,
He turned him to the food that thereby lay,
And ate and drank with none to say him nay;
And on the floor at last he laid him down,
Midst heaps of unknown tawny skins and brown.

There all the night in dreamless sleep he lay,
But rose again at the first streak of day,
And looking round about rejoiced to see
The uncouth image of his enemy,
Silent for ever, with wide mouth agape
E'en as he died; and thought, 'Who now shall 'scape
When I am angry, while this gift I have?
How well my needy lovers I may save

While this dread thing still hangeth by my side!'
  Then out he passed: a plain burnt up, and wide,
He saw before him, bare of any trees,
And much he longed for the green dashing seas,
And merry winds of the sweet island shore,
Fain of the gull's cry, for the lion's roar.
  Yet, glad at heart, he lifted up his feet
From the parched earth, and soon the air did beat,
Going north-east, and flew forth all the day,
And when the night fell still was on the way;
And many a sandy plain did he pass o'er,
And many a dry much-trodden river shore,
Where thick the thirsty beasts stood in the night.
The stealthy leopard saw him with afright,
As whining from the thicket it crept out;
The lion drew back at his sudden shout
From off the carcass of some slaughtered beast;
And the thin jackals waiting for the feast
Stinted their hungry howls as he passed by;
And black men sleeping, as he came anigh
Dreamed ugly dreams, and reached their hands to seize
The spear or sword that lay across their knees.

  So at the last the sea before him lay,
And yet, therefore, he made not any stay,
But flew on till the night began to wane,
And the grey sea was blue and green again;
Until the sunlight on his wings shone fair,
And turned to red the gold locks of his hair.
Then in a little while he saw no land,
But all was heaving sea on every hand,
Driven this way and that way by the wind.
  Still fast he flew, thinking some coast to find,
And so, about the middle of the day,
Far to the east a land before him lay,
And when unto it he was come anigh
He saw the sea beat on black cliffs and high,
With green grass growing on the tops of them,
Binding them round as gold a garment's hem.
  Then slowly alongside thereof he flew
If haply by some sign the land he knew,
Until a ness he reached, whereon there stood
A tower new-built of mighty beams of wood;
So nigh he came that, unseen, he could see
Pale haggard faces peering anxiously
From out its well-barred windows that looked forth
Into a bay that lay upon the north;
But inland over moveless waves of down
Shone the white walls of some great royal town.
Now underneath the scarped cliffs of the bay
From horn to horn a belt of sand there lay

Fast lessening as the flood-tide swallowed it,
There all about did the sea-swallows flit,
And from the black rocks yellow hawks flew down,
And cormorants fished amidst the sea-weed brown,
Or on the low rocks nigh unto the sea,
While over all the fresh wind merrily
Blew from the sea, and o'er the pale blue sky
Thin clouds were stretched the way the wind went by,
And forward did the mighty waters press
As though they loved the green earth's stedfastness.
Nought slept, but everything was bright and fair
Beneath the bright sun and the noon-day air.
Now hovering there, he seemed to hear a sound
Unlike the sea-bird's cry, and, looking round,
He saw a figure standing motionless
Beneath the cliff, midway 'twixt ness and ness,
And as the wind lull'd heard that cry again,
That sounded like the wail of one in pain;
Wondering thereat, and seeking marvels new
He lighted down, and toward the place he drew,
And made invisible by Pallas' aid,
He came within the scarped cliff's purple shade,
And found a woman standing lonely there,
Naked, except for tresses of her hair
That o'er her white limbs by the breeze were wound,
And brazen chains her weary arms that bound
Unto the sea-beat overhanging rock,
As though her golden-crowned head to mock.
But nigh her feet upon the sand there lay
Rich raiment that had covered her that day,
Worthy to be the ransom of a king,
Unworthy round such loveliness to cling.

  Alas, alas! no bridal play this was,
The tremors that throughout her limbs did pass,
Her restless eyes, the catching of her breath,
Were but the work of the cold hand of death,
She waited for, midst untold miseries,
As, now with head cast back, and close-shut eyes
She wailed aloud, and now all spent with woe
Stared out across the rising sea, as though
She deemed each minute brought the end anigh
For which in her despair she needs must cry.

  Then unseen Perseus stole anigh the maid,
And love upon his heart a soft hand laid,
And tender pity rent it for her pain,
Nor yet an eager cry could he refrain,
As now, transformed by that piteous sight,
Grown like unto a god for pride and might,
Down on the sand the mystic cap he east

And stood before her with flushed face at last,
And grey eyes glittering with his great desire
Beneath his hair, that like a harmless fire
Blown by the wind shone in her hopeless eyes.
  But she, all rigid with her first surprise,
Ceasing her wailing as she heard his cry,
Stared at him, dumb with fear and misery,
Shrunk closer yet unto the rocky place
And writhed her bound hands as to hide her face;
But sudden love his heart did so constrain,
With open mouth he strove to speak in vain
And from his heart the hot tears 'gan to rise;
But she midst fear beheld his kind grey eyes,
And then, as hope came glimmering through her dread,
In a weak voice he scarce could hear, she said,
"O Death! if thou hast risen from the sea,
Sent by the gods to end this misery,
I thank them that thou comest in this form,
Who rather thought to see a hideous worm
Come trailing up the sands from out the deep,
Or suddenly swing over from the steep
To lap me in his folds, and bone by bone
Crush all my body: come then, with no moan,
Will I make ready now to leave the light.
  "But yet—thy face is wonderful and bright;
Art thou a god? Ah, then be kind to me!
Is there no valley far off from the sea
Where I may live alone, afar from strife
Nor anger any god with my poor life?
Or do the gods delight in misery
And art thou come to mock me ere I die?
Alas, must they be pitiless, when they
Fear not the hopeless slayer of the day!
Speak, speak! what meanest thou by that sad smile?
  "O, if the gods could be but men awhile
And learn such fearful things unspeakable
As I have learned this morn, what man can tell
What golden age might wrap the world again—
Ah, dost thou love me, is my speech not vain?
Did not my beauty perish on this morn
Dost thou not kiss me now for very scorn?
Alas, my shame, I cannot flee from thee!
Alas, my sin! no green-stemmed laurel tree
Shall mock thy grasp, no misty mountain stream
Shall wake thee shuddering from a lovely dream,
No helping god shall hear, but thou alone!—
Help me, I faint! I see not! art thou gone?
Alas! thy lips were warm upon my brow,
What good deed will it be to leave me now!
  "Oh, yet I feel thy kind and tender hand
On my chained wrist, and thou wilt find some land

Where I may live a little, free from fear?
   "And yet, and yet, if thou hast sought me here
Being but a man, no manly thing it is,
Nor hope thou from henceforth to live in bliss,
If here thou wrongest me, who am but dead."
   Then as she might she hung adown her head,
Her bosom heaved with sobs, and from her eyes
Long dried amidst those hopeless miseries
Unchecked the salt tears o'er her bosom ran
As love and shame their varying strife began.
   But overwhelmed with pity, mad with love
Stammering, nigh weeping spoke the son of Jove,—
"Alas, what land is this, where such as thou
Are thus tormented? look upon me now,
And cease thy fear! no evil man am I,
No cruel god to mock thy misery;
But the gods help me, and their unmoved will
Has sent me here to save thee from some ill,
I know not what; to give thee rest from this,
And unto me unutterable bliss,
If from a man thou takest not away
The gift thou gavest to a god to-day;
But I may be a very god to thee,
Because the gods are helpful unto me,
Nor would I fear them aught if thou wert nigh,
Since unto each it happeneth once to die.
   "Speak not, sweet maid, till I have loosed thine hands
From out the grasp of these unworthy bands."
   So straight, and ere her lips could frame a word,
From out its sheath he drew the gleaming sword,
And while she shut her dazzled eyes for fear
To see the glittering marvel draw anear,
Unto her side her weary arms feel freed;
Then must she shrink away, for now indeed
With rest and hope and growing love there came
Remembrance of her helplessness and shame,
Weeping she said, "My fate is but to die,
Forget the wild words of my misery,
Take a poor maiden's thanks, and leave this place,
Nor for thy pity die before my face,
As verily thou wilt if thou stay'st here;
Because, however free thou art from fear,
What hopest thou against this beast to do,
My death, and thine unconquerable foe?
When all a kingdom's strength has had no hope
With this strange horror, God-endowed, to cope,
But deemed it good to give up one poor maid
Unto his wrath, who makes the world afraid."
   "Nay," said he, "but thy fate shall be my fate,
And on these sands thy bane will I await,
Though I know nought of all his mightiness:

For scarcely yet a man, I none the less
Such things have done as make me now a name,
Nor can I live a loveless life of shame,
Or leave thee now, this day's most god-like gain,
To suffer some unknown and mortal pain."

  She, hurrying as he spoke, with trembling hands
Had lifted up her raiment from the sands,
And yet therewith she was not well arrayed,
Before she turned round, ghastly white, and said,
"Look seaward and behold, my death draw nigh,
Not thine—not thine—but kiss me ere I die;
Alas! how many things I had to tell,
For certainly I should have loved thee well."
  He came to her and kissed her as she sank
Into his arms, and from the horror shrank,
Clinging to him, scarce knowing he was there;
But through the drifting wonder of her hair,
Amidst his pity, he beheld the sea,
And saw a huge wave rising mightily
Above the smaller breakers of the shore,
Which in its green breast for a minute bore
A nameless horror, that it cast aland,
And left, a huge mass on the oozing sand,
That scarcely seemed a living thing to be,
Until at last those twain it seemed to see,
And gathering up its strange limbs, towards them passed.
And therewithal a dismal trumpet-blast
Rang from the tower, and from the distant town
The wind in answer brought loud wails adown.
  Then Perseus gently put the maid from him,
Who sank down shivering in her every limb,
Silent despite herself for fear and woe,
As down the beech he ran to meet the foe.
  But he, beholding Jove's son drawing near,
A great black fold against him did uprear,
Maned with grey tufts of hair, as some old tree
Hung round with moss, in lands where vapours be;
From his bare skull his red eyes glowed like flame,
And from his open mouth a sound there came,
Strident and hideous, that still louder grew
As that rare sight of one in arms he knew:
But godlike, fearless, burning with desire,
The adamant jaws and lidless eyes of fire
Did Perseus mock, and lightly leapt aside
As forward did the torture-chamber glide
Of his huge head, and ere the beast could turn,
One moment bright did blue-edged Herpe burn,
The next was quenched in the black flow of blood;
Then in confusèd folds the hero stood,
His bright face shadowed by the jaws of death,

His hair blown backward by the poisonous breath;
But all that passed, like lightning-lighted street
In the dark night, as the blue blade did meet
The wrinkled neck, and with no faltering stroke,
Like a god's hand the fell enchantment broke,
And then again in place of crash and roar,
He heard the shallow breakers on the shore,
And o'er his head the sea-gull's plaintive cry,
Careless as gods for who might live or die.

  Then Perseus from the slimy loathsome coil
Drew out his feet, and then with little toil
Smote off the head, the terror of the lands,
And, dragging it along, went up the sands,
Shouting aloud for joy, "Arise, arise,
O thou whose name I know not! Ope thine eyes
To see the gift, that I, first seen to-day,
Am hastening now before thy feet to lay!
Look up, look up! What shall thy sweet face be,
That I have seen amidst such misery,
When thou at last beginnest to rejoice."
  Slowly she rose, her burdened heart found voice
In sobs and murmurs inarticulate,
And clean forgetting all the sport of fate,
She scarce could think that she should ever die,
As locked in fearless, loving, strait embrace,
They made a heaven of that lone sandy place.
  Then on a rock smoothed by the washing sea
They sat, and eyed each other lovingly.
And few words at the first the maiden said,
So wrapped she was in all the goodlihead
Of her new life made doubly happy now:
For her alone the sea-breeze seemed to blow,
For her in music did the white surf fall,
For her alone the wheeling birds did call
Over the shallows, and the sky for her
Was set with white clouds, far away and clear;
E'en as her love, this strong and lovely one
Who held her hand, was but for her alone.
  But after loving silence for a while,
She, turning round to him her heavenly smile,
Said, "Tell me, O my love, what name is thine,
What mother brought thee forth so nigh divine,
Whence art thou come to take away my shame?"
  Then said he, "Fair love, Perseus is my name,
Not known of men, though that may come to be;
And her that bore me men call Danaë,
And tales of my begetting people tell
And call my father, Jove: but it befell
Unto my mother, when I first was born,
That she, cast out upon the sea, forlorn

Of help of men, unto Seriphos came;
And there she dwells as now, not gathering shame,
But called a Queen; and thence I come indeed,
Sent by the gods to help thee in thy need."
    Then he began and told her everything
Down to the slaying of the monstrous king,
She listening to him meanwhile, glad at heart
That he had played so fair and great a part.
But all being told, she said, "This salt pool nigh
Left by the tide, now mirrors well the sky,
So smooth it is, and now I stand anear
Canst thou not see my foolish visage clear,
Yea, e'en the little gems upon my hands?
May I not see this marvel of the lands
So mirrored, and yet live—make no delay
The sea is pouring fast into the bay,
And we must soon be gone."
                                "Look down," he said,
"And take good heed thou turnest not thine head."
Then gazing down, with shuddering dread and awe,
Over her imaged shoulder, soon she saw
The head rise up, so beautiful and dread,
That, white and ghastly, yet seemed scarcely dead
Beside the image of her own fair face,
As, daring not to move from off the place,
But trembling sore, she cried, "Enough, O love!
What man shall doubt thou art the son of Jove;
I think thou wilt not die:" then with her hand
She hid her eyes, and trembling did she stand
Until she felt his lips upon her cheek;
Then turning round, with anxious eyes and meek,
She gazed upon him, and some doubtful thought
Up to her brow the tender colour brought,
And sinking somewhat down her golden head,
Stammering a little now these words she said,
    "O godlike man, thou dost not ask my name,
Or why folk gave me up to death and shame;
Dost thou not dread I am some sorceress,
Whose evil deeds well earned me that distress?"
    "Tell me thy name," he said; "yet as for thee
I deem that thou wert bound beside the sea,
Because the gods would have the dearest thing
Thy land possessed for its own ransoming."
    She said, "O love, the sea is rising fast,
And time it is that we henceforth were past;
The only path that leadeth to the down
Is far, and thence a good way is the town;
Come then, and on our journey will I tell
How all these things, now come to nought, befell."
    "Lead me," he said, and lifted from the sand
The monster's head; and therewith, hand in hand,

Together underneath the cliffs they went,
The while she told her tale to this intent.

   "This is the Syrian land, this town anigh
Is Joppa, and Andromeda am I,
Daughter of him who holds the sceptre there,
King Cepheus and Cassiope the fair.
   "She, smit by cruel madness, brought ill fate,
Upon the land to make it desolate;
For by the place whence thou deliveredst me,
An altar to the daughters of the sea
Erewhile there stood, and we in solemn wise,
Unto the maids were wont to sacrifice,
And give them gifts of honey, oil, and wine,
That we might have the love of folk divine;
And so it chanced that on a certain day,
When from that place the sea was ebbed away,
Upon the firm sands I and many a maid
About that altar went, while the flutes played
Such notes as sea-folk love; and as we went
Upon the wind rich incense-clouds we sent
About the hallowed stone, whereon there lay
Fruits of the earth for them to bear away;
Thus did we maids, as we were wont to do,
And watching us, as was their wont also,
Our mothers stood, my own amidst the rest.
   "But ere the rites were done, as one possessed
She cried aloud, 'Alas, what do we now,
Such honour unto unseen folk to show!
To spend our goods, our labour, and our lives,
In serving these the careless sea-wind drives
Hither and thither through the booming seas;
While thou Andromeda art queen of these,
And in thy limbs such lovely godhead moves,
That thou shalt be new Mother of the Loves;
Thou shalt not die! Go child, and sit alone,
And take our homage on thy golden throne;
And I that bore thee will but be thy slave,
Nor shall another any worship have.'
   "Trembling awhile we stood with heads downcast,
To hear those words, then from the beach we passed.;
And sick at heart each went unto her home
Expecting when the fearful death should come,
Like those of Thebes, who, smit by arrows, fell
Before the feet of her who loved too well.
   "And yet stayed not my mother's madness there;
She caused men make a silver image fair
Of me unhappy, round the base she writ
'Fairest of all,' and bade men carry it,
With flowers and music, down unto the sea,
Who on the altar fixed it solidly

Against the beating of the winds and waves.
  "But we, expecting now no quiet graves,
Trembled at every murmur of the night,
And if a cloud should hide the noon sun bright
Grew faint with terror; yet the days went by
Harmless above our great iniquity,
Until one wretched morn I woke to hear,
Down in the street loud wails and cries of fear,
And my heart died within me, nor durst I
Ask for the reason of that bitter cry,
Though soon I knew it—nigh unto the sea
Were gathered folk for some festivity;
When, at the happiest moment of their feast,
Forth from the deep there came a fearful beast
No man could name, who quickly snatched away
Their fairest maid, and with small pain did slay
Such men as there in arms before him stood;
For unto him was steel as rotten wood,
And darts as straw—nor grew the story old,
Day after day e'en such a tale was told.
Kiss me, my love! I grow afraid again;
Kiss me amid the memory of my pain.
Draw me to thee, that I thine arms may feel,
A better help than triple brass or steel!
  "Alas, love! folk began to look on me
With angry eyes, and mutter gloomily,
As pale and trembling through the streets I passed;
And from the heavy thunder-cloud, at last
The dreadful lightning quivered through the air:
For on a day the people filled the square
With arms and tumult, and my name I heard,
But heard no more; for, shuddering and afeard,
Unto my far-off quiet bower I fled,
And from that moment deemed myself but dead.
How the time passed I know not, what they did
I know not now; for like a quail half hid,
When the hawk's pinions shade the sun from him,
Crouching adown, I felt my life wax dim.
  "The gods have made us mighty certainly
That we can bear such things and yet not die.
This morn—Ah, love, and was it yet this year,
Wherein thou camest to me, kind and dear?—
This morn they brought me forth, they did on me
This mocking raiment bright with bravery;
They mocked my head with gold, with gems my feet,
My heart with lovely songs and music sweet.
Thou wouldst have wept to see me led along
Amidst that dreary pomp with flowers and song,
But if folk wept, how could I note it then;
Most vain to me were grown all ways of men.
  "They brought me to mine image on the sands,

They took it down, they bore it in their hands
To deck mine empty tomb, I think, and then—
O cruel is the fearfulness of men,
Striving a little while to 'scape death's pain!—
My naked body they spared not to chain,
Lest I should 'scape the death from which they fled,
Then left me there alone and shamed—and dead—
While to his home each went again, to live
Such vain forgetful life as fate might give.

   "O love, to think that love can pass away,
That, soon or late, to us shall come a day
When this shall be forgotten! e'en this kiss
That makes us now forget the high God's bliss,
And sons of men with all their miseries."

   "Turn round," he said, "and let your well-loved eyes
Behold the sea from this high grassy hill,
And thou shalt see the risen waves now fill
The bay from horn to horn of it: no more
Thy footprints bless the shell-strewn sandy shore,
The vale the monster scooped as 'neath my sword
He writhed, the black stream that from out him poured,
The rock we sat on, and the pool wherein
Thou sawest the gods' revenge for heedless sin—
How the green ripples of the shallow sea
Cover the strife and passion peacefully,
Nor lack the hallowing of the low broad sun.

   "So has love stolen upon us, lovely one,
And quenched our old lives in this new delight,
And if thou needs must think of that dull night
That creepeth on no otherwise than this,
Yet for that thought hold closer to thy bliss,
Come nigher, come! forget the more thy pain."

   So there of all love's feasting were they fain,
Words fail to tell the joyance that they had,
And with what words they made each other glad.

So, as it drew to ending of the day,
Unto the city did they take their way,
And when they stood before its walls at last
They found the heavy gate thereof shut fast,
And no one on the walls for very shame;
Then to the wicket straightway Perseus came,
And down the monster's grinning head he threw,
While on the horn a mighty blast he blew,
But no one answered; then he cried aloud,
"Come forth, O warders, and no more shrink cowed
Behind your battlements! one man alone
Has dared to do what thousands have not done,
And the great beast besides the sea lies dead:
Come forth, come forth! and gaze upon this head!"

Then opened was the door a little way,
And one peered forth and saw him with the may,
And turning round some joyous words he cried
Unto the rest, who oped the great gates wide,
And through them Perseus the saved maiden led.
Then as the folk cast eyes upon the head,
They stopped their shouts to gaze thereon with fear,
And timidly the women drew anear;
But soon, beholding Perseus' godlike grace,
His mighty limbs, and flushed and happy face,
Cried out unto the maid, "O happy thou,
Who art well paid for every trouble now,
In winning such a godlike man as this."
And many there were fain his skirts to kiss;
But he smiled down on them, and said, "Rejoice,
O girls, indeed, but yet lift heart and voice
Unto the gods to-day, and not to me!
For they it was who sent me to this sea.
And first of all fail not to bless the Maid
Through whom it came that I was not afraid."
   So through the streets they went, and quickly spread
News that the terror of the land was dead.
And folk thronged round to see the twain go by,
Or went before with flowers and minstrelsy,
Rejoicing for the slaying of their shame.

   Thus harbinger'd the happy lovers came
Unto King Cepheus' royal house of gold.
To whom by this the joyful cries had told
That all was changed and still his days were good,
So, eager in his well-built porch he stood,
No longer now in mournful raiment clad.
   But when they met, then were those two more glad
Than words can say; there came her mother, too,
And round about her neck fair arms she threw,
Weeping for joy; and all about the King
The great men stood and eyed the fearful thing
That lay at Perseus' feet: then the King said,
"O thou, who on this day hast saved my maid,
Wilt thou rule half my kingdom from to-day?
Or wilt thou carry half my wealth away?
Or in some temple shall we honour thee,
Setting thine image up beside the sea?
Ask what thou wilt before these mighty lords,
And straightway is it thine without more words."
   Then in his heart laughed Perseus: and, "O King,"
He said, "I ask indeed a mighty thing;
Yet neither will I take thy wealth away,
Or make thee less a King than on this day,
And in no temple shall mine image stand
To look upon the sea that beats this land,

For fear the God who now is friend to me
Thereby should come to be mine enemy;
And yet on this day am I grown so bold,
I ask a greater gift than power or gold;
Give me thy maiden saved, to be my bride,
And let me go, because the world is wide,
And the gods hate me not, and I am fain
Some fertile land with these my hands to gain.
Nor think thereby that thou wilt get thee shame,
For if thou askest of my race and name,
Perseus I am, the son of Danaë,
Born nigh to Argos, by the sounding sea,
And those that know, call me the son of Jove,
Who in past days my mother's face did love."

   Then, glad at heart, the King said, "Poor indeed
Were such a gift, to give thee to thy meed
This that thine own unconquered hands have won.
O ye! bring now the head and cast thereon
Jewels and gold from out my treasury,
Till nothing of its grimness men can see;
And let folk bring round to the harbour's mouth
My ship that saileth yearly to the south;
That to his own land since it is his will
This Prince may go; nor yet without his fill
Of that which all men long for everywhere,
Honour, and gold, and women kind and fair.
And ye, O lords, to-morrow ere midday,
Come hither to my house in great array,
For then this marriage will we solemnize,
Appeasing all the gods with gifts of price."

   Then loud all shouted, and the end of day
Being come, Andromeda was led away
Unto her bower, and there within a while
She fell asleep, and in her sleep did smile,
For on the calm of that forgetfulness
Her bliss some happy longings did impress.

   But in the Syrian King's adorned hall
Sat Perseus till the shadows 'gan to fall
Shorter beneath the moon, and still he thought
Amid the feast of what a day had brought
Unto his heart, a foolish void before,
And for the morrow must he long so sore
That all those joyances and minstrelsy
Seemed unto him but empty things to be.

   Early next morn the city was astir,
And country folk came in from far and near
Hearing the joyous tidings that the beast
Was dead, and fain to see the marriage feast,
And joyous folk wandered from street to street
Crowned with fair flowers and singing carols sweet.

Then to the maiden's chamber maidens came,
And woke her up to love and joyous shame,
And as the merry sun streamed through the room
Spread out unequalled marvels of the loom,
Stored up for such an end in days long done,
Ere yet her grey eyes looked upon the sun,
Fine webs like woven mist, wrought in the dawn,
Long ere the dew had left the sunniest lawn,
Gold cloth so wrought that nought of gold seemed there,
But rather sunlight over blossoms fair;
You would have said that gods had made them, bright,
To hide her body from the common light
Lest men should die from unfulfilled desire.
　Gems too they showed wrought by the hidden fire
That eats the world, and from the unquiet sea
Pearls worth the ransom of an argosy.
　Yet all too little all these riches seemed
In worship of her, who as one who dreamed,
By her fair maidens' hands was there arrayed,
Then, with loose hair, ungirded as a maid
Unto the threshold of the house was brought,
But when her hand familiar fingers caught—
And when that voice, that erst amidst her fear
She deemed a god's, now smote upon her ear
Like one new-born to heaven she seemed to be.
　But dreamlike was the long solemnity,
Unreal the joyous streets, where yesterday
She passed half dead upon her wretched way;
And though before the flickering altar flame
She trembled when she thought of that past shame,
And midst the shouting knit her brows to think
Of what a cup these men had bidden her drink,
Unreal they seemed, forgotten as a tale
We cannot tell, though it may still avail
For pensive thoughts betwixt the day and night.
　All things unto the gods were done aright;
Beside the sea the flame and smoke uprose
Over rich gifts of many things to those
A woman's tongue had wounded; golden veils
And images, and bowls wrought o'er with tales,
By all the altars of the gods were laid;
On this last day of maidenhood the maid
Had stood before the shrines, and there had thrown
Sweet incense on the flame, and through the town
The praises of immortals had been sung,
And sacred flowers about the houses hung;
And now the last hours of the dreamlike day
Amid great feasting slowly passed away.

　But in that land there was a mighty lord,
To whom erewhile the King had pledged his word

That he should wed Andromeda, and he
Heard through sure friends of this festivity
And raged thereat, and thought that eve to come
Unbidden to the feast and bear her home;
Phineus his name was, great amidst great men.
  He setting out, came to the great hall when
The sun was well-nigh down, all armed was he,
And at his back came on tumultuously
His armed men-slaves, and folk that loved him dear.
  Beholding him, the King rose up in fear,
And all about the place scared folk uprose
As men surprised at feast by deadly foes;
But Perseus laughing said, "What feat do ye
This eve in honour of my sweet and me?
Or are ye but the servants of the King
Returned from doing for him some great thing
In a far land? then sit here and be glad,
For on this day the king feeds good and bad."
  Then inarticulate with rage and grief
Phineus turned on him, snatching at a sheaf
Of darts that hung against a pillar there,
And hurled one at him, that sung through his hair
And smote a serving man down by his side;
Then finding voice, he faced the King and cried,
"What dost thou drinking with this robber here,
Who comes to steal that which I hold so dear
That on my knees I prayed for her to thee?
Speak, Cepheus! wilt thou give her yet to me
And have good peace withal, or wilt thou die?
Ho, friends, and ye that follow, cry my cry!"

  Then straight the hall rang with a mighty shout
Of "Phineus," and from sheath and belt leapt out
The gleaming steel, and Cepheus stammering
Took heart to say, "Think well upon this thing;
What should I do? the man did save her life,
And her he might have made his slave, as wife
He asks for now; take gifts and go thy way
Nor quench in blood the joyance of this day."
  Then forth stood Perseus with a frowning face
Before them all, and cried out from his place,
"Get ye behind my back, all friends to me!
And ere the lamps are lighted ye shall see
A stranger thing than ye have ever dreamed;"
And as he spake in his left hand there gleamed
The gold-wrought satchel; but amazed and cowed
Did the King's friends behind the hero crowd,
Who, ere from out the bag he drew the head,
Unto that band of fierce new-comers said;
"Will ye have life or death? if life, then go
And on the grass outside your armour throw,

And then returning, drink to my delight
Until the summer sun puts out the night."
  But loud they shouted, swaying to and fro,
And mocked at him, and cried aloud to know
If in his hand Jove's thunderbolt he had,
Or Mars' red sword that makes the eagles glad;
But Phineus, raging, cried, "Take him alive,
That we for many an hour the wretch may drive
With thongs and clubs until he longs to die!"
  Then all set on him with a mighty cry,
But, with a shout that thrilled high over theirs,
He drew the head out by the snaky hairs
And turned on them the baleful glassy eyes;
Then sank to silence all that storm of cries
And clashing arms; the tossing points that shone
In the last sunbeams, went out one by one
As the sun left them, for each man there died,
E'en as the shepherd on the bare hill-side,
Smitten amid the grinding of the storm;
When, while the hare lies flat in her wet form,
E'en strong men quake for fear in houses strong,
And nigh the ground the lightning runs along.
  But upright on their feet the dead men stood,
In brow and cheek still flushed the angry blood;
This smiled, the mouth of that was open wide,
This other drew the great sword from his side,
All were at point to do this thing or that.

  As silent in the hall the living sat
As those dead men, till Perseus turned at last
And over all a kingly look he cast,
And said, "O friends, drink yet one cup to me,
And then to-morrow will I try the sea
With this my love; and, sweet Andromeda,
Forgive me that I needs must play this play;
Forget it, sweet! thou wilt not see again
This land of thine, upland, or hill, or plain;
There where we go shall all be new to thee
Except the love that thou hast won from me."
Then to her frightened face there came a smile,
And in her cheeks within a little while
Sweet colour came again; but right few words
Upon that night were said of king or lords.

  But soon again the lovers were alone
Of all the sons of men remembering none,
Forgetting every god but him whose bow
About the vexed and flowery earth doth go.

So on the morn, when risen was the sun
About the capstan did the shipmen run,

Warping the great ship to the harbour mouth
That yearly went for treasures to the south,
And thither from the palace did men bear
Bales of rich cloth, and golden vessels rare,
And gold new coined, and silver bars of weight.
And women-slaves with bodies slim and straight
Stood on the snow-white deck, and strong men-slaves
Brought from some conquered land beyond the waves
Bore down rich burdens; so when all things due
Were laid on ship-board, and to noon it grew
Thither came Perseus with his new-wed wife,
And she, as losing somewhat of her life
Was pensive now, and silent, and regret
Must move her that her heart must soon forget
All folk and things where first her life began,
Yea, e'en the mother, whose worn face and wan,
Tearless and haughty, yet looked o'er the sea,
As though the life wherein no good could be
She still would hear in every god's despite—
Ah, folk forget; the damsel's heart grew light
E'en while her country's cliffs she yet could see.
Should she remember, when so lovingly
That cheek touched hers, and he was hers alone?

  Love while ye may; if twain grow into one
'Tis for a little while; the time goes by,
No hatred 'twixt the pair of friends doth lie,
No troubles break their hearts—and yet, and yet—
How could it be? we strove not to forget;
Rather in vain to that old time we clung,
Its hopes and wishes round our hearts we hung,
We played old parts, we used old names—in vain,
We go our ways, and twain once more are twain;
Let pass—at latest when we come to die
Thus shall the fashion of the world go by.
  But these, while still at brightest love's flame burned,
Were glad indeed, as towards Seriphos turned
Bright shone their gilded prow against the sun.

  Meanwhile the folk of Joppa, one by one,
Took Phineus' people and their master dead
All turned to stone as they had seen the head,
And in a lonely place they set them down,
Upon a hill that overlooked the town,
And round about them built a wall, four-square,
And at each corner raised a temple fair,
And therein altars made they unto Jove,
Pallas, and Neptune, and the God of Love;
And in Jove's temple carved that history,
That those who came there after them might see,
From first to last, how all these things were done,

And how these men last looked upon the sun.

  But the two lovers going on their way
Grew happier still, as bright day followed day;
And, the wind favouring, in a little while
They reached the low shore of the well-loved isle;
And, having beached the well-built keel, took land
Where Danae's boat first touched the yellow sand.
Then cityward alone did Perseus go
His fatal gift unto the King to show;
And, passing through the fair fields hastily,
Reached the green precinct, where he thought to see
His mother, he had left alive and well;
But from inside upon his ears there fell
A noise of shrieks and clashing arms and shouts;
Thereto he ran beset with many doubts,
Since Polydectes' evil wiles he knew,
And what a fate he erst had doomed him to;
So, hurrying through, he reached the shrine at last,
And there beheld his mother, her arms cast
About Minerva's image, and by her
Good Dictys, who, with shield and glittering spear,
Abode the onslaught of an armed band,
At head of whom did Polydectes stand.
  Then to her side sprang Perseus with a cry,
And at that sight and sound she joyfully
Said, "Com'st thou, long desired? nought fear I now,
This kingly traitor soon shall lie alow."
Then the King tottered backward, and awhile
Stood staring at him: but an evil smile
Soon hid his fear, as, turning, he beheld
The glittering weapons that his stout slaves held,
And he cried out, "Yea, art thou back again?
And was my story forged for thee in vain?
Be merry then, but give me place or die!
I am not one to meet thee fearfully.
But thee, O brother, must I then slay thee,
And in our house must one more story be?
Give back! nor for a woman's foolishness,
Bring curses on the name thou shouldest bless.
Set on at once then! take the three of them!"
  Then once more clashed the spears, but on the hem
Of that dread satchel Perseus set his hand,
And put his friend aside, and took his stand
Betwixt his mother and the island men;
And terribly he cried, "Thus take thou then
The gift thou badst me bring to thee! nor ask
Of any man again another task,
Except to cast on thee a little sand
That thou may'st reach in peace the shadowy land."
His mocking speech he ended with a shout,

And from the bag the dreadful head drew out,
And shook it in the King's bewildered face;
Who unto him yet strove to make one pace
With feebly brandished spear and drooping shield,
Then unto stony death his heart did yield,
And without any cry upright he died,
With fallen arms and fixed eyes staring wide.
But of his men the bravest turned and fled,
And on the ground some trembled, well-nigh dead
For very fear, till Perseus cried, "Arise,
Lay down your arms and go! Henceforth be wise;
Nor at kings' biddings 'gainst the just gods strive."
But as they slunk away, too glad to live
To need more words, and shivering with their dread,
Once more did Perseus hide the fearful head,
And toward his mother turned; who, with pale face,
Stood trembling there, remembering that embrace
Within the brazen house; but now he threw
His arms about her as he used to do
When her own arms his little body bore;
And smiling, even as he smiled of yore,
He said, "O mother, fear me not at all,
But yet bethink thee of the brazen wall
And golden Jove, nor doubt from him I came;
And no more now shall I be called thy shame,
But thy defence and glory everywhere.

   "But now to lovely Argos let us fare,
Too small a land this is become for thee,
And I may hope a greater sovereignty,
Who, by God's help, have done such mighty things,
Which I will tell thee of, while the wind sings
Amongst the shrouds of my rich-laden keel,
While by thy feet a god-given gift shall kneel,
My bride new won; in such-like guise will we
Come back to him who gave us to the sea,
And make our peace and all ill blood forget,
That through long happy years thou mayst live yet."
   Then did he take good Dictys by the hand,
And said, "O righteous man, we leave this land,
Nor leave thee giftless for the welcoming
Thou gav'st us erst, nor for this other thing
That thou hast wrought for us this happy tide;
Therefore do thou as King herein abide,
And win Jove's love by helping in such wise
As thou didst us, folk sunk in miseries."
   So gave he kingdoms, as he took away,
For strong the God was in him on that day,
And the gods smiled to hear him; yea, and she
Who armed him erst, then dealt so lovingly,
She caused the people's hearts towards him to yearn,

Who, thronging round, began somehow to learn
The story of his deeds, and cried aloud,
"Be thou our King!" Then showed he to the crowd
Dictys his friend, and said, "Ito my kin
Must go, mine heritage and goods to win,
And a king, deal with kings; but yet see here
This royal man, my helpful friend and dear;
Loved of the gods, surely he is of worth
For greater things." So saying he went forth
And 'mid their reverence, leading by the hand
His happy mother, turned unto the strand;
And still the wondering folk with them must go,
And now such honour unto him would show,
That rather they would make him God than King;
But while fresh carols round him these did sing
They came unto the low, sea-beaten sand;
And Danae took the Syrian by the hand
And kissed her, full of joy that such an one
Should bear brave children to her godlike son:
Then Perseus gave commands, and on the shore
Great gifts they laid from out his plenteous store,
To glad King Dictys' eyes withal, and then
Bade farewell to him and his island men;
And all took ship, and hoisting sail straightway,
Departed o'er the restless plain and grey.

   Now fair the wind was for a day and night,
But on the second day as it grew light,
And they were thinking that they soon should be
At Argos, rose a tempest on the sea,
And drave them from their course unto a land
Far north thereof. So on the yellow sand
They hauled their ship, and thereto presently
The good folk of the country drew anigh,
To make their market; and being asked, they said
That this was Thessaly, that strait paths led
Through rugged mountains to a fertile plain
Peneus watered, rich with many a fane:
That following down the stream they soon should come
Unto a mighty people's glorious home,
A god-loved ancient city, called of men
Larissa, and the time was fitting then
To go thereto, and there should they have rest,
For now each corner was an honoured guest,
Because Teutamias, the Thessalian king,
His father dead with games was honouring.
   Then to that city Perseus fain would go,
His might unto the gathered men to show;
Desiring, too, to gather tidings there
Of how the old Acrisius yet might fare,
And if unto his scarce-seen Argive home

He in good peace might venture now to come.
So of the country folk he took fair steeds
And gave them gold, and goods for all their needs,
And with a trusty band with this intent
Through the rough passes of the hills he went,
Bearing his mother, and the Syrian may:
As of a king's men deemed of his array,
When to the fertile peopled fields he came;
But yet he bade that none should tell his name.
So coming to Larissa, all men thought,
That he who with him such great marvels brought
Was some great king, though scanty was his band;
So honour did he get on every hand.
But when the games began, and none could win
A prize in any, if he played therein,
A greater name they gave him, saying, "What worth
In this poor age is left upon the earth
To do such deeds? Surely no man this is,
But some god weary of the heavenly bliss."

   At last, when all the other games were done,
Men fell to play at casting of the stone;
And strong men cast it, mighty of their hands,
Bearers of great names in the Grecian lands:
But Perseus stood and watched the play alone,
Nor did he move when every man had thrown.
Then cried Teutamias, "Nameless one! see now
How mightily these strong-armed heroes throw:
Canst thou prevail in this as in the rest?"

   "O King!" said Perseus, "now I think it best
To try the Fates no more; I must be gone:
Therefore to-day thou seest me thus alone,
For in the house my white-armed damsels stay
To order matters for our homeward way."

   "Nay, stranger," said the King, "but rather take
This golden garland for Teutamias' sake,
And try one cast: look, here I have with me
A well-loved guest, who is most fain to see
Thy godlike strength, yea we will draw anigh
To watch the heavy stone like Jove's bolt fly
Forth from thine hand." Then Perseus smiled and said,
"Nay then, be wary, and guard well thine head.!
For who of mortals knoweth where and when
The bolts of Jove shall smite down foolish men?"

   So said he, and withal the King drew nigh,
And with him an old man, who anxiously
Peered round him as if looking for a foe;
Then Perseus made him ready for the throw,
But even as he stooped the stone to raise,
The old man said, "That I the more may praise
This hero's cast, come to the other end
And we shall see the hill of granite send

The earth and stones up as its course is spent."
So then beyond the furthest cast they went
By some three yards, and stood aside; but now
Since it was evening and the sun was low
Its beams were in their eyes, nor could they see
If Perseus moved or not, then restlessly
Looking this way or that, the ancient man,
Gathering his garments up, in haste began
To cross the place, but when a warning shout
Rang in his ears, then wavering and in doubt
He stopped, and scarcely had he time to hear
A second cry of horror and of fear,
Ere crushed, and beaten down upon the ground,
The end of all his weary life he found.

    Then women shrieked, and strong men shouted out,
And Perseus ran to those that drew about
The slain old man, and asked them of his name,
But the King, eyeing him as nigh he came,
Said, "This we know, and thy hid name we know,
For certainly thou art his fated foe,
His very daughter's strange-begotten son,
The child the sea cast up, the dreaded one.
This was Acrisius, who for fear of thee
Shut up thy mother by the sounding sea;
This was the man, who, for the very dread
Of meeting thee, from lovely Argos fled
To be my guest. Nay, let thy sharp sword bide
Within its sheath, the world is fair and wide,
Nor have we aught to do to thee for this;
Go then in peace, and live in woe or bliss
E'en as thou may'st, but stay with us no more,
Because we fear the gods may plague us sore
For this thy deed, though they would have it so."

    Then soberly thenceforth did Perseus go
Unto his folk, and straightly told them all
That on that luckless day had chanced to fall;
Wondering thereat, there made they no delay
But down unto the sea they took their way;
And much did Danae ponder as they went
How the high gods had wrought out their intent,
And thinking on these things she needs must sigh
For pity of her sweet life passing by.
    But when they reached the border of the sea,
Then Perseus said, "Though all unwittingly
I slew this man, and though perchance of right
His throne is mine, yet never will I fight
Against the just gods, and I fear the stain
Of kindred blood, if slaying him I gain
His kingdom and the city of my birth:

Now, therefore, since the gods have made the earth
Most fair in many places, let us go
Where'er the god-sent fated wind shall blow
The ship, that carries one the high gods love.
But first the armed lovely Maid of Jove
Here let us worship, on this yellow beach,
That her, my helper erst, we may beseech
To grant us much, and first of all things, this,
A land where we may dwell awhile in bliss."

   They heard him gladly, for the most of those
Were young, nor yet by mishaps and by foes
Had learned to think the world a dreary thing;
So round about the altar did they sing
And feasted well, and when the day came round
Once more, they went a-shipboard to the sound
Of trumpets and heart-moving melody,
And gave their rich keel to the restless sea.

   Then for four days before the wind they drove,
Until at last in sight a new land hove
Their pilot called the coast of Argolis,
That rich in cattle and in horses is.

   But landing there had Perseus' godlike fame
Gone on before him, and the people came
And cried upon him for their king and lord,
The people's saving shield and conquering sword;
So in that land he failed not to abide,
And there with many rites he purified
His fated hands of that unlooked-for guilt:
And there a town within a while he built
Men call Mycenæ. Peaceful grew the land
The while the ivory rod was in his hand,
For robbers fled, and good men still waxed strong,
And in no house was any sound of wrong,
Until the Golden Age seemed there to be,
So steeped the land was in felicity.

   Time past, and there his wife and mother died,
And he, no god, must lie down by their side,
While Alceus his first son reigned after him,
A conquering king, and fair, and strong of limb.

   But long ere this he did not fail to lay
The sacred things that brought him on his way
Within Minerva's temple; there with awe
'Twixt silver bars, all folk these marvels saw,
But not for long, for on the twentieth day
From the fair temple were they snatched away
Though by the armed priests guarded faithfully.
But still the empty wallet there did lie
Wherein had Perseus borne the head with him,
Which still when his great deeds were waxing dim,

Hung in the Maiden's temple near the shrine,
And folk would pour before it oil and wine.

   And know besides, that from that very year
Those who are wise say that the Maid doth bear
Amidst her shield that awful snaky head
Whereby so many heedless ones are dead.

Before the last words of his tale were done
The purple hills had hidden half the sun,
But when the story's death a silence made
Within the hall, in freshness and in shade
The trembling blossoms of the garden lay.
   Few words at first the elder men could say,
For thinking how all stories end with this,
Whatever was the midway gain and bliss:
"He died, and in his place was set his son;
He died, and in a few days every one
Went on their way as though he had not been."
   Yet with the pictures that their eyes had seen,
As still from point to point that history past,
And round their thoughts its painted veil was cast,
Their hearts were softened,—far away they saw
That other world, that 'neath another law
Had lived and died; when man might hope to see
Some earthly image of Divinity,
And yet not die, but, strengthened by the sight,
Cast fear away, and go from might to might,
Until to godlike life, though short, he came,
Amidst all losses winning hope of fame,
Nor losing joy the while his life should 'dure,
For that at least his valiant strife made sure,
That still in place of dreamy, youthful hope,
With slow decay and certain death could cope.
So mused the Wanderers, and awhile might deem
That world might not be quite an empty dream,
But dim foreshadowings of what yet might come
When they perforce must leave that new-gained home;
Foreshadowings mingled with the images
Of man's misdeeds in greater days than these.

   With no harsh words their musing was undone,
The garden birds sang down the setting sun,
A rainy wind from 'twixt the trees arose,
And sang a mournful counterpoint to those;
And, ere the rain amidst the dark could fall,
The minstrel's song was ringing through the hall.

   When April-tide was melting into May,
Within a hall that midst the gardens lay
These elders met, and having feasted well,

The time came round the wonted tale to tell.
Then spake a Wanderer: "Sirs, it happed to me,
Long years agone, to cross the narrow sea
That 'twixt us Drontheimers and England lies;
Young was I then, and little thought these eyes
Should see so many lands ere all was done.
  "But this land was a fair and fertile one,
As at that time, for April-tide it was,
Even as now; well, sirs, it came to pass
That to this town or that we took our way,
Or in some abbey's guesten-chamber lay,
And many tales we heard, some false, some true,
Of the ill deeds our fathers used to do
Within that land; and still the tale would end,
'Yet did the Saint his Holy House defend;'
Or, 'Sirs, their fury all was nought and vain,
And by our Earl the pirate-king was slain.'
God wot, I laughed full often in my sleeve,
And could have told them stories, by their leave,
With other endings: but I held my tongue.
Let each king's deeds in his own land be sung,
And then will lies stretch far. Besides, these men
Were puffed up with their luck and glory then,
For at that tide, within the land of France,
Unto their piping must all people dance.—
But let that pass, for Captain Rolf has told
How, on the way, their king he did behold.

  "For other tales they told, and one of these
Not all the washing of the troublous seas,
Not all the changeful days whereof ye know,
Has swept from out my memory; even so
Small things far off will be remembered clear
When matters both more weighty, and more near,
Are waxing dim to us. I, who have seen
So many lands, and midst such marvels been,
Clearer than these abodes of outland men,
Can see above the green and unburnt fen
The little houses of an English town,
Cross-timbered, thatched with fen-reeds coarse and brown,
And high o'er these, three gables, great and fair,
That slender rods of columns do upbear
Over the minster doors, and imagery
Of kings, and flowers no summer field doth see,
Wrought on those gables.—Yea, I heard withal,
In the fresh morning air, the trowels fall
Upon the stone, a thin noise far away;
For high up wrought the masons on that day,
Since to the monks that house seemed scarcely well
Till they had set a spire or pinnacle
Each side the great porch. In that burgh I heard

This tale, and late have set down every word
That I remembered, when the thoughts would come,
Of what we did in our deserted home,
And of the days, long past, when we were young,
Nor knew the cloudy woes that o'er us hung.
And howsoever I am now grown old,
Yet is it still the tale I then heard told
Within the guest-house of that minster-close,
Whose walls, like cliffs new-made, before us rose."

THE PROUD KING

ARGUMENT

A certain King, blinded by pride, thought that he was something more than man, if not equal to God; but such a judgment fell on him that none knew him for king, and he suffered many things, till in the end, humbling himself, he regained his kingdom and honour.

In a far country that I cannot name,
And on a year long ages past away,
A King there dwelt, in rest and ease and fame,
And richer than the Emperor is to-day:
The very thought of what this man might say,
From dusk to dawn kept many a lord awake,
For fear of him did many a great man quake.

   Young was he when he first sat on the throne,
And he was wedded to a noble wife,
But at the daïs must he sit alone,
Nor durst a man speak to him for his life,
Except with leave: nought knew he change or strife,
But that the years passed silently away,
And in his black beard gathered specks of grey

   Now so it chanced, upon a May morning,
Wakeful he lay when yet low was the sun,
Looking distraught at many a royal thing,
And counting up his titles one by one,
And thinking much of things that he had done;
For full of life he felt, and hale and strong,
And knew that none durst say-when he did wrong.

   For no man now could give him dread or doubt,
The land was 'neath his sceptre far and wide,
And at his beck would well-armed myriads shout.
Then swelled his vain, unthinking heart with pride,
Until at last he raised him up and cried,
"What need have I for temple or for priest,
Am I not God, whiles that I live at least."

And yet withal that dead his fathers were,
He needs must think, that quick the years pass by;
But he, who seldom yet had seen death near
Or heard his name, said, "Still I may not die
Though underneath the earth my fathers lie;
My sire indeed was called a mighty king,
Yet in regard of mine, a little thing

"His kingdom was; moreover his grandsire
To him was but a prince of narrow lands,
Whose father, though to things he did aspire
Beyond most men, a great knight of his hands,
Yet ruled some little town where now there stands
The kennel of my dogs; then may not I
Rise higher yet, nor like poor wretches die?

"Since up the ladder ever we have gone
Step after step nor fallen back again;
And there are tales of people who have won
A life enduring, without care or pain,
Or any man to make their wishes vain;
Perchance this prize unwitting now I hold;
For times change fast, the world is waxen old."

So 'mid these thoughts once more he fell asleep,
And when he woke again, high was the sun,
Then quickly from his gold bed did he leap,
And of his former thoughts remembered none,
But said, "To-day through green woods will we run,
Nor shall to-day be worse than yesterday,
But better it may be, for game and play."

So for the hunt was he apparelled,
And forth he rode with heart right well at ease;
And many a strong, deep-chested hound they led,
Over the dewy grass betwixt the trees,
And fair white horses fit for the white knees
Of Her the ancients fabled rides a-nights
Betwixt the setting and the rising lights.

Now following up a mighty hart and swift
The King rode long upon that morning tide,
And since his horse was worth a kingdom's gift,
It chanced him all his servants to outride,
Until unto a shaded river-side
He came alone at hottest of the sun,
When all the freshness of the day was done.

Dismounting there, and seeing so far adown
The red-finned fishes o'er the gravel play,

It seemed that moment worth his royal crown
To hide there from the burning of the day,
Wherefore he did off all his rich array,
And tied his horse unto a neighbouring tree,
And in the water sported leisurely.

  But when he was fulfilled of this delight
He gat him to the bank well satisfied,
And thought to do on him his raiment bright
And homeward to his royal house to ride;
But 'mazed and angry, looking far and wide
Nought saw he of his horse and rich attire,
And 'gainst the thief 'gan threaten vengeance dire.

  But little help his fury was to him,
So lustily he 'gan to shout and cry;
None answered, still the lazy chub did swim
By inches 'gainst the stream; away did fly
The small pied bird, but nathless stayed anigh,
And o'er the stream still plied his fluttering trade,
Of such a helpless man not much afraid.

  Weary of crying in that lonely place
He ceased at last, and thinking what to do,
E'en as he was, up stream he set his face,
Since not far off a certain house he knew
Where dwelt his ranger, a lord leal and true,
Who many a bounty at his hands had had,
And now to do him ease would be right glad.

  Thither he hastened on, and as he went
The hot sun sorely burned his naked skin,
The whiles he thought, "When he to me has lent
Fine raiment, and at ease I sit within
His coolest chamber clad in linen thin,
And drinking wine, the best that he has got,
I shall forget this troublous day and hot."

  Now note, that while he thus was on his way,
And still his people for their master sought,
There met them one who in the King's array
Bestrode his very horse, and as they thought
Was none but he in good time to them brought,
Therefore they hailed him King, and so all rode
From out the forest to his fair abode.

  And there in royal guise he sat at meat,
Served, as his wont was, 'neath the canopy,
And there the hounds fawned round about his feet,
And there that city's elders did he see,
And with his lords took counsel what should be;

And there at supper when the day waxed dim
The Queen within his chamber greeted him.

Leave we him there; for to the ranger's gate
The other came, and on the horn he blew,
Till peered the wary porter through the grate
To see if he, perchance, the blower knew,
Before he should the wicket-gate undo;
But when he saw him standing there, he cried,
"What dost thou friend, to show us all thine hide?

   "We list not buy to-day or flesh or fell;
Go home and get thyself a shirt at least,
If thou wouldst aught, for saith our vicar well,
That God hath given clothes e'en to the beast."
Therewith he turned to go, but as he ceased
The King cried out, "Open, O foolish man!
I am thy lord and King, Jovinian;

   "Go now, and tell thy master I am here
Desiring food and clothes, and in this plight,
And then hereafter need'st thou have no fear,
Because thou didst not know me at first sight."
"Yea, yea, I am but dreaming in the night,"
The carle said, "and I bid thee, friend, to dream,
Come through! here is no gate, it doth but seem."

   With that his visage vanished from the grate;
But when the King now found himself alone,
He hurled himself against the mighty gate,
And beat upon it madly with a stone,
Half wondering midst his rage, how any one
Could live, if longed-for things he chanced to lack;
But midst all this, at last the gate flew back,

   And there the porter stood, brown-bill in hand,
And said, "Ah, fool, thou makest this ado,
Wishing before my lord's high seat to stand;
Thou shalt be gladder soon hereby to go,
Or surely nought of handy blows I know.
Come, willy nilly, thou shalt tell this tale
Unto my lord, if aught it may avail."

   With that his staff he handled, as if he
Would smite the King, and said, "Get on before!
St Mary! now thou goest full leisurely,
Who, erewhile, fain wouldst batter down the door.
See now, if ere this matter is passed o'er,
I come to harm, yet thou shalt not escape,
Thy back is broad enow to pay thy jape."

Half blind with rage the King before him passed,
But nought of all he doomed him to durst say,
Lest he from rest nigh won should yet be cast,
So with a swelling heart he took his way,
Thinking right soon his shame to cast away,
And the carle followed still, ill satisfied
With such a wretched losel to abide.

Fair was the ranger's house and new and white,
And by the King built scarce a year agone,
And carved about for this same lord's delight
With woodland stories deftly wrought in stone;
There oft the King was wont to come alone,
For much he loved this lord, who erst had been
A landless squire, a servant of the Queen.

Now long a lord and clad in rich attire,
In his fair hall he sat before the wine
Watching the evening sun's yet burning fire,
Through the close branches of his pleasance shine,
In that mood when man thinks himself divine,
Remembering not whereto we all must come,
Not thinking aught but of his happy home.

From just outside loud mocking merriment
He heard midst this; and therewithal a squire
Came hurrying up, his laughter scarcely spent,
Who said, "My lord, a man in such attire
As Adam's, ere he took the devil's hire,
Who saith that thou wilt know him for the King,
Up from the gate John Porter needs must bring.

"He to the King is nothing like in aught
But that his beard he weareth in such guise
As doth my lord: wilt thou that he be brought?
Perchance some treason 'neath his madness lies."
"Yea," saith the ranger, "that may well be wise,
But haste, for this eve am I well at ease,
Nor would be wearied with such folk as these."

Then went the squire, and coming back again,
The porter and the naked King brought in,
Who thinking now that this should end his pain,
Forgat his fury and the porter's sin,
And said, "Thou wonderest how I came to win
This raiment, that kings long have ceased to wear,
Since Noah's flood has altered all the air?

"Well, thou shalt know, but first I pray thee, Hugh,
Reach me that cloak that lieth on the board,
For certes, though thy folk are leal and true,

It seemeth that they deem a mighty lord
Is made by crown, and silken robe, and sword;
Lo, such are borel folk; but thou and I
Fail not to know the signs of majesty.

   "Thou risest not! thou lookest strange on me!
Ah, what is this? Who reigneth in my stead?
How long hast thou been plotting secretly?
Then slay me now, for if I be not dead
Armies will rise up when I nod my head.
Slay me!—or cast thy treachery away,
And have anew my favour from this day."

   "Why should I tell thee that thou ne'er wast king?
The ranger said, "Thou knowest not what I say;
Poor man, I pray God help thee in this thing,
And, ere thou diest send thee some good day;
Nor hence unholpen shalt thou go away.
Good fellows, this poor creature is but mad,
Take him, and in a coat let him be clad;

   "And give him meat and drink, and on this night
Beneath some roof of ours let him abide,
For some day God may set his folly right."
Then spread the King his arms abroad and cried,
"Woe to thy food, thy house, and thee betide,
Thou loathsome traitor! Get ye from the hall,
Lest smitten by God's hand this roof should fall;

   "Yea, if the world be but an idle dream,
And God deals nought with it, yet shall ye see
Red flame from out these careen windows stream.
I, I, will burn this vile place utterly,
And strewn with salt the poisonous earth shall be,
That such a wretch of such a man has made,
That so such Judases may grow afraid."

   Thus raving, those who held him he shook off
And rushed from out the hall, nigh mad indeed,
And gained the gate, not heeding blow or scoff,
Nor longer of his nakedness took heed,
But ran, he knew not where, at headlong speed.
Till, when at last his strength was fully spent,
Worn out, he fell beneath a woody bent.

   But for the ranger, left alone in peace,
He bade his folk bring in the minstrelsy;
And thinking of his life, and fair increase
Of all his goods, a happy man was he,
And towards his master felt right lovingly,
And said, "This luckless madman will avail

When next I see the King for one more tale."

Meanwhile the real King by the road-side lay,
Panting, confused, scarce knowing if he dreamed,
Until at last, when vanished was the day,
Through the dark night far off a bright light gleamed;
Which growing quickly, down the road there streamed
The glare of torches, held by men who ran
Before the litter of a mighty man.

These mixed with soldiers soon the road did fill,
And on their harness could the King behold
The badge of one erst wont to do his will,
A counsellor, a gatherer-up of gold,
Who underneath his rule had now grown old:
Then wrath and bitterness so filled his heart,
That from his wretched lair he needs must start;

And o'er the clatter shrilly did he cry,
"Well met, Duke Peter! ever art thou wise;
Surely thou wilt not let a day go by
Ere thou art good friends with mine enemies;
O fit to rule within a land of lies,
Go on thy journey, make thyself more meet
To sit in hell beneath the devil's feet!"

But as he ceased a soldier drew anear,
And smote him flatling with his sheathed sword,
And said, "Speak louder, that my lord may hear,
And give thee wages for thy ribald word!
Come forth, for I must show thee to my lord,
For he may think thee more than mad indeed,
Who of men's ways hast taken wondrous heed."

Now was the litter stayed midmost the road,
And round about, the torches in a ring
Were gathered, and their flickering light now glowed
In gold and gems and many a lordly thing,
And showed that face well known unto the King,
That, smiling yesterday, right humble words
Had spoken midst the concourse of the lords.

But now he said, "Man, thou wert cursing me
If these folk heard aright; what wilt thou then,
Deem'st thou that I have done some wrong to thee,
Or hast thou scathe from any of my men?
In any case tell all thy tale again
When on the judgment-seat thou see'st me sit,
And I will give no careless ear to it."

"The night is dark, and in the summer wind

The torches flicker; canst thou see my face?
Bid them draw nigher yet, and call to mind
Who gave thee all thy riches and thy place—
Well;—if thou canst, deny me, with such grace
As by the fire-light Peter swore of old,
When in that Maundy-week the night was cold—

   "—Alas! canst thou not see I am the King?"
So spoke he, as their eyes met mid the blaze,
And the King saw the dread foreshadowing
Within the elder's proud and stony gaze,
Of what those lips, thin with the lapse of days,
Should utter now; nor better it befell;—
"Friend, a strange story thou art pleased to tell;

   "Thy luck it is thou tellest it to me,
Who deem thee mad and let thee go thy way:
The King is not a man to pity thee,
Or on thy folly thy fool's tale to lay:
Poor fool! take this, and with the light of day
Buy food and raiment of some labouring clown,
And by my counsel keep thee from the town,

   "For fear thy madness break out in some place
Where folk thy body to the judge must hale,
And then indeed wert thou in evil case—
Press on, sirs! or the time will not avail."
There stood the King, with limbs that 'gan to fail,
Speechless, and holding in his trembling hand
A coin new stamped for people of the land;

   Thereon, with sceptre, crown, and royal robe,
The image of a King, himself, was wrought;
His jewelled feet upon a quartered globe,
As though by him all men were vain and nought.
One moment the red glare the silver caught,
As the lord ceased, the next his hurrying folk
The flaring circle round the litter broke.

   The next, their shadows barred a patch of light,
Fast vanishing, all else around was black;
And the poor wretch, left lonely with the night,
Muttered, "I wish the day would ne'er come back,
If all that once I had I now must lack:
Ah God! how long is it since I was King,
Nor lacked enough to wish for anything?"

   Then down the lonely road he wandered yet,
Following the vanished lights, he scarce knew why,
Till he began his sorrows to forget,
And, steeped in drowsiness, at last drew nigh

A grassy bank, where, worn with misery,
He slept the dreamless sleep of weariness,
That many a time such wretches' eyes will bless.

But at the dawn he woke, nor knew at first
What ugly chain of grief had brought him there,
Nor why he felt so wretched and accursed;
At last remembering, the fresh morning air,
The rising sun, and all things fresh and fair,
Yet caused some little hope in him to rise,
That end might come to these new miseries.

  So looking round about, he saw that he
To his own city gates was come anear;
Then he arose and going warily,
And hiding now and then for very fear
Of folk who bore their goods and country cheer,
Unto the city's market, at the last
Unto a stone's-throw of the gate he passed.

  But when he drew unto the very gate,
Into the throng of country-folk he came
Who for the opening of the door did wait,
Of whom some mocked, and some cried at him shame,
And some would know his country and his name;
But one into his waggon drew him up,
And gave him milk from out a beechen cup,

  And asked him of his name and misery;
Then in his throat a swelling passion rose,
Which yet he swallowed down, and, "Friend," said he,
"Last night I had the hap to meet the foes
Of God and man, who robbed me, and with blows
Stripped off my weed and left me on the way:
Thomas the Pilgrim am I called to-day.

  "A merchant am I of another town,
And rich enow to pay thee for thy deed,
If at the King's door thou wilt set me down,
For there a squire I know, who at my need
Will give me food and drink, and fitting weed.
What is thy name? in what place dost thou live?
That I some day great gifts to thee may give."

  "Fair Sir," the carie said, "I am poor enow,
Though certes food I lack not easily;
My name is Christopher a-Green; I sow
A little orchard set with bush and tree,
And ever there the kind land keepeth me,
For I, now fifty, from a little boy
Have dwelt thereon, and known both grief and joy.

"The house my grandsire built there has grown old,
And certainly a bounteous gift it were
If thou shouldst give me just enough of gold
To build it new; nor shouldst thou lack my prayer
For such a gift." "Nay, friend, have thou no care,"
The King said: "this is but a little thing
To me, who oft am richer than the King."

Now as they talked the gate was opened wide,
And toward the palace went they through the street,
And Christopher walked ever by the side
Of his rough wain, where midst the May-flowers sweet
Jovinian lay, that folk whom they might meet
Might see him not to mock at his bare skin:
So shortly to the King's door did they win.

Then through the open gate Jovinian ran
Of the first court, and no man stayed him there;
But as he reached the second gate, a man
Of the King's household, seeing him all bare
And bloody, cried out, "Whither dost thou fare?
Sure thou art seventy times more mad than mad,
Or else some magic potion thou hast had,

"Whereby thou fear'st not steel or anything."
"But," said the King, "good fellow, I know thee;
And can it be thou knowest not thy King?
Nay, thou shalt have a good reward of me,
That thou wouldst rather have than ten years' fee,
If thou wilt clothe me in fair weed again,
For now to see my council am I fain."

"Out, ribald!" quoth the fellow: "What say'st thou?
Thou art my lord, whom God reward and bless?
Truly before long shalt thou find out how
John Hangman cureth ill folk's wilfulness;
Yea, from his scourge the blood has run for less
Than that which now thou sayest: nay, what say I?
For lighter words have I seen tall men die.

"Come now, the sergeants to this thing shall see!"
So to the guard-room was Jovinian brought,
Where his own soldiers mocked him bitterly,
And all his desperate words they heeded nought;
Until at last there came to him this thought,
That never from this misery should he win,
But, spite of all his struggles, die therein.

And terrible it seemed, that everything
So utterly was changed since yesterday,

That these who were the soldiers of the King,
Ready to lie down in the common way
Before him, nor durst rest if he bade play,
Now stood and mocked him, knowing not the face
At whose command each man there had his place.

"Ah, God!" said he, "is this another earth
From that whereon I stood two days ago?
Or else in sleep have I had second birth?
Or among mocking shadows do I go,
Unchanged myself of flesh and fell, although
My fair weed I have lost and royal gear?
And meanwhile all are changed that I meet here;

"And yet in heart and nowise outwardly."
Amid his wretched thoughts two sergeants came,
Who said, "Hold, sirs! because the King would see
The man who thus so rashly brings him shame,
By taking his high style and spotless name,
That never has been questioned ere to-day.
Come, fool! needs is it thou must go our way."

So at the sight of him all men turned round,
As 'twixt these two across the courts he went,
With downcast head and hands together bound;
While from the windows maid and varlet leant,
And through the morning air fresh laughter sent;
Until unto the threshold they were come
Of the great hall within that kingly home.

Therewith right fast Jovinian's heart must beat,
As now he thought, "Lo, here shall end the strife;
For either shall I sit on mine own seat,
Known unto all, soldier and lord and wife,
Or else is this the ending of my life,
And no man henceforth shall remember me,
And a vain name in records shall I be."

Therewith he raised his head up, and beheld
One clad in gold set on his royal throne,
Gold-crowned, whose hand the ivory sceptre held;
And underneath him sat the Queen alone,
Ringed round with standing lords, of whom not one
Did aught but utmost reverence unto him;
Then did Jovinian shake in every limb.

Yet midst amaze and rage to him it seemed
This man was nowise like him in the face;
But with a marvellous glory his head gleamed,
As though an angel sat in that high place,
Where erst he sat like all his royal race,

But their eyes met, and with a stern, calm brow
The shining one cried out, "And where art thou?

  "Where art thou, robber of my majesty?"
"Was I not King," he said, "but yesterday?
And though to-day folk give my place to thee,
I am Jovinian; yes, though none gainsay,
If on these very stones thou shouldst me slay,
And though no friend be left for me to moan,
I am Jovinian still, and King alone."

  Then said that other, "O thou foolish man,
King was I yesterday, and long before,
Nor is my name aught but Jovinian,
Whom in this house the Queen my mother bore,
Unto my longing father, for right sore
Was I desired before I saw the light;
Thou, fool, art first to speak against my right.

  "And surely well thou meritest to die;
Yet ere that I bid lead thee unto death,
Hearken to these my lords that stand anigh,
And what this faithful Queen beside me saith,
Then may'st thou many a year hence draw thy breath,
If these should stammer in their speech one whit:
Behold this face, lords, look ye well on it!

  "Thou, O fair Queen, say now whose face is this!"
Then cried they, "Hail O Lord Jovinian
Long mayst thou live!" and the Queen knelt to kiss
His gold-shod feet, and through her face there ran
Sweet colour, as she said, "Thou art the man
By whose side I have lain for many a year,
Thou art my lord Jovinian lief and dear."

  Then said he, "O thou wretch, hear now and see!
What thing should hinder me to slay thee now?
And yet indeed, such mercy is in me,
If thou wilt kneel down humbly and avow
Thou art no King, but base-born, as I know
Thou art indeed, in mine house shalt thou live,
And as thy service is, so shalt thou thrive."

  But the unhappy King laughed bitterly,
The red blood rose to flush his visage wan
Where erst the grey of death began to be;
"Thou liest, "he said, "I am Jovinian,
Come of great Kings; nor am I such a man
As still to live when all delight is gone,
As thou might'st do, who sittest on my throne."

No answer made the other for a while,
But sat and gazed upon him steadfastly,
Until across his face there came a smile,
Where scorn seemed mingled with some great pity.
And then he said, "Nathless thou shalt not die,
But live on as thou mayst, a lowly man
Forgetting thou wast once Jovinian."

Then wildly round the hall Jovinian gazed,
Turning about to many a well-known face,
But none of all his folk seemed grieved or mazed,
But stood unmoved, each in his wonted place;
There were the Lords, the Marshal with his mace,
The Chamberlain, the Captain of the Guard,
Grey-headed, with his wrinkled face and hard,

That had peered down so many a lane of war;
There stood the grave ambassadors arow,
Come from half-conquered lands; without the bar
The foreign merchants gazed upon the show,
Willing new things of that great land to know;
Nor was there any doubt in any man
That the gold throne still held Jovinian.

Yea, as the sergeants laid their hands on him,
The mighty hound that crouched before the throne,
Flew at him fain to tear him limb from limb,
Though in the woods, the brown bear's dying groan,
He and that beast had often heard alone.
"Ah!" muttered he, "take thou thy wages too
Worship the risen sun as these men do."

They thrust him out, and as he passed the door,
The murmur of the stately court he heard
Behind him, and soft footfalls on the floor,
And, though by this somewhat his skin was seared,
Hung back at the rough eager wind afeard;
But from the place they dragged him through the gate,
Wherethrough he oft had rid in royal state.

Then down the streets they led him, where of old,
He, coming back from some well-finished war,
Had seen the line of flashing steel and gold
Wind upwards 'twixt the houses from the bar,
While clashed the bells from wreathed spires afar;
Now moaning, as they haled him on, he said,
"God and the world against one lonely head!"

But soon, the bar being past they loosed their hold,
And said "Thus saith by us our Lord the King,
Dwell now in peace, but yet be not so bold

To come again, or to thy lies to cling,
Lest unto thee there fall a worser thing;
And for ourselves we bid thee ever pray
For him who has been good to thee this day."

Therewith they turned away into the town,
And still he wandered on and knew not where,
Till, stumbling at the last, he fell adown,
And looking round beheld a brook right fair,
That ran in pools and shallows here and there,
And on the further side of it a wood,
Nigh which a lowly clay-built hovel stood.

Gazing thereat, it came into his mind
A priest dwelt there, a hermit wise and old,
Whom he had ridden oftentimes to find,
In days when first the sceptre he did hold,
And unto whom his mind he oft had told,
And had good counsel from him, though indeed
A scanty crop had sprung from that good seed.

Therefore he passed the brook with heavy cheer,
And toward the little house went speedily,
And at the door knocked, trembling with his fear,
Because he thought, "Will he remember me?
If not, within me must there surely be
Some devil who turns everything to ill,
And makes my wretched body do his will."

So, while such doleful things as this he thought,
There came unto the door the holy man,
Who said, "Good friend, what tidings hast thou brought?"
"Father," he said, "knowest thou Jovinian?
Knowst thou me not, made naked, poor, and wan?
Alas, O father! am I not the King,
The rightful lord of thee and everything?"

"Nay, thou art mad to tell me such a tale!"
The hermit said; "if thou seek'st soul's health here,
Right little will such words as this avail;
It were a better deed to shrive thee clear,
And take the pardon Christ has bought so dear,
Than to an ancient man such mocks to say
That would be fitter for a Christmas play."

So to his hut he got him back again,
And fell the unhappy King upon his knees,
And unto God at last he did complain,
Saying, "Lord God, what bitter things are these?
What hast thou done, that every man that sees
This wretched body, of my death is fain?

O Lord God, give me back myself again!

"E'en if therewith I needs must die straightway.
Indeed I know that since upon the earth
I first did go, I ever day by day
Have grown the worse, who was of little worth
E'en at the best time since my helpless birth.
And yet it pleased thee once to make me King,
Why hast thou made me now this wretched thing?

"Why am I hated so of every one?
Wilt thou not let me live my life again,
Forgetting all the deeds that I have done,
Forgetting my old name, and honours vain,
That I may cast away this lonely pain?
Yet if thou wilt not, help me in this strife,
That I may pass my little span of life,

"Not made a monster by unhappiness.
What shall I say? thou mad'st me weak of will,
Thou wrapped'st me in ease and carelessness,
And yet, as some folk say, thou lovest me still;
Look down, of folly I have had my fill,
And am but now as first thou madest me,
Weak, yielding clay to take impress of thee."

So said he weeping, and but scarce had done,
When yet again came forth that hermit old,
And said, "Alas! my master and my son,
Is this a dream my wearied eyes behold?
What doleful wonder now shall I be told,
Of that ill world that I so long have left?
What thing thy glory from thee has bereft?"

A strange surprise of joy therewith there came
To that worn heart; he said, "For some great sin
The Lord my God has brought me unto shame;
I am unknown of servants, wife, and kin,
Unknown of all the lords that stand within
My father's house; nor didst thou know me more
When e'en just now I stood before thy door.

"Now since thou know'st me, surely God is good,
And will not slay me, and good hope I have
Of help from Him that died upon the rood,
And is a mighty lord to slay and save:
So now again these blind men will I brave,
If thou wilt give me of thy poorest weed,
And some rough food, the which I sorely need;

"Then of my sins thou straight shalt shrive me clean."

Then weeping said the holy man, "Dear lord,
What heap of woes upon thine head has been;
Enter, O King, take this rough gown and cord,
And scanty food, my hovel can afford;
And tell me everything thou hast to say;
And then the High God speed thee on thy way."

   So when in coarse serge raiment he was clad,
He told him all his pride had made him think;
And showed him of his life both good and bad;
And then being houselled, did he eat and drink,
While in the wise man's heart his words did sink,
For, "God be praised!" he thought, "I am no king,
Who scarcely shall do right in anything!

Then he made ready for the King his ass,
And bade again, God speed him on the way,
And down the road the King made haste to pass
As it was growing toward the end of day,
With sober joy for troubles passed away;
But trembling still, as onward he did ride,
Meeting few folk upon that even-tide.

So to the city gate being come at last,
He noted there two ancient warders stand,
Whereof one looked askance as he went past,
And whispered low behind his held-up hand
Unto his mate, "The King, who gave command
That if disguised he passed this gate to-day,
No reverence we should do him on the way."

   Thereat with joy, Jovinian smiled again,
And so passed onward quickly down the street;
And well nigh was he eased of all his pain
When he beheld the folk that he might meet
Gaze hard at him, as though they fain would greet
His well-known face, but durst not, knowing well
He would not any of his state should tell.

   Withal unto the palace being cone,
He lighted down thereby and entered,
And once again it seemed his royal home,
For folk again before him bowed the head;
And to him came a Squire, who softly said,
"The Queen awaits thee, O my lord the King,
Within the little hall where minstrels sing,

   "Since there thou badst her meet thee on this night."
"Lead on then!" said the King, and in his heart
He said, "perfay all goeth more than right
And I am King again;" but with a start

He thought of him who played the kingly part
That morn, yet said, "if God will have it so
This man like all the rest my face will know."

  So in the Little Hall the Queen he found,
Asleep, as one a spell binds suddenly;
For her fair broidery lay upon the ground,
And in her lap her open hand did lie,
The silken-threaded needle close thereby;
And by her stood that image of the King
In rich apparel, crown and signet-ring.

  But when the King stepped forth with angry eye
And would have spoken, came a sudden light,
And changed was that other utterly;
For he was clad in robe of shining white,
Inwrought with flowers of unnamed colours bright,
Girt with a marvellous girdle, and whose hem
Fell to his naked feet and shone in them;

  And from his shoulders did two wings arise,
That with the swaying of his body, played
This way and that; of strange and lovely dyes
Their feathers were, and wonderfully made:
And now he spoke, "O King, be not dismayed,
Or think my coming here so strange to be,
For oft ere this have I been close to thee.

  "And now thou knowest in how short a space
The God that made the world can unmake thee,
And though He alter in no whit thy face,
Can make all folk forget thee utterly,
That thou to-day a nameless wretch mayst be,
Who yesterday woke up without a peer,
The wide world's marvel and the people's fear.

  "Behold, thou oughtest to thank God for this,
That on the hither side of thy dark grave
Thou well hast learned how great a God He is,
Who from the heavens countless rebels drave,
Yet turns himself such folk as thee to save;
For many a man thinks nought at all of it,
Till in a darksome land he comes to sit,

  "Lamenting everything: so do not thou!
For inasmuch as thou thoughtst not to die
This thing may happen to thee even now,
Because the day unspeakable draws nigh,
When bathed in unknown flame all things shall lie;
And if thou art upon God's side that day,
Unslain, thine earthly part shall pass away.

"Or if thy body in the grave must rot,
Well mayst thou see how small a thing is this,
Whose pain of yesterday now hurts thee not,
Now thou hast come again to earthly bliss,
Though bitter-sweet thou knowest well this is,
And thou no coming day canst ever see
Ending of happiness where thou mayst be.

"Now must I go, nor wilt thou see me more,
Until the day, when, unto thee at least,
This world is gone, and an unmeasured shore,
Where all is wonderful and changed, thou seest:
Therefore, farewell! at council and at feast
Thy nobles shalt thou meet as thou hast done,
Nor wilt thou more be strange to anyone."

So scarce had he done speaking, ere his wings
Within the doorway of the hall did gleam,
And then he vanished quite; and all these things
Unto Jovinian little more did seem
Than some distinct and well-remembered dream,
From which one wakes amidst a feverish night,
Taking the moonshine for the morning light.

Silent he stood, not moving for a while,
Pondering o'er all these wondrous things, until
The Queen arose from sleep, and with a smile,
Said, "O fair lord, your great men by your will
E'en as I speak the banquet-chamber fill,
To greet thee amidst joy and revelling,
Wilt thou not therefore meet them as a King?"

So from that place of marvels having gone,
Half mazed, he soon was clad in rich array,
And sat thereafter on his kingly throne,
As though no other had sat there that day;
Nor did a soul of all his household say
A word about the man, who on that morn
Had stood there, naked, helpless, and forlorn.

But ever day by day the thought of it
Within Jovinian's heart the clearer grew,
As o'er his head the ceaseless time did flit,
And everything still towards its ending drew,
New things becoming old, and old things new;
Till, when a moment of eternity
Had passed, grey-headed did Jovinian lie

One sweet May morning, wakeful in his bed;
And thought, "That day is thirty years a-gone

Since useless folly came into my head,
Whereby, before the steps of mine own throne,
I stood in helpless agony alone,
And of the wondrous things that there befell,
When I am gone there will be none to tell:

  "No man is now alive who doubts that he,
Who bade thrust out the madman on that tide,
Was other than the King they used to see:
Long years have passed now, since the hermit died,
So must I tell the tale, ere by his side
I lie, lest it be unrecorded quite,
Like a forgotten dream in morning light.

  "Yea, lest I die ere night come, this same day
Unto some scribe will I tell everything,
That it may lie when I am gone away,
Stored up within the archives of the King;
And may God grant the words thereof may ring
Like His own voice in the next corner's ears!
Whereby his folk shall shed the fewer tears."

  So it was done, and at the King's command
A clerk that day did note it every whit,
And after by a man of skilful hand
In golden letters fairly was it writ;
Yet little heed the new King took of it
That filled the throne when King Jovinian died,
So much did all things feed his swelling pride.

  But whether God chastised him in his turn,
And he grew wise thereafter, I know not;
I think by eld alone he came to learn
How lowly on some day must be his lot.
But ye, O Kings, think all that ye have got
To be but gawds cast out upon some heap,
And stolen the while the Master was asleep.

The story done, for want of happier things,
Some men must even fall to talk of kings;
Some trouble of a far-off Grecian isle,
Some hard Sicilian craftsman's cruel guile
Whereby he raised himself to be as God,
Till good men slew him; the fell Persian rod
As blighting as the deadly pestilence,
The brazen net of armed men from whence
Was no escape; The fir-built Norway hall
Filled with the bonders waiting for the fall
Of the great roof whereto the torch is set;
The laughing mouth, beneath the eyes still wet
With more than sea-spray, as the well-loved land

The freeman still looks back on, while his hand
Clutches the tiller, and the eastern breeze
Grows fresh and fresher: many things like these
They talked about, till they seemed young again,
Remembering what a glory and a gain
Their fathers deemed the death of kings to be.
  And yet amidst it, some smiled doubtfully
For thinking how few men escape the yoke,
From this or that man's hand, and how most folk
Must needs be kings and slaves the while they live,
And take from this man, and to that man give
Things hard enow. Yet as they mused, again
The minstrels raised some high heroic strain
That led men on to battle in old times;
And midst the glory of its mingling rhymes,
Their hard hearts softened, and strange thoughts arose
Of some new end to all life's cruel foes.

William Morris - A Short Biography

British poet, author, thinker and publisher William Morris was born in 1834 in Walthamstow, Essex. The eldest son of wealthy Londoners Emma Shelton Morris and William Morris, the younger Morris would become one of the most influential people in the cultural landscape of Victorian England.

Educated at home and at a nearby preparatory school, Morris's childhood was one of privilege, with books, leisurely excursions and ponies for personal use. The idyll ended (to an extent) with the sudden death of Morris Senior in 1847 when the younger Morris was just 14 years old. The next year, Morris began his formal studies at Marlborough College in Wiltshire. After three years of bullying and homesickness, Morris returned to his family home and was thereafter privately tutored.

In 1852, Morris entered Oxford University to study the Classics. While there he also became interested in medieval-era history and architecture. Morris would come to identify with medievalist ideals, as did a growing socio-political movement in England that rejected the values of the prevailing Victorian capitalist system. Morris would become even more politically active later in life, embracing the socialist values that he had recognized in medievalism as an undergraduate.

Morris made several important and life-long friends while at Exeter College at Oxford, most notably the artist and designer Edward Burne-Jones. Morris and Burne-Jones became part of a group of Oxford thinkers (most of them from the industrial city of Birmingham) who would be known historically as "The Birmingham Set." The group included divinity student William Fulford, poet and theologian Richard Watson Dixon, mathematician Charles Faulkner and scholar Cormell Price – internally they called themselves "The Brotherhood." The members of the group shared literary interests as well as values and were huge fans of Alfred Lord Tennyson, art critic John Ruskin, the Arthurian legends and William Shakespeare.

In 1856, Morris helped fund and start up the *Oxford and Cambridge Magazine*, the first of many cooperative projects in which he took an active role. Twelve issues were published. Also in 1856 – upon completion of his Bachelor of Arts degree - Morris was apprenticed briefly to the Oxford based Gothic revival architect George Edmund Street. Morris would use lessons learned from Street, and supervising architect Philip Webb, during the design process for his own Red House in Kent. Morris lived there with his new family – wife Jane Burdon, who he married in 1859, and daughters Jenny and Mary – until 1865.

In 1858 Morris published *The Defence of Guenvere*, an innovative volume of lyric and dramatic verse, which nonetheless was not well received critically. Morris would not publish again until 1867 when Bell and Dandy published the epic romantic poem *The Life and Death of Jason*. The printing was financed by Morris himself; happily, the book was well received and Morris received a fee for the second edition.

From 1861 Morris commuted from The Red House to London where he had opened a decorative arts firm with Burne-Jones, Webb, Faulkner and other friends: the Pre-Raphaelite painter Dante Gabriel Rossetti, Ford Madox Brown and Peter Paul Marshall. The company – known publicly as Morris, Marshall, Faulkner & Co. and privately as "The Firm" – specialized in locally produced fabrics, furniture, tapestries, wallpaper, architectural carving and stained glass windows. In 1875, Morris assumed total control of the company, now named Morris & Co. Though known in his lifetime chiefly for being a poet, Morris would also achieve posthumous acclaim as a chief architect of the "Arts and Crafts" British design movement.

In 1865, Morris sold The Red House and moved to Bloomsbury in London with his family. By 1870, he was a cultural fixture in that city and a celebrity of some stature.

From 1865 to 1870, Morris worked on another epic poem, *The Earthly Paradise*. Designed as homage to Chaucer, it consists of 24 stories, each with a different narrator from a different cultural background. Set in the late 14th century, it is about a group of Norsemen who flee the Black Death by sailing away from Europe, on the way discovering an island where the inhabitants continue to venerate an ancient Greek god. Published in four parts by F. S. Ellis, the epic gained a cult following and established Morris' reputation as a major poet.

Greatly influenced by his friendship with Icelandic theologian Eiríkr Magnússon and several visits to Iceland, Morris produced a series of English-language translations of the Icelandic Eddas and Sagas (old Norse poems and stories). Morris also taught himself calligraphy and created hand written copies of Nordic tales in translation, including *Frithiof the Bold* and *Halfden the Black*. It was the continuation of a life-long devotion to craft, a feature of many of his subsequent works, including the poetic drama *Love is Enough*, published in 1872 with woodcut illustrations by Burne-Jones.

Though leading a rich life in London, Morris did find the city unhealthy for his young family. He came across and fell in love with a 16th century manor house in Oxfordshire. The Morris family would share Kelmscott Manor with Morris' friend Rossetti (who, it is said, had developed a close relationship with Morris' wife Jane) until their friendship eventually disintegrated. Kelmscott also lent its name to another of Morris' achievements – the Kelmscott Press, which he co-founded, with Emery Walker, in 1891. The bespoke publishing house was dedicated to publishing limited edition, illuminated style fine art books, in keeping with Morris' devotion to the craft of making books as beautiful objects. The Press dovetailed with Morris' continuing design work with Morris & Co. Over the next seven years, it would publish 66 volumes, the first of which was Morris' own novel, *The Story of the Glittering Plain*, in 1891. The Kelmscott Press would go on to publish 23 of Morris' books, but also editions of works by Keats, Shelley, Ruskin, and Swinburne, as well as copies of various Medieval texts. Kelmscott's magnum opus would turn out to be the Kelmscott Chaucer, published in 1896; it took several years to complete and included 87 illustrations and decorative borders from Burne-Jones.

In 1883, Morris joined England's first socialist organization, the Democratic Federation, later renamed the Socialist Democratic Federation (SDF). This was the beginning of years of overt activism on behalf of workers and the poor. In 1884, Morris and a large group of SDF members seceded in order to form the brand new Socialist League (SL). For the rest of the decade, Morris worked tirelessly for the cause; he met several times each week with his comrades from the SL and delivered hundreds of lectures. He was arrested in 1885 for disorderly conduct at the trial of several Socialist protesters, wrote for and edited SL's newspaper, *The Commonweal* and wrote a long series of socialist literary works, including the song collection *Chants for Socialists* (1884); a narrative poem, *The Pilgrims of Hope* (1885); the historical meditation *A Dream of John Ball* (1887); and his most influential work, *News from Nowhere* (1890), a pastoral utopian communist vision of England in the twenty-first century.

Morris also continued as a poet and prose writer. In December 1888, the Chiswick Press published his *The House of the Wolfings*, a fantasy story set in Iron Age Europe, which provides a reconstructed portrait of the lives of Germanic-speaking Gothic tribes. The book contains both prose and poetic verse and was followed by a two-volume sequel, *The Roots of the Mountains*, in 1899.

Morris also embarked on a translation of the quintessential Anglo-Saxon tale, *Beowulf*. Because he could not fully understand Old English, his poetic translation was based largely on that already produced by A.J. Watts. *The Tale of Beowulf* was not well received.

In the last nine years of his life, Morris wrote a series of imaginative fictions usually referred to as the "prose romances." These novels – including *The Wood Beyond the World* and *The Well at the World's End* (1896) – have been credited as important milestones in the history of fantasy fiction, because, while other writers wrote of foreign lands, or of dream worlds, or the future (as Morris had already done in the utopian *News from Nowhere*), Morris's works were the first to be set in an entirely invented neo-medieval fantasy world.

By 1896, Morris was an invalid, not working much but being visited by friends and family at his home. The great man died of tuberculosis on October 4th, 1896. Morris' funeral was held on October 6th, his corpse carried from Kelmscott House, his home in Hammersmith, to Paddington rail station, where it was transported to Oxford, then to Kelmscott, where it was buried in the churchyard of St. George's Church.

Morris lives on with the legacy of the Arts and Crafts movement, in his many fine literary works, essays and translations and through his homes, which have been preserved by the UK's National Trust and the William Morris Society as monuments to the man and the epic period of cultural history in which he flourished.

William Morris - A Concise Bibliography

Collected Poetry, Fiction, and Essays
The Hollow Land (1856)
The Defence of Guenevere, and other Poems (1858)
The Life and Death of Jason (1867)
The Earthly Paradise (1868–1870)
Love is Enough, or The Freeing of Pharamond: A Morality (1872)
The Story of Sigurd the Volsung and the Fall of the Niblungs (1877)
Hopes and Fears For Art (1882)

The Pilgrims of Hope (1885)
A Dream of John Ball (1888)
A Tale of the House of the Wolfings, and All the Kindreds of the Mark. In Prose and in Verse (1889)
The Roots of the Mountains (1890)
Poems By the Way (1891)
News from Nowhere (or, An Epoch of Rest) (1890)
The Story of the Glittering Plain (1891)
The Wood Beyond the World (1894)
Child Christopher and Goldilind the Fair (1895)
The Well at the World's End (1896)
The Water of the Wondrous Isles (1897)
The Sundering Flood (1897)
A King's Lesson (1901)
The World of Romance (1906)
Chants for Socialists (1935)

Translations
Grettis Saga: The Story of Grettir the Strong with Eiríkr Magnússon (1869)
The Saga of Gunnlaug the Worm-tongue and Rafn the Skald with Eiríkr Magnússon (1869)
Völsung Saga: The Story of the Volsungs and Niblungs, with Certain Songs from the Elder Eddawith Eiríkr Magnússon (1870) (from the Volsunga saga)
Three Northern Love Stories & Other Tales with Eiríkr Magnússon (1875)
The Odyssey of Homer Done into English Verse (1887)
The Aeneids of Virgil Done into English (1876)
Of King Florus and the Fair Jehane (1893)
The Tale of Beowulf Done out of the Old English Tongue (1895)
Old French Romances Done into English (1896)

Published Lectures and Papers
Lectures on Art delivered in support of the Society for the Protection of Ancient Buildings (Morris lecture on The Lesser Arts). London, Macmillan, 1882
Architecture and History & Westminster Abbey". Papers read to SPAB in 1884 and 1893. Printed at The Chiswick Press. London, Longmans, 1900
Communism: a lecture London, Fabian Society, 1903

www.ingramcontent.com/pod-product-compliance
Lightning Source LLC
LaVergne TN
LVHW051630080426
835511LV00016B/2279